POLITICAL OPINION POLLING

POLITICAL OPINION POLLING

An International Review

Edited by

ROBERT M. WORCESTER

President
World Association for
Public Opinion Research

St. Martin's Press　　New York

© Robert M. Worcester 1983

All rights reserved. For information, write:
St. Martin's Press, Inc., 175 Fifth Avenue, New York, NY 10010

Printed in Great Britain

First published in the United States of America in 1983

ISBN 0–312–62321–6

Library of Congress Cataloging in Publication Data

Main entry under title:

Political opinion polling.

Includes index.
1. Public opinion polls. I. Worcester, Robert M.
HM261.P565 1983   303.3′8   82–21438
ISBN 0–312–62321–6

Contents

List of Illustrations

Notes on the Contributors

Ian McNair

Joined McNair Anderson in 1952 and is now its chairman. He holds a B.Econ. degree from the University of Sydney, where he graduated with honours in statistics, and an M.Sc. from Columbia University, New York, majoring in marketing. He is a fellow of the Market Research Society of Australia, and a member of the Executive of the Constitutional Association of Australia and various professional bodies. At McNair Anderson one of his responsibilities is the organisation of Australian public opinion polls, which are published by the *Herald* and *Weekly Times* Group.

Frank Teer

Joint managing director of McNair Anderson, with overall responsibility for the group's many marketing and management research services. Before joining the board of McNair Anderson in 1978 he was successively managing director of two of the leading six research organisations in Great Britain: Research Surveys of Great Britain Ltd for five years and NOP Market Research Ltd for six. A graduate of the London School of Economics, he has lectured and broadcast widely on marketing research and opinion polling. He was joint author with J. D. Spence of *Political Opinion Polls* (London: Hutchinson, 1976) and a contributor to *The Consumer Market Research Handbook*, ed. R. M. Worcester (London: Van Nostrand Reinhold, 1978). He is a former chairman of the UK Market Research Society, a fellow of the Royal Statistical Society and a member of the Market Research Society of Australia.

Jean Stoetzel

Chairman of Faits et Opinions, Paris, having been founder (in 1938) and for many years chairman of L'Institut Français d'Opinion Publique (IFOP). He was, in 1947, the first president of the World Association for Public Opinion Research (WAPOR) and still serves on the WAPOR

Council, as liaison with UNESCO. He was formerly professor of social psychology at the Sorbonne (University of Paris) in the Faculty of Letters and in the Faculty of Science. He graduated from the Sorbonne in 1937 and taught at Columbia University.

Elisabeth Noelle-Neumann
Head of the Institut für Demoskopie Allensbach and a director of the Institut für Publizistik at the University of Mainz. She studied philosophy, history, journalism and American studies at universities in Germany and the USA and received a Ph.D. at the University of Berlin in 1940. That year she began work as a journalist, and in 1947, together with her husband, Erich Peter Neumann (d. 1973), founded the first German survey research institute – the Institut für Demoskopie Allensbach. From 1961 to 1964 she was a lecturer in communication research at the Free University of Berlin, and in 1964 was appointed to the newly established professorship in communication research at the University of Mainz. She was visiting professor in the Department of Political Science at the University of Chicago in 1978 and 1980. Professor Dr Noelle-Neumann was president of the World Association for Public Opinion Research from 1978 to 1980 and currently serves as a member of the WAPOR Executive Committee. She is a member of the Steering Committee of the International Association for Mass Communication Research; of the German UNESCO Commission Committee for Communication Research; and of the boards of the Stiftervereinigung der Presse e.V. and the Deutsche Lesegesellschaft e.V.

Robert M. Worcester
Chairman and managing director of Market & Opinion Research International Ltd (MORI) and has for over a decade served as public opinion polling adviser to the Labour Party in Great Britain. MORI polls are published in the *Sunday Times*, *The Times*, the *Daily Express*, the *Daily Star*, the *Standard*, *The Scotsman* and for the BBC. An American by birth, Mr Worcester is a graduate of the University of Kansas and was an officer of the Opinion Research Corporation, Princeton, New Jersey, before moving to London to establish MORI in 1969. He is currently president of the World Association for Public Opinion Research, is on the International Advisory Board of the Roper Centre and recently convened seminars for ESOMAR and WAPOR in Bonn on 'Opinion Polls', and for the Political Studies Association at the University of Newcastle on 'Political Communications and the 1979 General Election'. He is co-editor with Martin Harrop of *Political*

Communications (London: Allen & Unwin, 1982) and with John Downham of *Consumer Market Research Handbook* (London: Van Nostrand Reinhold, 1978).

John F. Meagher

Chairman and managing director of Irish Marketing Surveys Ltd (IMS). He has spent virtually all his working life in market research. From 1957 to 1963 he was with International Surveys Ltd, Toronto. He then returned to his native Ireland to set up IMS in 1963. He is also chairman of Lansdowne Market Research, Dublin, and a director of Irish Tam. He is a former chairman of the Market Research Society of Ireland and of the Marketing Society of Ireland. He served for eight years as national representative for Ireland to ESOMAR and was one of the contributors to the ESOMAR/WAPOR seminar on 'Opinion Polls' held in Bonn in January 1980.

Pierpaolo Luzzatto-Fegiz

Born in Trieste, Italy, he began his academic career as an assistant lecturer in economics, but has subsequently devoted himself to applied statistics, writing several books and over two hundred scientific papers on demography, economics and social statistics. From 1931 to 1969 he was professor of statistics at the University of Trieste (where he served also as dean of the Department of Economics and Business Administration). In 1961 he was appointed professor at the University of Rome. In 1946 he founded the Institute for Statistical Research and Public Opinion Analysis in Milan (DOXA), of which he is still managing director. He is a member of the Accademia dei Lencei, of the International Institute of Statistics and of other learned societies, and an honorary member of ESOMAR.

Sigeki Nisihira

Director of the Training School at the Institute of Statistical Mathematics in Tokyo since 1966. He graduated with a B.Sc. in mathematics at the University of Hokkaido in 1947. He has been a member of staff at the Institute of Statistical Mathematics since 1949 and has also held the posts of part-time lecturer in sociology at the University of Tokyo and in political science at the University of Waseda, and that of visiting professor at the University of Paris V (René Descartes). He has written or contributed to numerous books, articles, reports and surveys published in Japanese, English and French. He currently serves as member-at-large on the Council of the World Association for Public Opinion Research.

Jan Stapel
Director of the Netherlands Institute of Public Opinion (NIPO) which
he co-founded with Wim J. de Jonge in 1945. He is also a founding
member of ESOMAR and of the Dutch Association of Market
Researchers, and a former president of the World Association for Public
Opinion Research; and is currently on the board of directors of the
Gallup Organization Inc., USA, and of FISA A.G., Switzerland. He has
published a number of articles in Europe and the USA and is the author
of *Measuring Advertising Results for Marketing* (Amsterdam: Samsom,
1972), published in Dutch. He is the winner (1981) of the Helen
Dinnerman Award of WAPOR for his contribution to the methodology
of public opinion research.

Juan Antonio Giner
Professor of public opinion at the School of Journalism, University of
Navarra (Pamplona, Spain). Since 1979 he has been editor-in-chief of
Nuestro Tiempo, a monthly current affairs magazine published by
EUNSA, the University of Navarra Press. A native of Barcelona, Dr
Giner received a B.A. in Law from the University of Barcelona in 1970, a
B.A. in journalism from the Official School of Journalism in Madrid in
1975, a Ph.D. in law from the University of Navarra in 1978 and an
M.A. in journalism from the University of Navarra in 1980. He was a
Ford Foundation post-doctoral fellow and visiting scholar at the
Graduate School of Journalism, Columbia University, New York, in
1978–9. He is a member of the board of editors of *Investigación y
Marketing*, the journal of the Spanish Association of Market and
Opinion Studies (AEDEMO), as well as a member of WAPOR, the
American Association of Public Opinion Research (AAPOR) and
AEDEMO. He has also been a regular contributor to *La Vanguardia*
and *El país*. His doctoral thesis, 'Legal and ethical regulation of public
opinion polls', is currently being prepared for publication. Since
October 1981 he has been the Vice-Dean of the School of Journalism. He
is co-author with Kenneth Maxwell of *Press and the Rebirth of Iberian
Democracy* (Westport, Connecticut: Greenwood Press, 1982).

Mervin D. Field
Chairman of the Field Research Corporation, a director of the
California Poll and president of the Field Institute; he was founder of
each of these organisations in 1946, 1947 and 1975, respectively. In the
early 1940s he also worked for the US Maritime Service, the Gallup Poll
and the Opinion Research Corporation (the last two in Princeton, New

Jersey). His other academic and professional activities have included membership of the American Association for Public Opinion Research; the National Council of Published Polls (as a trustee); the Advisory Council of the Roper Public Opinion Research Center, University of Connecticut; the Council of American Survey Research Organizations (of which he was a founding director); and the American Marketing Association; the Advisory Committee of the Survey Research Center, University of California. He was also director of the Advertising Research Foundation in 1977/8. He is author of over 1100 reports for the California Poll on various aspects of Californian public opinion, attitudes and behaviour, and has written numerous articles and reports for journals as well as contributing to seminars and conferences throughout the USA. His study *A Post-Election Review of the 1970 British Elections with Particular Reference to the Performance and Role of the Public Opinion Polls. A Transatlantic View* was published by the Survey Research Centre at the University of Strathclyde, Glasgow.

Introduction

Political opinion polling is very much a national rather than an international activity. In each democratic country polling has developed its own institutes, history of political polls, use of polling in both the public (press, radio and television) and the private (political parties and individual politicians) sectors and, to some degree, differing national methodologies. Yet there are many aspects of the methodological basis of polling that cross national borders. Question techniques translate, as do sampling procedures and data processing programmes for cross-tabulation of results and multivariate analysis. Also, many of us involved in the practice of political opinion polling naturally have an interest in what our counterparts in other countries are doing in their work for their clients, the media and the political parties.

For the most part this interest has been expressed through the meetings, seminars, conferences and correspondence between members of the World Association for Public Opinion Research (WAPOR). The purpose of WAPOR is to establish a worldwide meeting ground for those working in the area of survey research. Through its activities, WAPOR unites the world of survey research within the universities and the world of survey research within private institutes – two worlds which far too often are still strictly separated. It is the express goal of WAPOR to bridge the gap existing between practitioners of social research in commercial institutes and academic theoreticians. WAPOR was founded in Williamstown, Massachusetts, USA, in 1947. Jean Stoetzel was its first elected president. In 1948 the association had 129 members; today the number of formal members is around 450. New members may enrol at a cost of $30.00 on application to WAPOR Secretariat, c/o The Roper Centre, Yale University, PO Box 1732, Yale Station, New Haven, Conn. 06520, USA.

This book is the first transnational record of political opinion polling ever compiled. In some countries, e.g. the USA, the history of opinion polling covers the full fifty or so years of the practice itself. In several others it is a relatively new phenomenon. An example of each type of

1

experience has been included in this volume. It is inevitably a symposium, as no single individual exists, not even George Gallup who can fairly be described as the father of political opinion polling, who could review its history and present state in as many as ten countries.

There are obvious omissions in both the geographical and the historical coverage. There is no contribution from Scandinavia, which has a long tradition of polling; nor from Belgium, Switzerland, Israel, Africa, or South-East Asia. Having carried out what I understand to be the first national opinion poll ever published in Portugal, in 1972, I am particularly sorry that space limitation precluded the inclusion of a chapter on the recent history of polling in that country. Further, even in the countries which are included, space limitations prevented all but sketchy coverage of the history of polls, their problems and prospects for the future. None the less, it is hoped that this book will help to lay the groundwork for a history of political opinion polling across national borders while many of its founding practitioners are still alive and active in their work. In the future, it will be difficult to reconstruct what the pioneers can now offer.

In the summer of 1982 Dr Henry Durrant, the founder of British Gallup, died, taking with him much of the early history of the first British polling organisation. In the last few years election polling in a number of countries has been chronicled in the series of election studies edited by Howard Penniman and funded by the American Enterprize Institute (AEI) in Washington DC; each country has at least one contemporary historian who has covered election polls to a greater or lesser degree in a history of his or her country's elections (e.g. David Butler since 1945 in Great Britain; Theodore White since 1960 in America). Polling archives in the individual institutes and in such places as the Roper Center and the Survey Research Consultants Institute (SRCI) in America, the SSRC survey archives in England and the Barswitz Institute in the Netherlands are rich sources of polling data, for the most part under-utilised. Several books in various countries, either by institutes or by individual writers, have been devoted to some aspects of political opinion polls. Examples of the former are Demoskopie Allensbach's *The Germans* in two volumes covering polls carried out from 1946 to 1980 in West Germany; the Gallup Poll's *Gallup International Public Opinion Polls, Great Britain 1937–1975* and *The Gallup Poll Public Opinion 1972–1977*; and, over the past few years, the SRCI's annual *Index . . . to International Public Opinion*, which has broadened the field of coverage immeasurably. Notable books by individual writers are Leo Bogart's *Silent Politics* (New York: Wiley-

Inter-Science, 1972) and Roll-Cantrill's *Polls* (Cabin John, Maryland: Seven Locks Press, 1972).

In preparing the manuscript for publication I wish to thank the authors for their patience, my secretary, Rena McMeeking, for her long hours and Cathy Hopkins for her thoughtful and careful job of editing.

Robert M. Worcester
London
May 1982

1 Political Opinion Polling in Australia

IAN McNAIR AND FRANK TEER

There are four major polling organisations in Australia:

The Roy Morgan Research Centre Pty Ltd produces the Morgan Gallup Poll which is published in the Australian weekly news magazine *The Bulletin* and also (at federal election times only) in *The Australian* and *The Weekend Australian*. The organisation is the Australian Gallup Poll affiliate and has been conducting political opinion polls ever since it was formed in 1941 by Roy Morgan. Up to and including the 1969 federal election, this was the only organisation that regularly conducted political polls. Until 1973 the poll was known as the Australian Gallup Poll and was published in various newspapers throughout Australia.

McNair Anderson Associates Pty Ltd does the fieldwork and data processing for Australian Public Opinion Polls (using the Gallup Method). These polls are published in *The Herald* and *The Sun News-Pictorial* (Melbourne), *The Sun* and *The Sun-Herald* (Sydney), *The Courier-Mail* (Brisbane), *The Advertiser* (Adelaide), *The West Australian* (Perth) and *The Mercury* (Hobart) and have by far the greatest exposure of any Australian poll. Majority ownership in the company is now held by the UK's AGB Research Ltd. The organisation has been conducting regular political polls since 1973, when it was awarded the APOP Gallup contract in place of Morgan Research. The organisation is the result of a merger in 1973 between McNair Surveys and the Anderson Analysis, which were formed in 1944 by Bill McNair and George Anderson respectively.

ANOP (Australian Nationwide Opinion Polls) produces a poll of the same name, which was published for the 1980 federal election in the

Australian Financial Review. Prior to this, the poll was published at different times in the *National Times* and *The Australian* and reported on the Australian Broadcasting Commission's television programme *Four Corners*. The organisation began taking polls of voting intention in 1971.

Irving Saulwick and Associates produces the *Herald* Survey/*Age* Poll, which is published in the *Sydney Morning Herald* and *The Age* (Melbourne). This organisation has been conducting polls since 1971, continuously under the direction of Saulwick but originally under the name of Australian Sales Research Bureau (ASRB). The poll is currently conducted in conjunction with Beacon Research Company Pty Ltd (a subsidiary of Unilever Pty Ltd) and the Department of Political Science at the University of Melbourne.

A fifth polling organisation commenced political polling in 1980:

Spectrum Research (NSW) Pty Ltd produced two telephone polls for *The Australian* just before the 1980 federal election. This organisation has been operating since 1978 and specialises in telephone surveys and qualitative research.

METHODS USED BY THE POLLS

Major differences in the methods currently used by each pollster are highlighted in Table 1.1. Three of the polls regularly offer sample coverage of both rural and urban regions in each State. ANOP does not always do this and usually restricts its sample coverage to marginal electorates or to the capital cities. Two of the polls use the electoral rolls as sampling frames while the other two randomly select clusters of dwellings in census collectors' districts (these are small districts which consist of about 200 or 300 dwellings and to which one collector is assigned at the time of each 10 yearly population census). For all polls, one person is interviewed per household.

Two of the polls (Morgan and APOP Gallup) use the simulated ballot box technique for recording an individual's voting intention. This involves the respondent in marking a 'ballot paper' which contains his or her party preference. The paper is placed in a small hand-held cardboard box and is later transcribed to the survey questionnaire. In this way the voter's intention can be cross-classified with other personal or

TABLE 1.1 *Survey methods used by Australian opinion polls*

	Morgan Gallup	APOP Gallup	ANOP	Herald Survey/ Age Poll
Sampling frame	Electoral roll	Census: occupied dwellings	Electoral roll	Census: occupied dwellings
Sample size (approximate)	2200	2200	1500 (marginal) electorates	2000
Respondent selection	Random selection of approximately 220 electors' addresses in all electorates; field selection of neighbouring electors to yield total cluster of 10	Random selection of 330 census collectors' districts distributed in all electorates of all states	Pre-stratified random selection of clusters of two electors' addresses in sample of 15 marginal electorates	Random selection of clusters of 7 dwellings in census collectors' districts in all electorates of all States
Collection of voting intention data	Simulated ballot box	Simulated ballot box	Face-to-face questioning using precoded questionnaire	Face-to-face questioning using precoded questionnaire

household characteristics or other information collected in the interview. In the case of ANOP and the *Herald* Survey/*Age* Poll, voting
intention questions are asked directly of the respondent and are
recorded by the interviewer on the questionnaire.

Until 1964 the Australian Gallup Poll (now Morgan Gallup) employed a quota sampling technique, but in that year a change to random
sampling was made which came into effect before the 1966 election. This
may have been prompted by the relatively poor performance of the poll
in providing predictions of the outcomes in 1961 and 1963; it may equally
have sprung from a desire to emulate the American Gallup organisation
which had adopted random sampling some years before.

Each of the polling organisations asks questions on the popularity of
the political leaders and on current political issues. The frequency with
which these and voting intention questions are asked varies from about
once every month for the Morgan and APOP Gallup Polls to very
spasmodically for ANOP and the *Herald* Survey/*Age* Poll.

Apart from published polls, each polling organisation also conducts
private unpublished political polls. For example, Morgan Gallup
provides private research for the Liberal Party and ANOP for the Labor
Party (ALP). McNair Anderson conducts election-day polls for the
Australian Broadcasting Commission, with the idea of finding out
reasons for voting behaviour. The work that has been done of an
academic nature was by Don Aitkin, Professor of Politics at the
Australian National University and reported in a book entitled *Stability
and Change in Australian Politics* (Canberra: Australian University
Press, 1977).

THE PERFORMANCE OF AUSTRALIAN POLLS

The performance of Australian political polls of voting intention has on
the whole been extremely good. This has been helped by the fact that
voting in Australia is compulsory and that usually about 92 per cent of
people on the electoral rolls turn out to vote.

Between 1946 and 1958 the Australian Gallup Poll performed
reasonably well. At each election it provided a reliable guide as to which
party would obtain a majority of the two-party preferred vote. Table 1.2
gives the details. The average error in the prediction of the final poll was
1.2 per cent, a figure which could be taken to show a high degree of
accuracy. The poll's best performance was, paradoxically, in 1954, when
it picked the 'wrong' winner.

TABLE 1.2 *The Gallup Poll performance 1946–58*

Year	Final poll 2-party preferred vote ALP (%)	Actual results 2-party preferred vote ALP (%)	Difference, final poll and actual (%)	Seats ALP/Lib–NCP
1946	55	53.9	+1.1	45/29
1949	49	48.6	+0.4	47/74
1951	47	49.2	−2.2	53/69
1954	51	50.9	+0.1	57/64
1955	46	46.2	−0.2	47/75
1958	49	45.9	+3.1	45/77

With the onset of the 1960s, unfortunately, the organisation experienced acute embarrassment. In 1961 the final Gallup Poll produced a two-party preferred vote of 47 per cent for the ALP. On polling day, however, the ALP obtained 50.5 per cent of the two-party preferred vote and for over a week the outcome of the election was unclear. The deviation between the final poll and the election, 3.5 per cent, was the biggest in the Gallup Poll's experience up to that time. In 1963 the final Gallup Poll, taken two days after the assassination of President Kennedy, showed an ALP two-party preferred vote of 51 per cent. Six days later, Sir Robert Menzies' Liberal–NCP government was comfortably returned to power with 52.6 per cent of the two-party preferred vote. On both occasions a late swing between the final poll and polling day seems to have accounted for the deviations between the figures. This was also the case in 1966, when the Gallup Poll overstated the Liberal vote by 3.1 per cent but, having demonstrably provided a correct indication of the landslide to the Holt government, the poll met with little criticism.

It was in the period leading up to the 1969 election that the increasing volatility of the Australian electorate was first clearly illustrated in the Gallup Poll. Up to June 1969 the coalition outpaced the ALP in the polls – in that month, indeed, the poll showed the Gorton Liberal – NCP government holding 57 per cent of the two-party preferred vote. By October this had been dramatically reversed in the poll, and the sample taken one week before polling day correctly depicted the slight Labor majority in the two-party preferred vote which was the final result.

The subjective impression of increased voter volatility which this dramatic movement created was reinforced by detailed study of the poll findings, which showed an increase in the proportion of 'swinging' voters between 1961 and 1969 of nearly 30 per cent – a development of obvious concern to those seeking to predict election outcomes from poll results.

The advent of the 1970s saw the phenomenon of competitive opinion polling in Australia. Yet the performance of the polls at the 1972 election could only have left observers somewhat perplexed. The Gallup Poll showed an improvement in the ALP's fortunes during the lead-up to the election, whereas the ANOP Poll and the ASRB Poll showed a decline in Labor's fortunes. Nevertheless, the last polls released by each organisation proved useful guides to the ultimate result – a victory for the ALP led by Gough Whitlam.

Up to 1974, with occasional exceptions, marked fluctuations in recorded support tended to be spread over a period of months. In the four most recent elections, however, opinion polls have recorded violent fluctuations in party support during the course of the six weeks leading up to the election – possible food for thought for those who deny that election campaigns exercise much influence on the electorate.

In 1974 the Liberal–National Country Party coalition went into the campaign with a good lead. However, Labor ran a very effective campaign, stressing that any judgement of its performance less than eighteen months after its original election was premature, an argument which the coalition was unable to counter effectively. Until the end of April the poll figures pointed to a Liberal–NCP win. Thereafter up to the election date (18 May) all polls correctly indicated a Labor win.

During 1975 the Whitlam Labor government plummeted in public esteem. With the decision of the opposition to defer consideration of the budget in the Senate, the stocks of the government appeared to rise, reflected especially in the APOP and Morgan Polls taken the weekend before the dismissal of the government on 11 November. With the dissolution of Parliament, Labor's support once again collapsed, although the party regained some of it at the end of the campaign when it concentrated on economic issues instead of seeking a sympathy vote. Table 1.3 shows final poll predictions.

During 1977 the Labor primary vote was slightly ahead of the government vote for most of the period between June and November. From this point on, support for Labor fell sharply, although all polls to varying degrees suggested a better result for Labor than was in fact achieved. This is shown in Table 1.4.

TABLE 1.3 *1975 federal election*

	APOP[a] Gallup (%)	Age (SMH)[b] Poll (%)	Morgan Gallup (%)	Actual results (%)
Liberal–NCP[c]	52	52.9	54.9	53.0
ALP[d]	42	40.0	41.0	42.8
DLP[e]	1	2.1	1.9	1.3
Aust. Party	1	2.0	0.9	0.4
Others	4	3.0	1.3	2.5

Notes: a. Australian Public Opinion Poll (McNair Anderson Assoc.)
      b. *Sydney Morning Herald*
      c. National Country Party
      d. Australian Labor Party
      e. Democratic Labor Party

TABLE 1.4 *1977 federal election*

	APOP Gallup (%)	Age (SMH) Poll (%)	Morgan Gallup (%)	ANOP (%)	Actual results (%)
Liberal–NCP	46	47.0	46	43.0	48.1
ALP	41	39.7	43	42.5	39.6
Aust. Demo- crats	10	10.8	9	11.0	9.4
Others	3	2.5	2	3.5	2.9

THE 1980 ELECTION

During the 1980 federal election campaign the political polls received more publicity and comment than at any previous election. Unfortunately for the polls, the performance of most of them was not nearly as good as in previous elections.

During the year most of the polls showed Labor ahead of the Liberal–NCP coalition on the primary vote. But a curious feature of the Australian electoral system is that Labor needed at least 51.6 per cent of the two-party preferred vote because the swing in its favour proved to be very uneven – quite high in Victoria and Western Australia and low in New South Wales and South Australia. In other words, the swing in its favour occurred in the wrong places as far as Labor was concerned. Had the swing been more uniform, Labor would have won some more marginal seats, particularly in New South Wales, and the final result would have been much closer.

Table 1.5 shows final poll predictions and the actual result. Even though Labor achieved almost as many votes as the Liberal–NCP coalition, and therefore even though it achieved almost half of the two-preferred vote, it in fact won only 52 of the 127 House of Representatives seats.

TABLE 1.5 *1980 federal election*

	APOP Gallup (%)	Age (SMH) Poll (%)	Morgan Gallup (%)	ANOP (%)	Spectrum (%)	Actual result (%)
Liberal–NCP	43	40.8	44.5	42.0	44.9	46.0
ALP	49	49.6	46.5	49.5	47.8	45.8
Aust. Democrats	7	9.0	8.5	7.5	7.3	6.5
Others	1	0.6	0.5	1.0	–	1.7

Poll figures leading up to the election showed that ALP support peaked on the weekend of 27–8 September, just before the major policy speeches. The public really became aware of this support on about 5 October, by which time there was a reaction back in favour of the government. Some people who said they might vote ALP or Democrat began to realise that the ALP might in fact win. These people were not entirely happy about the government's performance, but felt it was better on reflection to 'keep with the devil they knew rather than the devil they didn't know', and to opt for stability and the status quo rather than for radical change.

The final week of the campaign was particularly critical. The government's campaign strategy changed, with less emphasis on the leaders and on the government's past performance, and more emphasis on positive policies. The coalition also emphasised the possible introduction by a Labor government of a capital gains tax or wealth tax. None of the polls predicted the full extent of the swing back to the government between the end of September and the election date (18 October).

So was the election really a 'surprise'? Yes, in the sense that there had been wholesale misinterpretation of what the opinion polls meant. The pollsters had suggested a national swing to Labor of about 6–7%, which is roughly what happened. But this was assumed to predict a uniform national swing away from the government to Labor, whereas a good chunk of the Labor gain came from the small parties, and the polls had anyway not allowed for differences between constituencies and States. (*The Economist*, 25 October 1980)

The past four elections reinforce the view that polls should not be used indiscriminately to forecast election results. The potential of the electorate to swing right up to polling day has been clearly established by these recent results. This towers above other factors as the principal limitation of opinion polls. However, the opinion polls remain incomparably superior to all other sources of information in Australia about the mood of the electorate.

AUSTRALIAN POLLING COMPARED

Every country poses difficult problems for the pollster and (more rarely) compensations. As Australian Prime Minister Malcolm Fraser is repeatedly reminded, he once said 'Life wasn't meant to be easy'. While there are many problems facing the Australian pollster in a huge, sparsely populated country, there is one major compensation – voting is compulsory. Failure to vote at any election is punishable by a not inconsiderable fine and consequently, whatever the interest or excitement level for a particular campaign, or however dull the polemic, voters will turn out. Furthermore, to make life easier for the voter, all polling takes place on a Saturday and even the weather is in the politicians' favour, as most campaigns are fought in the Australian summer. Car ownership levels are high and even in country districts it is not too hard to get to the polling booths.

The pollster therefore has little to fear from differential abstention. In many countries, particularly the UK and the USA, this is a major cause for concern. The level of voter turn-out can vary considerably from one election to another and supporters of the various parties do not necessarily turn out to vote on a *pro rata* basis. In Australia, if the pollster can get the level of sentiment right, he is likely to make a reasonable forecast of voting behaviour, because his respondents are much more likely to go to the polls.

Although differential abstention is an irrelevance in Australia, this does not mean that compulsory voting is a total blessing to the pollster. It could be argued that it has consequences that operate to his detriment. Because voting is compulsory, the parties tend to concentrate their efforts on exhortation through the media, rather than at the grass roots. Local electoral information, in terms of leaflets, canvassing and even posters, is at a minimum. This phenomenon applies in the densely populated cities just as much as in country districts, where such activities could well be too difficult. This lower level of grass-roots activity arises because there is a less pressing need to get the faithful out to vote. As a consequence, there is considerable electoral ignorance about candidates and parties standing in particular electorates. When there are a large number of names on the ballot paper confusion can be considerable, and weakly aligned voters may be so ill-informed that they are unable to exercise the 'right' choice at the ballot box. It is well known that in elections for the Senate, where the constituency is the State, and in consequence there are a large number of names on the paper, there are considerable advantages in being drawn at the head of the list. These problems are further exacerbated by the relatively high proportion of voters, around 10 per cent, whose native tongue is not English. Once again, while their voting preferences may be clear to them in party terms, the translation of that preference into the right vote at the polling booth may not be perfect. Whether these factors are all a consequence of compulsory voting may be debatable, but they must create some degree of uncertainty as to whether a stated party preference will be frustrated by ignorance.

There is a further major problem for the Australian pollster resulting from the preferential voting system. In this system, electors have to put the list of candidates in order of preference. If there are more than two candidates standing, then the second preferences of the candidate with the least number of votes are distributed to the other candidates. The pollster therefore has to assess the likely impact of second preferences on the result.

The Australian electoral system therefore has advantages and disadvantages for the pollster. The size of the country is an added disadvantage. There are 125 electorates in Australia. Of these, 81 are mainly in the six State capital cities and Canberra, and 44 are mainly in country areas. Some of these country electorates are vast in area. To give them adequate representation in a representative sample of all electorates is a daunting task. Conventionally, cities and country districts are selected *pro rata* to the number of electors, so the thinly populated country electorates form a relatively small proportion of the total sample. However, they must be represented and the costs and communication problems of including them are considerable. Furthermore, the distance between cities is such that the transmission of interview materials and the return of results is also a sizeable problem. It is over 2500 miles from Sydney to Perth; and from Perth (the capital of Western Australia) to the Pilbara, a growing mineral resources area in the north of that State, is 1105 miles. These distances bring taxing problems in terms of obtaining a quick feedback of results or indeed a fast transmission of questions to be asked. Since many of these remote areas are insignificant in marketing terms, they would not normally be part of a market research company's target population, and while the sampled numbers are small for election surveys, they have to be covered for this purpose, in circumstances where there is little, if any, supervisory infrastructure.

The Achilles heel of the Australian pollster is therefore a late change in electoral sentiment, because it is extremely difficult to arrange for last-minute surveys on a door-to-door basis to assess the effect of 'late change'. Most of the polling organisations use the telephone to call back on voters interviewed in earlier surveys, in order to assess any changes in sentiments. However, the telephone, even with an average home penetration of around 75 per cent, represents a less than satisfactory sampling method, especially if that late change is related to deeply socially divisive issues. With the recent unemployment problems and dissatisfaction resulting from the growing divide between rich and poor, this could become a greater problem in the future than it has been in the past.

One further factor differentiating political polling in Australia and the UK is the public's attitude to being interviewed about politics. In the UK and Australia the respective market research societies have examined public opinion on different types of research. Table 1.6 summarises the types of research which UK and Australian respondents like most and like least.

While the general pattern of response in the two countries is not dissimilar, it is worth noting that 24 per cent of Australians nominate political polls as the least liked form of research compared with 11 per

TABLE 1.6 *Public attitudes to opinion research*

	Australia		United Kingdom	
	Like best (%)	Like least (%)	Like best (%)	Like least (%)
Being interviewed at home	45	8	46	3
Being interviewed in the street	8	35	6	28
Being interviewed on the phone	7	37	1	41
Trying new products at home	34	4	21	1
Political opinion polls	8	24	1	11

cent of British people. Why Australians should dislike political polls more than British people do is not clear, but the response to the question has obvious implications for refusal rates in political surveys.

THE FUTURE

Opinion polls received greater attention at the 1980 federal elections than ever before. A large number of polls were published, were highlighted in the media and were frequently referred to by the politicians.

The high level of exposure was due to two main factors. In the first place the polls, especially those early in the campaign, pointed to the possibility of Labor cutting back an apparently unassailable Liberal majority to the point of a Labor victory. Whilst Labor had been narrowly in the lead in the polls for some time, general expectations were that this would be dramatically cut back as the campaign developed. The expected revival in Liberal support did not take place and the possibility of a Labor victory ensured added attention to each published poll. In the second place, the Liberal campaign based on 'the government's record' lacked sparkle. The debate between the two parties was less than stimulating and the press therefore found the polls of more interest.

This increased exposure for the opinion polls is likely to be a continuing feature of Australian elections. It could be argued that the attention given to the polls in Australia has, in the past, been rather less than elsewhere, notably the USA and the UK. In the 1970s, polls achieved more prominence in the UK than ever before and the level of media and public interest in the polls appears to be a continuing feature of British elections. This pattern seems likely to be repeated in Australia and the pollsters must expect and be prepared for a greater spotlight of publicity to be focused on them at election times in the future. This means that they should agree on a code of conduct and prepare themselves for public exposure.

It could be argued that media exposure of the polls might be inhibited in future because of the currently expressed view of the media and the politicians that the polls got the 1980 election 'wrong'. That the polls were all left of target is unarguable but the probability is that even if the experts had been presented with the actual national voting figures before seeing the constituency results they would have forecast a very small Liberal–NCP majority in the House of Representatives instead of the 23-seat majority that occurred. However, UK experience since 1970 suggests that the possibility of polls being wrong enhances media exposure rather than the opposite.

Not surprisingly, the prominence of the polls in 1980 led to the resurgence of the 'ban the polls' lobby and the call for a prohibition on the publication of polls for some or all of the campaign period. This issue is of course not new to anyone involved in opinion polling and generally it appears to be accepted that banning the publication of 'objective' polls with a reputation for reliability would lead to greater evils than their publication – evils in the form of leaked private polls commissioned by the parties, rumours of poll results and the like. It seems unlikely that the move to ban polls will gather strength in Australia but it is possible that, in a country where there is already a complete blackout on political news on radio and television in the forty-eight hours before an election, a movement to ban the publication of opinion polls could gain ground.

The debate on whether polls should be banned is of course related to the question of whether polls influence voters. We would continue to argue that the case is unproven and that if there is an influence it is unpredictable. The argument in favour of banning polls could only really have force if it could be shown that polls can be used to produce a particular influence on voters. Robert Worcester has recently argued that polls can influence behaviour and it seems likely that the abundance of polls showing that the ALP had a chance of winning the 1980 Australian federal election influenced some voters to change allegiance. Apparently the 'protest' voters returned to the Liberal fold when they saw the risk of returning an ALP government.

In terms of methodology the most likely consequence of the 1980 election is to make the opinion pollsters look harder at how to carry out meaningful polls immediately before election day. This may mean greater emphasis on telephone interviewing, possibly with panels of electors who might be recruited to minimise bias and who could on a longitudinal basis indicate trends.

Little work seems to have been done on the conditioning effect of empanelling respondents, the main question being 'Are respondents reluctant to change their expressed voting intention once they have made a statement about it to an interviewer?'.

If personal interviewing is to play a part in last-minute polls, a considerable effort will have to be made to ensure a faster transmission of results from the field. The use of telephone or facsimile machines to transmit interviewers' results to base may well be essential here. If the micro-chip makes possible the provision of hand-held recorders for interviewers to register their results on an interview-by-interview basis it will undoubtedly solve many of these problems.

Given the patchy nature of the swing in the 1980 Australian election, more attention may have to be paid in future to marginal electorates. Historically, polls in marginal electorates have not been a great success. They have generally been a worse predictor of election results than national surveys. Why this should be so is not clear. If there is considerable variation in swing between marginal electorates, then clearly the selection of marginals for sampling could in itself lead to considerable bias in the results. The other problem is that being marginal is itself a variable and difficult to predict from one election to the next. It seems likely, therefore, that to be successful relatively large samples might be needed in each marginal electorate sampled and the cost might prove prohibitive.

Change in opinion polling methods has generally been slow and only minor changes in methods seem likely in Australia in the foreseeable future.

REFERENCES

Beed, Terence W., Goot, Murray, Hodgson, Stephen, and Ridley, Peggy, *Australian Opinion Polls 1941–1977* (Sydney: Hale & Iremonger University of Sydney Sample Survey Centre, 1978).
Goot, Murray, 'Part Science and a Hell of a Lot of Human Judgement', reprinted in SSC newsletter, 1982.
Mackerras, M., *Elections 1980* (Sydney: Angus & Robertson, 1980), particularly Part X by Bill Maley, 'The opinion polls'.
McNair, I. W., 'Three years of Labor – some reasons why Labor was elected and defeated', *Australian Quarterly*, September 1977.
Teer, F., and Spence, J., *Political Opinion Polls* (London: Hutchinson, 1972).

2 Political Opinion Polling in France

JEAN STOETZEL

Political polling in France today is more than an institution; it is a kind of fact of nature. It is something the French expect to find when they look out into the world, just as when you and I walk out into the street we expect to step upon a pavement.

What the French expect from political polling is, on the evening of election day, at 8 p.m. exactly when the last polling station closes, to be told on radio and television the name of the winning party or candidate and, correct to the first decimal place, the percentage distribution of the votes cast.

Until 1977, when a law was passed banning the publication of political poll results during the week preceding an election, the French expected to be given a quantitative preview of the winning side up to the last day, sometimes with astonishing accuracy. Between elections they are used to finding in their newpapers, both graphically and numerically, the ups and downs of the voting intentions of their fellow citizens, the popularity of the main leaders, and the positions on the issues of the day taken by the public as a whole and in their subdivisions. Opinion is news; everybody expects to have toll-free access to this news, as if that access were an additional article to the Bill of Rights.

THE PRESENT-DAY SITUATION

The younger generation may find it hard to believe that this situation is the outcome of a long-fought battle against indifference, incredulity and irate opposition, but before turning to the pioneering years, I shall first describe the present-day situation.

An election for the President of France took place in April–May 1981. The French were informed, at the moment the last vote was cast, of the outcome of the election, thanks to the work of the Société Française de Recherches et d'Etudes par Sondages (SOFRES), a polling agency, and Honeywell-Bull, a computer agency. At the same time the Institut Français d'Opinion Publique (IFOP) was conveying its own estimation to a private but large audience.

Before the election IFOP, SOFRES, Publimétrie, Démoscopie, Public SA, Louis Harris-France and one or two other agencies released through various mass media their findings on the preferences of the voters for the likely, and later actual, candidates. Some agencies had done so as early as 1978.

In *France-Soir* and *Le Point*, and in *Figaro* and *Figaro-Magazine*, tables are published periodically on the popularity of prominent political figures. More work commissioned by clients for more or less private use is or will be carried out by the same agencies and by others such as Cofremca, BVA and Novaction.

The National Political Science Foundation, operating through its Centre d'Etudes de la Vie Politique Française Contemporaine under the directorship of Professor Alain Lancelot since 1962, has been active as one of the sponsors of surveys, as well as performing political sampling surveys of its own. Its sixteen publications which have appeared so far, either as books or as papers for learned journals or congresses, are worthy contributions to the understanding of many phases of French political opinion. It is hoped that Professor Lancelot's work will continue.

Some of the above-mentioned polling organisations are relatively new in the field, though this does not mean that they lack experience. Such is the case with Louis Harris-France, which was registered in 1977 jointly by Louis Harris-International and SOFRES (the latter with a minority share). In fact the managing director is Pierre Weill, the president of SOFRES.

Louis Harris-France is independently engaged in practically the same activities as SOFRES, except that it does not study the variations in popularity of politicians. It surveyed the general elections in 1978 and 1981; its findings are released through the daily newspaper *Le Matin* and two weeklies, *L'Express* and *Télérama*.

The first political publications of the Institut Français de Démoscopie (director Yves Rickebusch) appeared in late 1976. The company was officially founded in 1977 by Cofremca (described below). Démoscopie's occasional publications on voting intentions and images of political personalities appear in the daily *Quotidien de Paris* and various magazines.

Three more agencies were founded during the same decade: Novaction (1971), BVA (1970) and Publimétrie (1970). Novaction (directors Jean Bounine and Jean-Mathieu Paoli) polled for private clients during the presidential election of 1974 and the general elections of 1973 and 1978. An interesting article by J.-M. Paoli can be found in *European Research*, vol. 7, July 1979, under the title 'Designing social organisations for the people such as they are'.

Michel Brulé and Jean-Pierre Ville (BVA Associates), who had previously worked for IFOP for about ten years, took part in studies of the 1981 presidential contest.

Publimétrie (director Roland Muraz) is the third best-known French polling institute (12 per cent, after IFOP's 66 per cent and SOFRES' 54 per cent, in November 1978). It has studied voting intentions since 1972, and has a good record of pre-election surveys. Its work is mostly published in the daily newspaper *L'Aurore*.

Cofremca, founded as the Bureau de Psychologie et de Sociologie Appliquées and later renamed Cofremca, under the leadership of its president Alain de Vulpain and other psychologists, entered the field of political studies in 1954. Since 1955, although it does not refuse to undertake quantitative work, the bulk of its research has been of a qualitative nature; its studies are mostly confidential. For this reason it is little known to the general public.

SOFRES is recognised as one of the major French polling agencies. Founded in 1962 by D. Lindon, as a subsidiary of SEMA (Societé d'Etudes de Mathématiques Appliquées under the sponsorship of the Banque de Paris et des Pays-Bas), the company entered the political field in 1965 under the directorship of Pierre Weill and at once became the main competitor of IFOP.

Since the presidential election of 1965 SOFRES has been active, with undeniable success and authority, in all elections – presidential, general and local. In the questionnaire for this chapter which was sent to all the above-mentioned organisations, SOFRES answered 'yes' to every item: it engages in political polling both for publication and confidentially for clients; it performs pre-electoral studies at the local level as well as at the national level; it occasionally assesses the popularity of political figures.

SOFRES' results on political popularity are a regular feature of *Figaro* and *Figaro-Magazine*, and other findings are disclosed also in the provincial daily press and in the weekly *Nouvel Observateur*. Besides these publications for the general public, scientific discussions on methodology and substantial problems in political matters are found in books and journal articles by such authors as D. Lindon, P. Weill, A. Lancelot and J. Jaffré. In addition in 1977 SOFRES published a yearbook, *L'Opinion française en 1977* (edited by J. Jaffré).

Last on the list, but certainly not least, comes IFOP. Everything that has been said of SOFRES also applies to IFOP. IFOP was founded and registered as a company in 1938 and has been functioning now for over forty years. Since early 1979 there have been major changes in the company: the resignation of its president who led the development of the company for more than twenty years and the loss of a good third of the technical staff through dismissal or voluntary resignation.

THE BEGINNINGS OF FRENCH POLITICAL POLLING

As the first polling company to be established on the Continent of Europe, IFOP not only broke new ground, but set the framework for all following research. Although some rather primitive market research existed in France in the early 1930s, it is now hard to believe that when I came back in May 1938 from a one-year stay at Columbia University as a teacher, and started experimenting with sample surveys, no one else in France seemed to be aware of what had attracted America's attention to the pre-election pollings of 1936. A French word had to be coined to convey the meaning and nature of this unprecedented operation; it was necessary to have recourse to a metaphor: *sondage*, a 'sounding'.

It is not easy to set the birth date of political polling in France. Some say that IFOP was born several times: in July 1938 when the first political survey was successfully attempted, or possibly in November when IFOP was incorporated as a company. It could also be set at the date of the first issue of *Sondages* in June 1939 (there have been 218 to date), published on behalf of the Association des Amis de l'Institut Français d'Opinion Publique, a voluntary association of which the original officers were Henri Paoletti, Pierre Borie, Louis de Chauvigny, Pierre Laroque, Didier Lazard and Pierre Lelong. They were the first to believe in the scientific validity of the method, in the feasibility of the operation and in the public usefulness of the findings. To that list one must add at least the names of Pierre Denoyers, a prominent journalist who published early in the spring of 1939 in *Le Petit Parisien* the first record of the popularity curves of the political personalities of the day,

and Yves Chataigneau, head of the Prime Minister's office, who did not
fail to notice that if the majority of the French were 'ready to die for
Danzig', the younger age-groups were less inclined to do so, a bad omen
in view of the coming war.

After the apparent slumber of the Occupation years, a new birth of
IFOP, perhaps better termed a reawakening, or even a coming of age,
occurred in the late summer of 1944 when an Anglo-American task-
force from SHAEF arrived in Paris to discover in the daily *Libération*
the report of the first opinion survey carried out among the liberated
Paris population. It showed that 72 per cent of the Parisians wanted the
re-election of President Roosevelt, that 61 per cent thought that the
USSR had contributed the most to German defeat, but that 69 per cent
expected the USA to contribute most to France's recovery. The divided,
possibly contradictory, international feelings of the French were evident
at the time; they were to make France, as Hadley Cantril later called it,
'the Difficult Ally'. An unexpected outcome of this released report was
that Colonel Elmo C. Wilson and Majors Jerome S. Bruner and Pierre
M. Turquet became the first clients of IFOP.

Almost exactly a year later, in October 1945, IFOP predicted that the
'yes' answers to the two questions of the referendum of 21 October
would be respectively 93 per cent and 67 per cent. The actual figures were
96 per cent and 66 per cent. In a country which had been disorganised by
the war, in which the demographic structure had been deeply modified,
and of which public sentiments were a completely unknown quantity, it
was a brilliant feat. It was also the final proof that the French were not at
variance with the Americans and could readily accept being asked
political questions and answer them sincerely, a much-debated point
since 1938. As a matter of fact, General de Gaulle, the head of the
government of the time, was so impressed that he offered IFOP either
official status or a state subsidy (an offer which was politely turned down
to protect IFOP's independence).

During the next twenty years IFOP carried on independently, testing
new methods, pioneering new operations, monitoring trends of opinions
and of politicians' popularity, publishing pre-electoral data, and so on.
Then came the first round of the presidential election of December 1965.
(The non-French reader should be reminded of the rather unusual two-
round French electoral system in operation since 1958. The system is
designed to winnow out fringe candidates in the first-round vote, so that
only larger parties survive for the second round. In the case of a
presidential election, a minimum of one vote in excess of 50 per cent of
the votes cast is necessary to nominate the winner.) Now, would Charles

de Gaulle, who was running for President against a number of competing candidates, be elected in the first round?

Until that particular day, 5 December 1965, election night used to be for many French citizens a somewhat festive occasion. After the closing of the polling booths at 8 p.m., results of the local vote would be parsimoniously released – the bad results being withheld as long as possible – by the Ministry of the Interior. The consolidated results and the name of the winner would not be known until the next morning. People would gather at friends' homes, and comment upon the partial results, discussing them and betting on them till the small hours.

During the eleven previous weeks IFOP had published the results of six successive electoral surveys. They showed a decrease in the intentions to vote for General de Gaulle: from 68 per cent in late September to 43 per cent in the first days of December. However, no one had paid much attention to these public opinion polls. After all, during the seven years of Charles de Gaulle's presidency his popularity had consistently (except in the middle months of 1963) exceeded the 50 per cent mark, with an average of some 60 per cent.

At 9.30 p.m. on election day, after careful checking and rechecking of its calculations, IFOP announced over the radio that candidate de Gaulle would not get more than 48 per cent of the vote, and that there would be a second round to the election; surprise mixed with incredulity and indignation seized the listening populace.

At 10.50 p.m., cautiously taking into account the confidence limits involved, IFOP made a final announcement: de Gaulle would get between 43 and 45 per cent of the vote. The next day the official figure was 43.97 per cent. This performance turned the tables in favour of IFOP and generally of all political polling; it has been suggested that 5 December 1965 was the true birthday of IFOP.

THE RECORD OF ACCURACY

The pre-election polling of seven referendums and six general elections by IFOP during those twenty years of solitary performance had shown a fairly fine record of accuracy. However it was during the early part of that period, in May 1946, that IFOP made its only bad mistake. On the occasion of the second referendum of the Fourth Republic IFOP had found a majority of 54 per cent approving the new constitution. The actual vote was in the other direction, with only 47 per cent replying 'yes'. Very likely a change had occurred during the last few days; the polling had been stopped too early. A similar situation pertained in the British general election of 1970, as evidenced by late reinterviewings made by ORC. The lesson was not forgotten by IFOP. The record for the seven referendums appears in Table 2.1.

TABLE 2.1 *Referendums prior to 1965*

Date of vote		Final IFOP survey (%)	Actual result (%)
21 Oct. 1945:	1st question	93	96
	2nd question	67	66
5 May 1946		54	47
13 Oct. 1946		53	53
28 Sept. 1958		78	79
8 Jan. 1961		73	75
8 Apr. 1962		91	91
28 Oct. 1962		61	62

On general elections, only four publications are available. Since 1951 IFOP had concentrated on experimenting with new sampling methods, assessing voting intention changes, comparing differences in opinion demographically and linking political preferences with stands taken on current issues. The available records are shown in Table 2.2 in compact form.

TABLE 2.2 *General elections up to 1965*

Date of vote	Party	Final survey (%)	Actual results (%)	Particulars in Sondages
2 June 1946	Left	61	59	1949 p. 139
	Right	39	42	
10 Nov. 1946	Left	60	56	1951 (1) p. 45
	Right	40	44	
17 June 1951	Communists	32	33	1952 (2) p. 45
(Paris only)	Gaullists	24	27	
	Others	44	40	
2 Jan. 1956	No data			1955 (4) p. 5 sq.
23–30 Nov. 1958	No data			1960 (4) p. 12
18 Nov. 1962	Left	37	39	1963 (2) p. 110
	Centre	44	47	
	Right	19	14	

From 1965 on, first SOFRES, then other agencies joined IFOP in political polling. The available data on pre-electoral polling are summarised in Table 2.3.

SPECIAL FEATURES OF THE FRENCH STUDIES

Pre-election sample surveys, the findings of which are often mistakenly called forecasts, are now performed in many countries equipped with polling organisations. Less common are two rather different kinds of operation which are found in France. The first of these is that operation which on the evening of 5 December 1965 called the attention of the French to political polling. But it was not a poll as such, since nobody was interviewed. In the professionals' jargon, it was an 'estimation'.

An estimation operation is based on the fact that the polling stations do not all close at the same time – at 6 p.m. in the French villages, at 7 p.m. in the towns and at 8 p.m. in the cities – so that partial results are available in succession from these various sources. The estimation of the total is worked out in two stages. Well ahead of time, a baseline is established from the political records of a sample of polling stations, combined with the findings of the latest pre-electoral surveys. Then, on the evening of election day, this hypothetical estimation is gradually adjusted as the actual votes in the sampled polling stations come in over the telephone as soon as they are counted locally.

The number of polling stations in the sample has varied over the years from 300 to some 600. Originally the expected results, that is, the estimation was expressed in terms of confidence interval estimates based on three standard deviations, popularly known in France as the *fourchette*. After nine successful operations IFOP decided in 1972 to give straight figures and suppress the *fourchette*. In the second round of the presidential election of 19 May 1974, which was an extremely close contest, at 8 p.m. an estimated percentage of 50.63 per cent of the vote in favour of Valéry Giscard d'Estaing was announced by IFOP. The official percentage published the next day was 50.66.

Between 1965 and 1978 IFOP carried out sixteen estimation operations, all successfully. SOFRES joined in at the second round of the 1965 presidential election, and Honeywell-Bull at a later date. No electoral study based on probability laws is ever entirely safe, as was borne out by the estimation operations of the 1978 general election when IFOP was the only one to come out right. Still, estimating the share of votes on the evening of an election day is a much easier task than trying

Table 2.3 Pre-electoral poll findings and actual election results 1965–78

Date	Nature of election	Candidates, parties, or issues	Actual results (%)	IFOP: date findings		SOFRES: date findings		Publimétrie: date findings	Louis Harris: date findings
5 Dec. 1965	Presidential, 1st round	De Gaulle Mitterrand Lecanuet	43.97 32.04 15.78	2 Dec.	43 27 20				
19 Dec. 1965	Presidential, 2nd round	De Gaulle	54.49	16 Dec.	55				
5 Mar. 1967	General, 1st round	Left Centre Vth Rep.	43.51 12.79 37.15	2 Mar.	41 14 38	?	47 14 17		
23 June 1968	General, 1st round	Left Government	41.20 58.26	19 June	43 57				
27 Apr. 1969	Referendum	Yes	46.82	26 Apr.	46.5	24 Apr.	47		
1 June 1969	Presidential, 1st round	Pompidou Poher	43.95 23.42	29 May	41 25	?			
15 June 1969	Presidential, 2nd round	Pompidou	57.58	12 June	58	?			

23 Apr. 1972 Referendum

		20 Apr. 72	18 Apr. 74
Yes	67.70		

4 Mar. 1973 General, 1st round

		27 Feb.	24 Feb	23 Feb.
Communists	21.3	19	20	20
Soc. and allies	21.7	23	21	21
Government	36.7	36	37	37

5 May 1974 Presidential, 1st round

		2 May	30 Apr.	1 May
Mitterrand	43.35	45	44	43
Giscard	32.92	30	31	30
Chaban	14.55	15	17	17

12 May 1974 Presidential, 2nd round

		13 May	14 May	15 May
Mitterrand	49.33	50	50	49
Giscard	50.66	50	50	51

12 Mar. 1978 General, 1st round

		10 Mar.	28 Feb.	25 Feb	27 Feb.
United Left	48.4	51	49	48	49
Government	48.4	45.5	45	47	45
Ecologists	2.1	2.4	4	3	3
Others	1.1	1.1	2	2	3

to assess the number of seats won. This second distinctively French operation, called 'simulation', so far appears as a reckless venture.

Since a large number of seats are decided only in the second round of the election, it would seem that the eventual outcome rests on the way the votes cast in the first round are transferred in the second round, due to the winnowing out of several candidates present in the first round, according to the rules of the election process as explained above. This depends on the choice of candidates surviving to the second round, on the new grouping of parties, on the local tactics of the coalitions, and on the private strategies of the individual voters. This tightrope-walking operation was experimented with in the general election of 1967 and carried out with dubious success. Once more the polling agencies, towards which the press is always ambivalent, were apt to be made a laughing-stock by the newspapermen.

The techniques of IFOP and SOFRES, based on different rationales, are described and discussed in a paper by Bon and Michelat. Table 2.4 presents an example, condensed from published data.

TABLE 2.4 *Forecasts of seats in the French National Assembly after the 5–12 March 1967 general election (IFOP)*

Parties	4 March before first round	10 March after first round	12 March 11 p.m. election night	Actual results
Vth Republic	255–275	255–280	238–247	244
Leftist federation	95–110	95–110	115–119	116
Communist	40–55	55–58	73–77	74
Centre	40–55	29–40	37–40	38
PSU (Unified Soc.)		2–4	2–3	4
Others		12–16	10–11	10

BASIC SCIENTIFIC RESEARCH

Concluding their analysis of the simulations of seats worked out by IFOP and SOFRES in 1967, Bon and Michelat comment: 'It seems that their results would have been better if, instead of restricting their work to observing the effects of alleged laws, they had tried to analyse those laws.'

Blind empiricism is rarely successful when making predictions. Pollsters are well aware of the apodeictic nature of the laws of probability. They may be less sensitive to the existence of psycho-sociological laws in the field of political behaviour. The works of the late Paul F. Lazarsfeld should be remembered in this connection. In his political research he always was on the look-out for constructs, indicators, models, laws. As early as 1944 Lazarsfeld pointed out that a campaign may have five different effects on the public, the most important of which by a long way is reinforcement. It may very well be that de Gaulle lacked this effect during the first round of the 1965 election, when he had decided not to campaign at all.

In the same book Lazarsfeld submitted a hypothetical model of his Index of Political Predisposition (predisposition to vote Democrat). He was delighted to find confirmation of his model in the French election of 1965. It is interesting to compare the three sets of figures in Table 2.5.

TABLE 2.5 *Lazarsfeld's Model: France 1965*

(A)

	Protestant		Catholic	
	Rural	*Urban*	*Rural*	*Urban*
A, B	1	2	3	4
C+	2	3	4	5
C−	3	4	5	6
D	4	5	6	7

(B)

27	36	45	54
36	45	54	63
45	54	63	72
54	63	72	81

(C)

	Men		Women	
	Blue or white collars	*Others*	*Blue or white collars*	*Others*
1	25	36	46	54
2	44	50	52	68
3	46	56	62	71
4	50	69	64	79

The first (A) is found in *The People's Choice*, p. 174. The second (B) is derived from the first by a simple transformation:

$$X = (L+2) \times 9$$

where L stands for Lazarsfeld's figure, and X for the corresponding figure in the second part of the table. The third set of figures, (C), are attributable to chance by a probability exceeding 99 per cent, and they suggest an excellent fit of the above simple model.

Between 1938 and 1978 IFOP systematically invested in basic research. The transfer matrix used in the simulation of 1967 was no novelty for IFOP. The first published transfer matrix dated back to 1951. Popularity curves were studied as early as 1938–9. Popularity trends of Presidents and Prime Ministers have been a well-known feature of IFOP's political polling since 1947 (and were later to become a regular part of SOFRES's published work as well).

A number of general statements about political behaviour have been discovered, such as the fact that the level of religious affiliation and practice is the best single predictive factor; that the number of the changers tend to compensate each other, so that an apparent stability may often hide an actual mobility of attitudes, as was mathematically demonstrated by Lazarsfeld in a footnote in *Voting*. This last fact may well be related to personal influences, as Lazarsfeld thought. But it is also a fact that the politically active are found more often on the radical side than on the conservative side of the political scale; and that the distribution on that scale tends to be of a Gaussian nature when people are asked to position themselves upon it.

Still, the vast field of public opinion and political behaviour remains, if not totally virgin soil, at least mostly unexplored ground. More basic research in France and elsewhere is badly needed for further progress in political opinion research.

THE 1981 ELECTIONS AND THE PRESS

In the spring of 1981 eventful elections brought about major political and possibly everyday life changes in France. A Socialist was called to live in the presidential mansion on rue du Faubourg Saint-Honoré, a Socialist majority of Representatives was sent to the House, and eventually four Communists were appointed by the new President as ministers to sit in the Cabinet.

To many, these events came as a total surprise. Similarly François Mitterrand, the new President of the Republic, said the French were enjoying a honeymoon period (*l'état de grâce*). Actually what was going to happen could have been read in the poll results at least six months ahead of time, if the French public, political circles and media personnel had not been blind. But, as Raymond Aron said in his doctoral dissertation, referring to the philosophy of history: it is not the past which explains the present, it is the present which gives the past its meaning.

This section endeavours to outline briefly what actually happened, what were the performances of the polling agencies, how everybody could have been misled by the previous poll results and, fourthly, how these poll results were a sure basis for forecasting a Socialist victory in the spring of 1981.

Recalling the facts

According to the constitution of the Fifth Republic, the President is elected for seven years, the House (Assemblée Nationale) for five years. Valéry Giscard d'Estaing having been elected on 12 May 1974, a presidential election was automatically scheduled for the spring of 1981. On the other hand the House had been elected in March 1978. Consequently the term of the Assembly men would normally expire in 1983. However, the right of the President is to repeal the Assembly if he so wishes, and this is precisely what Mitterrand did as soon as he came into office.

The first round of the presidential election took place on April 26. At the end of 1980 a large number of people expressed their intention of running for the presidency. But since each of them had to find 500 sponsors, only ten eventually ran.

For the sake of brevity I shall omit the six candidates who received less than 4 per cent of the vote. The four who came out top are shown (in rounded figures) in Table 2.6 (a). The second round results (on 10 May) are shown in Table 2.6 (b). Then came the general (Assembly) elections on 14 and 21 June. The simplified list of runners is shown in Table 2.6 (c). The final result in the number of seats on 21 June is shown in Table 2.6 (d). Mitterrand got his majority of supporters in the House.

TABLE 2.6(a) *Presidential election 1981 first round (%)*

Giscard	28
Mitterrand	26
Chirac	18
Marchais	15

TABLE 2.6(b) *Second round (%)*

Mitterrand	52
Giscard	48

TABLE 2.6(c) *General election 1981, first round (%)*

	First round	Second round
Communists	16	7
Socialists and Radicals	38	49
Total left	**56**	**57**
Giscardians	21	22
Chiraqnians	19	18
Total right	**43**	**43**
Ecologists	1	0

TABLE 2.6(d) *Second Round*

Communists	44
Socialists and Radicals	283
Giscardians	81
Chiraquians	83
Others: Left	6
Right	11

The performances of the polls

It is only fair to say that the polls did a very good job. Tables 2.7 and 2.8 show last published findings. It should be pointed out that, as was noted earlier, the law forbids publication of poll results during the week before election day.

It is everybody's privilege to comment upon the accuracy of those results and upon the validity of the techniques developed by the French polling agencies. However, let me add this. Especially important in a two-round electoral system is the estimation at an early date of the transfer of the votes cast in the first round to the candidates remaining in the second. As early as 18 April, that is, eight days before the first round of the presidential election, IFOP was able to publish the vote transfers shown in Table 2.9. It was on the basis of this transfer matrix that IFOP was able to publish at that early date the figures quoted above in

TABLE 2.7(a) *Presidential election 1981, first round (%)*

	Last published survey				Actual
	Public SA 26 Mar.	Louis Harris 13 Apr.	IFOP 14 Apr.	SOFRES 16 Apr.	vote 26 Apr.
Giscard	30	28.5	27.5	27.5	28
Mitterrand	24.5	24	23.5	22	26
Chirac	13	17	17	19.5	18
Marchais	16	17	17	18.5	15

TABLE 2.7(b) *Second round (%)*

	SOFRES 17 Apr.	IFOP 18 Apr.	Actual vote 10 May
Mitterrand	51.7	51.5	52
Giscard	48.3	48.5	48

TABLE 2.8(a) *General election 1981, first round (%)*

	Last published survey			Actual vote
	Harris 30 May	IFOP 2 Jun.	SOFRES 4 Jun.	14 Jun.
Communists	17	14	17.5	16
Socialists	34.5	35.5	33	38
Total left	**54**	**52.5**	**52.5**	**56**
Giscardians	18	21.5	20.5	19
Chiraquians	23	18	22	21
Total right	**44**	**43.5**	**44.5**	**43**
Ecologists	2	4	2	1

TABLE 2.8(b) *Second round*

	Estimation of seats on 15 June			Actual results
	SOFRES	Louis Harris	IFOP	21 June
Communists	34–45	30–35	40–45	44
Socialists and Radicals	260–320	260–330	280–290	283
Giscardians	54–74	50–80	55–60	81
Chiraquians	68–86	60–90	80–90	83

TABLE 2.9. Presidential election 1981, vote transfers

	Giscard	Chirac	Mitterrand	Marchais	Other right	Other left	Ecologists
Will vote in the second round for:							
Giscard	98	62	1	5	55	17	18
Mitterrand	1	23	98	73	23	75	50
N A	1	15	1	22	22	8	32

Table 2.9, showing that Giscard and Mitterrand would be the contenders in the second round.

Were the polls misleading?

The French election outcome was a total surprise in France and abroad.
Still, there had been a wide diffusion of the poll results. On Sunday 31
May I happened to be in Vancouver, BC. In the local paper, the
Province, I could read a column on French voting intentions to be
published the next day in *Le Point*. Were the polls so misleading? Let us
carefully review the possible public interpretations of some of the pre-
electoral publications.

Before the campaign officially started, on 16 February 1981, *Le Point*
published an IFOP survey on the dislikes scores for the main likely
candidates (fieldwork 3–7 Feb.). Giscard comes lowest (Table 2.10; my
computation).

TABLE 2.10 *Dislike scores (%)*

Giscard	11.5
Mitterrand	19
Chirac	45
Marchais	48

Between 23 and 29 February SOFRES asked ten questions concerning the performance of Giscard during his seven-year mandate. The
topics included preservation of the authority of the state, the upkeep of
public lifestyles, fighting racism and fighting violence. On the whole, 65
per cent of the public were able to find at least one good point in
Giscard's policy. Even 56 per cent of the Communists were able to
mention one good point. These findings were published by *Le Figaro* on
4 March. Translated into a liking score index the findings closely
approximate the votes in the first round presidential election (Table
2.11).

TABLE 2.11. *Liking score index and actual votes*

	Index (%)	Actual vote (%)
Giscard	27.8	28
Mitterrand	25.2	26
Chirac	17.5	18
Marchais	16.5	15

During the campaign SOFRES investigated (10–13 April, publication 19 April in *Le Figaro*) attitudes on various topics discussed by the main candidates. On a majority of items, Giscard's actions were commended. After the contest between Giscard and Mitterrand on television, the balance between the good and bad points in their appearances was strongly in favour of Giscard (Table 2.12). Twenty-three per cent said they would like to have Giscard for a friend; only 14 per cent mentioned Mitterrand. However, Mitterrand was considered to have greater psychological qualities by 29 per cent of respondents (Giscard 24.5 per cent) and 35 per cent said Mitterrand would be a more able president (Giscard 33 per cent) (IFOP survey 14–21 April, published by *Le Point* 27 April).

TABLE 2.12 *IFOP survey after television contest*

	Averages	
	Good points (%)	Bad points (%)
Giscard	38	38
Mitterrand	33	41

Between the first and the second round, on 23 April, SOFRES surveyed the images of the contestants (results published in *Figaro-Magazine* on 30 April; see Table 2.13). Once more Giscard came higher on three consolidated counts: psychological, such as likeable, trustworthy, faithful to his word; domestic policy (will keep political stability, etc.); foreign policy (independence *vis-à-vis* USA and USSR). In the headlines the press usually favoured Giscard, even when reporting adverse findings. To quote only a few from *Le Figaro*: 'Slow recovery' (7 March); 'Fewer pessimists' (4 April); 'Opinion mobilised: Giscard + 3, Barre + 3' (*Figaro-Magazine*, 4 April). Accordingly, until the last few days before the first round of the presidential election, the majority of the voters were expecting a Giscard victory.

TABLE 2.13 *Positive features (%)*

Positive scores favouring:	Psychology	Domestic	Foreign
Giscard	54.4	40.25	54.00
Mitterrand	47.8	33.50	22.25

The polls were predictive

It is easy now, when we know the outcome, to see how much the polls were predictive, and how much the perceptions of the public were selective or, to be more specific, pinpointed in time. It seems that they entirely neglected the trends. And yet the trends were repeatedly published by the media.

Take, for instance, the trend on expectations (see Figure 2.1). It starts in December 1980 at 70 per cent for Giscard and 10.5 per cent for Mitterrand, to reach on 11 April the point mentioned above. Taken independently from the trend, the April expectation figures establish

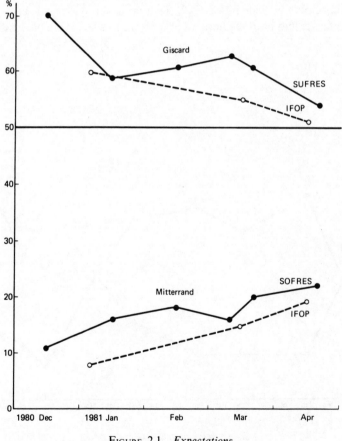

FIGURE 2.1 *Expectations*

that at that late date many more were still expecting Giscard to win in the presidential election. This is the first of my two points: the majority of the public who voted, who were about to turn away from Giscard, were unaware of the consequence of their own votes.

My second point is also sustained. Had the public considered the four-month trend, it would have become crystal clear that confidence in a Giscard victory had declined since December, by some 20 per cent. More available trends pointed to the same conclusion. Consider Figure 2.2, which is redrafted from *Le Point* (no. 448, p. 44, 18 April) – this chart, brought up to date, was dropped in a number of earlier issues. The question framed by IFOP was: 'If you had today to estimate the net balance of Giscard's action as President since 1974, would you say that this balance is on the whole positive or negative?' The trend lines show a turning-point in September 1980. They also show that the negative judgements had been regularly exceeding the positive since November.

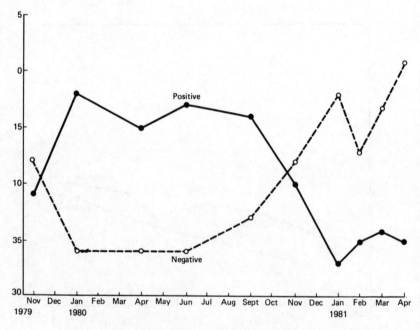

FIGURE 2.2   *The balance of Giscard's action*

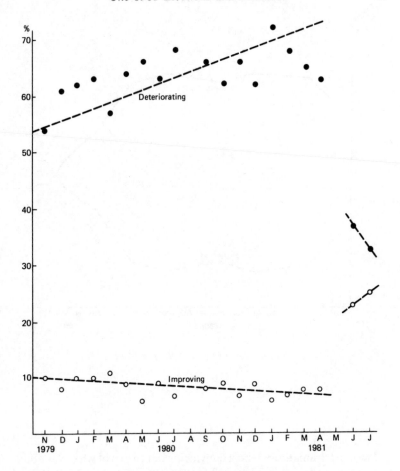

FIGURE 2.3 *The perceived situation is...*

Figure 2.3, described by *Le Figaro* as 'a chart of optimism–pessimism' shows, like Figure 2.1, but for a longer period, a growing discontent (from SOFRES data). Agreed there are in the trend, month after month, many ups and downs. But the linear model, which I computed by the least squares method, leaves no doubt about the direction of the trend.

Figure 2.4 (Penniman) is especially interesting. It sets the date of the decline of Giscard's popularity as November 1980. It agrees with data in Figure 2.2. It shows that the turning-point was exactly six months before the election.

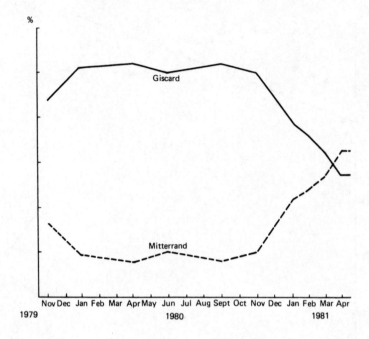

%

NovDec Jan Feb Mar AprMay Jun Jul Aug Sept Oct Nov Dec Jan Feb Mar Apr
1979   1980   1981

FIGURE 2.4 *Preference for president*

The most dramatic and most convincing indicators of what was about to happen are found in Figures 2.5(a), 2.5(b), 2.5(c) and 2.5(d). These summarise the findings of the three major French polling agencies concerning the voters' intentions more than six months before the election. It should be noted that these findings agreed more and more closely as election-day drew nearer. Figure 2.5(a) is particularly striking because of the nearly perfect curve shown by the IFOP's trend for Giscard. One wonders how it was that the last figure on Mitterrand's trend, Figure 2.5(b), broke the regularity of IFOP's upward curve. If this had not been the case, IFOP would probably have hit the bull's eye.

In summary, I cannot but agree with what Louis Harris wrote for the *Chicago Tribune* on 22 June: 'Had more heed been paid to the public opinion surveys, all of which accurately predicted the outcome of the election, much of the element of surprise would have been removed.'

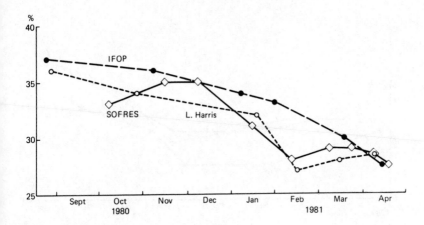

FIGURE 2.5(a)   *Giscard*

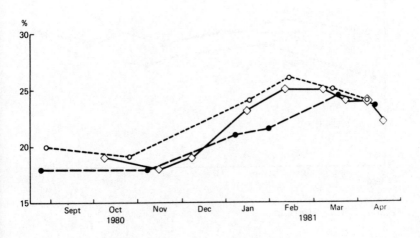

FIGURE 2.5(b)   *Mitterrand*

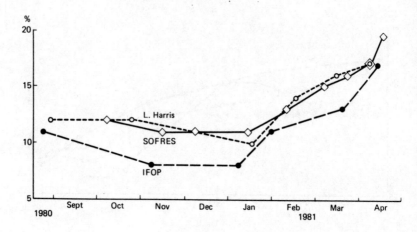

FIGURE 2.5(c)   *Chirac*

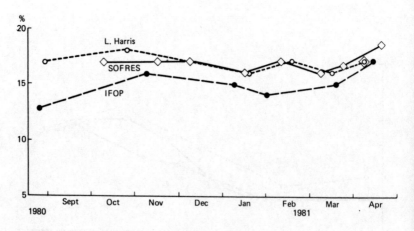

FIGURE 2.5(d)   *Marchais*

FIGURE 2.5   *Preference for president: the four candidates*

BIBLIOGRAPHY AND REFERENCES

On the history of IFOP:
H. Riffault, 'L'Institut Français d'Opinion Publique', in *Science et théorie de l'opinion publique, hommage à Jean Stoetzel, présenté par Raymond Boudon, François Bourricaud et Alain Girard*, ed. Boudin *et al.* (Paris: Retz, 1981).

On the technique of 'estimation':
Lucien Boucharenc, 'L'opération Europe n° 1 – IFOP', *Sondages*, vol. 27, no. 4, 1965, pp. 51–69.

On the technique of 'simulation':
B. R. Berelson, P. Lazarsfeld and W. H. McPhee, *Voting* (Chicago: University of Chicago Press, 1954).

Frédéric Bon and Guy Michelat, 'L'estimation des résultats des élections législatives, 5–12 mars 1967, par l'IFOP et la SOFRES', *Revue française de science politique*, June 1967, pp. 545–58.

Lucien Boucharenc, 'La simulation des élections législatives de mars 1967', *Sondages*, vol. 29, no. 4, 1967, pp. 65–78.

IFOP, *Les Français et de Gaulle, présentation et commentaire de Jean Charlot* (Paris: Plon, 1971).

IFOP, *Quand la gauche peut gagner. Les élections législatives des 4–11 mars 1973* (Paris: Alain Moreau, 1973).

J. Jaffré (ed.), *L'Opinion française en 1977* (Paris: SOFRES, 1978).

P. Lazarsfeld, B. Berelson and H. Gaudet, *The People's Choice* (New York: Columbia University Press, 1944).

R. Muraz, *La Parole aux français, cinq ans de sondages* (Paris: Dunod, 1977).

H. Penniman (ed.), *France at the Polls* (Washington, DC: American Enterprise Institute for Public Policy Research, 1981).

R. Aron, *Introduction à la philosophie de l'histoire: Essai sur les limites de l'objectivité historique*, (Paris: Gallimard, 1938); Translation: *Introduction to the philosophy of history* (London, Weidenfeld and Nicholson).

3 Political Opinion Polling in Germany

ELISABETH NOELLE-NEUMANN

After the capitulation of the Reich in 1945, German public opinion polling developed in an extremely peculiar manner in that part of Germany that first included the Western zones occupied by the UK, USA and France and then became the Federal Republic of Germany. The development had two roots, each almost completely independent of the other. There was also a more indirect third root, namely, the great German social inquiries of the nineteenth and early twentieth centuries. These inquiries involved written interviews with structured questionnaires and thousands of respondents on themes like 'Research on the State of the Farm Worker' (questionnaires dispatched to 15 000 landowners in 1874–5); 'The State of Factory Workers and Apprentices' (questionnaires to 7000 factory proprietors, workers and apprentices in 1875); 'The Morale in the Countryside' (questionnaires to 14 000 Protestant pastors in 1895); and so on (Oberschall, 1962). But this tradition was destroyed by the First World War. Again, in 1933, just as smaller inquiries were getting back on their feet in Germany, and even more widespread in Austria, the establishment of the Third Reich in Germany put an end to empirical social research (Jahoda *et al.*, 1933).

Both roots from which German public opinion research developed after 1945 arose under American influence. In 1937–8 I was a German exchange student in the School of Journalism at the University of Missouri and busy working on the dissertation topic I had been given at the University of Berlin: 'What do American newspapers do to captivate their readers?' With such a topic, I could not help but come across the works of George Gallup, who had graduated from the University of Iowa in 1928 after completing a dissertation on newspaper audiences (Gallup, 1928) and who, along with Archibald Crossley and Elmo Roper, had proved what surveys with representative samples and oral interviews could accomplish in the presidential election of 1936.

In 1940, after the war had begun, my dissertation appeared as a book in Germany under the title *Researching Opinion and the Masses in the USA: Surveys on Politics and the Press*. In 1946 a psychologist working for the French military government saw the book in the library of the University of Freiburg and sought out the author. He found me in the French occupation zone in Allensbach on Lake Constance and commissioned me to organise surveys among young people for the French occupational force. I finished seven surveys; publication of the results began in July 1947 (Noelle-Neumann, 1947a, 1947b). Early in 1948 the Allensbach Institut für Demoskopie was incorporated.

The second root of political opinion research was the Office of the Military Government of the United States (OMGUS) surveys in its zone (Merritt and Merritt, 1970). The American surveys began about two years before the first German ones, which were the Allensbach surveys of May 1947. First came the 'US Strategic Bombing Survey' in May 1945. The personnel of this survey were then taken over by the Opinion Survey section of the Information Control Division to be trained in random sample selection and fieldwork in the autumn of 1947. By the autumn of 1949 this organisation had conducted seventy-two surveys in the American zone. From 1949 until 1955 American surveys in Germany were conducted by the Reactions Analysis Staff of the Office of Public Affairs, Office of the US High Commission for Germany (HICOG).

American surveys had three notable effects on the development of public opinion research in Germany.

1. *The educational achievement.* Americans educated great numbers of Germans in how to organise surveys, how to construct random samples, in fieldwork and in data processing. The HICOG Reactions Analysis Group granted exchange fellowships to allow Germans to study polling techniques in the USA. In the 1950s several German institutes were founded by people who had previously worked with the Americans. The best-known of these institutes was Deutsches Institut für Volksumfragen (DIVO), in Frankfurt am Main.

2. *The contribution to the prestige of surveys.* It was probably the American military government's use of surveys that awakened the interest of German politicians in this medium of information. A good OMGUS prediction of voter participation in the first general election, in January 1946, made Germans believe that this procedure could function in Germany, too.

3. *Philosophy of random samples.* The situation in occupied Germany was ideal for drawing random samples. During the rationing of foodstuffs and other goods there was a card index of all German inhabitants that was immediately reliable at any time because it served as the distribution basis for food and supply cards. OMGUS surveys drew their samples from these card indexes. In turn, these ideal conditions for the first surveys led to a continuing strong trust in random surveys in Germany and to a corresponding contempt for the quota method. We see this mood indicated in the title a statistician gave to an article published in the official periodical *Allgemeines Statistisches Archiv*: 'When will the quota method be buried?' (Wendt, 1960).

All this created both favourable and unfavourable conditions for the development of public opinion polls in Germany. As one could have expected, this field established itself and spread very quickly. In 1980 the German news magazine *Der Spiegel* spoke of over a hundred institutes that conduct representative surveys, although it named only seven that regularly poll public opinion (*Der Spiegel*, 26, 1980). On the other hand, these two disparate roots never really worked towards a common growth and so, rather astonishingly, they have led to a situation of minimal contact, minimal sharing of experience between institutes.

The almost religious ardour with which random procedures were championed could not prevent the quota method from becoming generally accepted, largely because Allensbach election predictions proved its worth. Election predictions themselves became a point of dispute. There were strong efforts from outside Allensbach to come to a general agreement to forbid them altogether. These efforts were based principally on the fear that false election predictions would discredit the whole field; besides, people thought, a successful institute would obtain an advantage over its competition; officially, however, they reasoned that publicising election predictions could influence the decisions of voters. I will return later to the theme of election predictions.

In 1950 O. W. Riegel, a scientist who had been commissioned to visit the budding survey institutes in the Federal Republic of Germany, prepared the notes of his impressions for the Department of State in Washington, DC (Riegel, 1950). Read today, his report clearly explains why this field developed in such a divided way in Germany. Riegel warned of the development, but the American experts on public opinion research in Germany clung too tightly to their mistrust of Germans who had not learned directly from them. Riegel ended his notes with the prediction: 'This may be healthy for German public opinion research, in the long view, but it does not seem particularly favourable for an enlargement of American influence or example in the field of German polling.'

GOVERNMENTS, PARTIES AND ASSOCIATIONS AS CONTRACTORS OF POLITICAL SURVEYS

In the same year, 1950, Konrad Adenauer, the first German Chancellor of the Federal Republic, made a contract with the Allensbach Institute. It required the institute to include eight to ten questions for the federal government in its regular monthly omnibus questionnaires, and to report twice a month on the mood of the country. Sometimes Adenauer himself, or his head of the Federal Press and Information Office – the official partner in the agreement – suggested themes for the questions, but usually the Allensbach Institute had to decide for itself which topics were important. This contract has been renewed by every federal administration up to today. It established a tradition that is characteristic of the present situation of opinion polling in Germany. The federal, state and city governments, individual ministries, the political parties and both churches use surveys intensively as a medium of information. A summarising report of the late 1950s (Schmidtchen, 1959) shows how general that use had become only ten years after the first use of German political opinion research in 1950.

Today the German government, represented by the Federal Press and Information Office, has contracts with four opinion research institutes (Grünewald, 1980). Every state government has also signed such contracts. The controversy over whether the party not represented in the government at any given time should also receive information about the results of opinion research has been resolved by a decision not to provide the opposition party in question with such information. Often the chosen institute changes when the administration changes. As a matter of course the parties have concluded contracts with opinion research institutes. Some institutes even have close financial ties to a particular party, for example, the Institute for Applied Social Science in Bonn/Bad Godesberg (INFAS) with the Social Democratic Party (SPD). This very party that, as the governing party, today uses surveys so intensively, originally wanted nothing to do with them. One of the leading Social Democrats after the war, Carlo Schmid, describes how in 1949 he tried in vain to persuade Kurt Schumacher, the first party chairman, to work together with Allensbach (Schmid, 1976).

That political survey research in Germany nevertheless achieved such dominant political strength is due above all to the influence of the co-founder of the Allensbach Institute, Erich Peter Neumann. Neumann, born in 1912, became a political journalist at 18. He had experienced the prevailing undemocratic forces that brought the Weimar Republic to its end, and he promised himself that political survey research would have the effect of an early warning system; in the future it would prevent developments similar to those of the years 1930–33 – for which democratic politicians were unprepared – from ever occurring again (Neumann, 1951). With these thoughts, he convinced Adenauer. He advised the CDU/CSU during their successful election campaigns in 1953 and 1957; he was a personal adviser to Adenauer throughout his terms as Chancellor, until 1963. From 1961 to 1965 he was a CDU Representative in the German Parliament.

There was a similarly intimate connection between public opinion research and politics when, in 1969, Chancellor Willy Brandt appointed Klaus von Dohnanyi, a partner of the Infratest Institute, State Secretary and then later Minister of Education and Science.

But the great respect public opinion research in Germany now enjoys has a decided negative aspect as well. Political propagandists are attempting to use the results for their own ends. At the same time, politicians regard all results that do not stem from their own party with mistrust as a weapon for their political opponents. They publicly denounce all results that are disadvantageous to their political intentions as misleading. When journalists do not like the results of a survey, they present those results in the media with the name of the polling institute, adding that the institute leans towards the X or Y party, even when the institute in question works only very occasionally for the party named. For some time now, it has been a common practice for the German media to imply that survey results are coloured by the interests of the client.

ELECTION PREDICTIONS

In connection with the objectivity of results, election predictions naturally play a large role. Predictions intend above all to demonstrate that the reliability of an institute's work is independent of the interests of any party or contractor. The intention of election predictions, in other words, directly opposes the intentions of politicians, journalists, or competitors to discredit an institute as biased.

The history of election predictions in Germany has been stormy. From the outset, the Allensbach Institute concentrated on proving the reliability of its methods through election predictions. This was, first, because of its pioneering role. In the first seven years after the institute was founded, its most important task was to prove that the methods of public opinion research which many people considered appropriate only for the USA would work in Germany, too. Second, the Allensbach Institute for Demoscopy wanted to prove its reliability because it was using unconventional methods that were easy to attack. After a few field experiments, for example, it preferred the quota method to random sampling for its omnibus questionnaires; after one field experiment, it preferred to select interviewers through written tests, without personal examinations. Instead of checking its interviewer work through call-backs, the institute used so-called 'cheater questions', according to the principle and advice of Eric Stern, a German-American who organised surveys in Europe for the Marshall Plan beginning in 1949, commissioned work from the Allensbach Institute and, at that time, recommended this method of interviewer control.

Allensbach also departed from the usual methods in concentrating a large part of its effort on the development of questionnaires and intensive pre-tests. In these pre-tests, the managing personnel themselves tested questions under normal interviewer conditions, in the households of strangers. Tests continued until every instruction on how to present the questionnaire was foolproof and there would be no need to instruct the interviewer personally. One could not convincingly prove the usefulness of these Allensbach procedures with words alone; it required good election predictions. (For a detailed description and explanation of the methods used by the Allensbach Institute, see *Umfragen in der Massengesellschaft*, 17th edn, 1976).

After unofficial testing during the federal election in 1953, the Allensbach Institute publicised election predictions for every following general election, that is, beginning in 1957 (see Figure 3.1). At first these predictions were published in the *Frankfurter Allgemeine Zeitung*; from 1965 onwards the predictions were released on television immediately after the polls closed and before the broadcast of the first official returns.

From the beginning, Allensbach predictions showed a high degree of precision. Surprisingly, however, their accuracy makes them inappropriate for competition between institutes. For example, Emnid, the

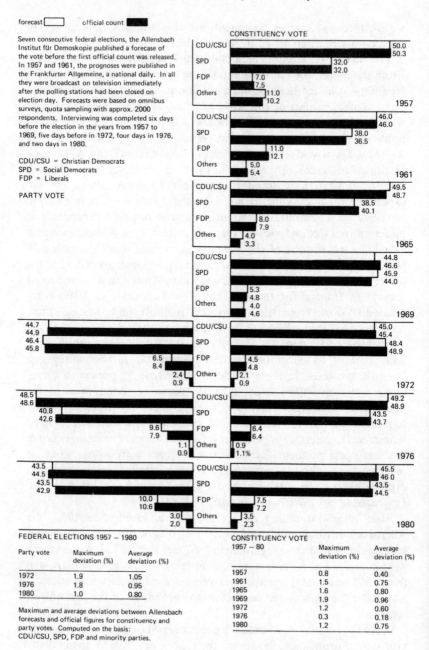

forecast ☐   official count ■

Seven consecutive federal elections, the Allensbach Institut für Demoskopie published a forecase of the vote before the first official count was released. In 1957 and 1961, the prognoses were published in the Frankfurter Allgemeine, a national daily. In all they were broadcast on television immediately after the polling stations had been closed on election day. Forecasts were based on omnibus surveys, quota sampling with approx. 2000 respondents. Interviewing was completed six days before the election in the years from 1957 to 1969, five days before in 1972, four days in 1976, and two days in 1980.

CDU/CSU = Christian Democrats
SPD = Social Democrats
FDP = Liberals

PARTY VOTE

CONSTITUENCY VOTE

1957
CDU/CSU 50.0 / 50.3
SPD 32.0 / 32.0
FDP 7.0 / 7.5
Others 11.0 / 10.2

1961
CDU/CSU 46.0 / 46.0
SPD 38.0 / 36.5
FDP 11.0 / 12.1
Others 5.0 / 5.4

1965
CDU/CSU 49.5 / 48.7
SPD 38.5 / 40.1
FDP 8.0 / 7.9
Others 4.0 / 3.3

1969
CDU/CSU 44.8 / 46.6
SPD 45.9 / 44.0
FDP 5.3 / 4.8
Others 4.0 / 4.6

1972
PARTY VOTE — CDU/CSU 44.7 / 44.9   CONSTITUENCY VOTE — CDU/CSU 45.0 / 45.4
SPD 46.4 / 45.8 — SPD 48.4 / 48.9
FDP 6.5 / 8.4 — FDP 4.5 / 4.8
Others 2.4 / 0.9 — Others 2.1 / 0.9

1976
CDU/CSU 48.5 / 48.6 — CDU/CSU 49.2 / 48.9
SPD 40.8 / 42.6 — SPD 43.5 / 43.7
FDP 9.6 / 7.9 — FDP 6.4 / 6.4
Others 1.1 / 0.9 — Others 0.9 / 1.1%

1980
CDU/CSU 43.5 / 44.5 — CDU/CSU 45.5 / 46.0
SPD 43.5 / 42.9 — SPD 43.5 / 44.5
FDP 10.0 / 10.6 — FDP 7.5 / 7.2
Others 3.0 / 2.0 — Others 3.5 / 2.3

FEDERAL ELECTIONS 1957 – 1980

Party vote	Maximum deviation (%)	Average deviation (%)
1972	1.9	1.05
1976	1.8	0.95
1980	1.0	0.80

Maximum and average deviations between Allensbach forecasts and official figures for constituency and party votes. Computed on the basis: CDU/CSU, SPD, FDP and minority parties.

CONSTITUENCY VOTE 1957 – 80	Maximum deviation (%)	Average deviation (%)
1957	0.8	0.40
1961	1.5	0.75
1965	1.6	0.80
1969	1.9	0.96
1972	1.2	0.60
1976	0.3	0.18
1980	1.2	0.75

FIGURE 3.1 *The Allensbach election forecasts 1957–80*

second oldest German institute for public opinion research twice, in 1957 and in 1961, readjusted its previously published final predictions after the final Allensbach results appeared. In 1965 Emnid accepted a challenge from Allensbach to deposit a prediction with the same lawyer in Bonn as Allensbach did two days before the election. On election day both predictions would be made public on television after the polls had closed. The Allensbach prediction showed a clear lead for the CDU/CSU and came within an average of 0.8 per cent of the exact official figures. The Emnid prediction showed both parties with approximately the same strength – practically repeating the last published Allensbach survey results from four weeks earlier – and was approximately 4.3 per cent off the actual results for both parties. A few months later, because of economic difficulties, the Emnid Institute was sold to the German market research institute Ifak, which still owns it today.

The other German opinion research institutes had refused to participate in the deposit of election predictions with a lawyer and the television announcement of the predictions on election night in 1965. After 1965 they tried to get all institutes to forgo election predictions, but Allensbach refused. From that time on, only the Allensbach prediction has been announced on television on election night after the polls close. Emnid still deposits a prediction with a lawyer but does not release the prediction on television. In the weeks preceding an election, all media try to obtain party strength figures from the various institutes; each party announces the figures from its own surveys when it finds them advantageous. However, the information publicised on the prospects for each party is not entirely disorganised. Since 1972, thus up to now for three elections, *Der Stern*, the largest German illustrated magazine (circulation currently around 2 million), has commissioned Allensbach to ascertain party strength and has published the Allensbach figures continuously for the six weeks preceding the election.

There are also two methodological problems connected with election predictions. The German election system gives every voter two votes, and the voter can give them to different parties. Voters take the so-called 'first [constituency] vote' particularly seriously, but it is in fact the 'second [party] vote' that determines the final number of seats each party receives in Parliament. Until the mid-1960s this created no problems because most voters voted twice for the same party. However, when at the end of the 1960s more and more people began splitting their votes, the methods of predicting elections had to be developed further in order to be able to predict this party vote as well. The problem was not easily solved because even a few weeks before the election most voters still did not know that they had two votes and what the second vote would mean.

A second problem lay in the fact that survey results, from the end of the 1960s on, no longer reflected the reality of voters' decisions. We were warned of this discrepancy by results in response to the question of which party the respondent had chosen in the last federal election. The strength of the discrepancy has varied, but the tendency from then until now has remained the same: clearly too few respondents say they voted for the CDU and clearly too many claim to have chosen the SPD (Noelle-Neumann, 1978a).

To explain this phenomenon, at the beginning of the 1970s I developed a theory of a spiral of silence, first presented at the Conference of Psychologists in Tokyo in 1972 (Noelle-Neumann, 1973). I proceeded from an assumption that had been supported empirically by survey results. The assumption was that people, because they do not want to become isolated, continuously and alertly observe their environment; they see which attitudes become more prominent and which less so. Persons who find their views strongly represented in public also acknowledge light-heartedly and openly that they hold those views. On the other hand, people who find their views presented with decreasing frequency in public tend to prefer to keep their views silent.

This sets a spiralling process in motion. The side that presents itself strongly in public opinion thereby appears to be stronger than it really is, while the other side appears to be weaker than it is because of its tendency to be silent. This public impression of relative strength in turn further motivates other people to speak out for the one side or, on the other, to lapse into silence.

A tendency to be silent about an issue creates a serious source of error for survey research, partly because the respondent who inclines towards silence will elude answering any question about his or her party loyalty and partly because that person will tend, at a higher than average rate, to refuse to be interviewed altogether. We assumed that, in the protective secrecy of the voting booth, even those who inclined towards silence in public would vote according to their personal conviction. On the basis of the unrealistic answers we received about how a respondent last voted, we weighted the figures in our punch cards to fill in what we estimated to be the missing number of CDU/CSU voters and, on the other hand, accordingly reduced the surplus number of SPD voters.

After weighting the cards in this manner we calculated the present party strength. We tested this procedure internally in two state elections and since 1972 have used it in all public predictions of state and federal elections. Tables 3.1 and 3.2 show for the last two federal elections how much accuracy is gained by this procedure. Other German institutes involved in public opinion research have, in the meantime, also adopted the procedure. A report on the pressure exerted by the climate of opinion and its possible causes has been published elsewhere (Noelle-Neumann, 1978b).

The assumptions we use as a starting-point are not yet empirically established. Likewise, no one can predict what further surprises the difficulties in dealing with climate-of-opinion pressure will bring us. However, one has to contradict persons who conclude from these uncertainties that we would do better to forgo all election forecasts. On the contrary, these difficulties have fostered genuine progress because attempts to solve them have led to a new understanding of the processes of public opinion.

Our studies on the concept of the spiral of silence also led to new political controversy about the role of public opinion research. In 1972 the federal election campaign showed how the spiral of silence works (Noelle-Neumann, 1974). During the six-week campaign the followers of the CDU/CSU were almost as strong in numbers as were the Social Democrats, but they were almost invisible in public. There was no better way of isolating oneself than by putting a CDU/CSU sticker on one's car or wearing a CDU/CSU badge. In the weeks immediately after the election, when asked whose badges and stickers they had seen most, 53 per cent of a representative cross-section of the adult population replied those of the SPD, 9 per cent those of the CDU/CSU.

The party strategists of the CDU/CSU immediately drew a lesson from the analysis of the spiral of silence and, beginning in 1974, they started to inform the party grass roots about its existence and to make preparations to prevent the 1972 situation from recurring in the 1976 federal election campaign (Conradt, 1978). Their success was evident. During the 1976 electoral campaign the two major parties were, by and large, equally strong. The question about whose badges and stickers had been seen most received a balanced answer: 29 per cent had seen more of the CDU/CSU, 31 per cent more of the SPD (Noelle-Neumann, 1978b).

At this point the concept of the spiral of silence came under fire. It had obviously been useful for the CDU/CSU – but there was also another reason. This second reason leads us into the delicate area of the relationship between public opinion research and the mass media.

TABLE 3.1 *Election forecasts: raw figures or weighted according to climate-of-opinion factors?*

Example: Federal election, September 1976

Question: 'If the federal election were to take place this Sunday, which party would you vote for?'

	Eligible voters in the Federal Republic of Germany with concrete party declaration, unweighted results (%)	Allensbach election forecast (constituency vote), results weighted by climate-of-opinion factors (%)	Official results (constituency vote, %)
Christian Democrats	44.9	49.2	48.9
Social Democrats	45.8	43.5	43.7
Liberals	8.5	6.4	6.4
Others	0.9	0.9	1.1
	100.1	**100.0**	**100.1**

TABLE 3.2 *Election forecasts: raw figures or weighted according to climate-of-opinion factors?*

Example: Federal election, September 1980

Question: 'Would you please tell me who you are going to give your constituency vote to in the next federal election?' (presentation of a list)

	Eligible voters in the Federal Republic of Germany with concrete party declaration, unweighted results (%)	Allensbach election forecast (constituency vote), results weighted by climate-of-opinion factors (%)	Official results (constituency vote, %)
Christian Democrats	41.4	45.5	46.0
Social Democrats	46.7	43.5	44.5
Liberals	8.2	7.5	7.2
Others	3.7	3.5	2.3
	100.0	**100.0**	**100.0**

PUBLIC OPINION AND THE MASS MEDIA

Since 1969 Allensbach election research has mainly been based on oral interviews with panels of approximately 1200 persons eligible to vote (Institut für Demoskopie Allensbach, 1969). Also in 1969, the second television network and the Allensbach Institute began a tradition of weekly half-hour television programmes on the development of voter preferences, each involving a panel being interviewed jointly by the network and Allensbach. The 1976 panel was particularly designed to observe the process of the spiral of silence throughout the election year.

During this year we made a peculiar discovery. We used the question which Lazarsfeld had already praised for its prognostic potential (Lazarsfeld *et al.*, 1944) – 'Who do you think will win the election?' – as a particularly important indicator of the strength or weakness of the climate of opinion. In March 1976 people who watched television a lot, a medium amount or only a little gave fairly similar replies to this question. Three months later, however, in July, the CDU/CSU had lost the sympathies of voters who watched a lot of television, the SPD had gained, while persons who watched only a little between March and July and based their attitudes on factors other than television had not noticed a shift in the climate of opinion (Noelle-Neumann, 1977, 1980a).

As this connection was also found in all examined subgroups, the probability increased that television spread a climate of opinion unfavourable to the CDU/CSU and favourable to the SPD. Since the CDU/CSU had lost the 1976 election by a very narrow margin (if 350 000 of approximately 40 million voters had not voted SPD, the CDU/CSU would have had an absolute majority), CDU policy-makers accused television of swinging the elections against their party. The call to control television more strictly grew among CDU/CSU politicians, and the controversy has continued to rage until the present day. The hard feelings were so strong that the 1980 Allensbach Election Prognosis could not be published on either of the two German television networks, but was broadcast by the Austrian television network, ORF, instead.

In the early summer of 1980 *Der Spiegel* invited seven German institutes to take part in a discussion of opinion polling, election research and election forecasts. The magazine published the discussion in two instalments (*Der Spiegel*, nos 26/7, 1980).

According to *Der Spiegel*, the seven institutes listed below all currently conducted public opinion polls in the Federal Republic of Germany:

Infratest, Munich (400 employees), directors Wolfgang and Dr Renate Ernst. At the *Spiegel* discussion Infratest was represented by the head of the two subsidiary institutes, Infratest Sozialforschung (Infratest Social Research) and Infratest Medienforschung (Infratest Media Research), Gerhard Unholzer. Infratest Social Research works for the SPD; another subsidiary institute, Infratest Wirtschaftsforschung (Infratest Economic Research), works for the CDU. Hence, Infratest is the only institute working for both the major political parties. Infratest has probably been particularly active for the federal government and the federal ministries ever since Willy Brandt assumed the chancellorship. Reports in the media about Infratest investigations are rare.

Institut für Demoskopie Allensbach, Allensbach (90 employees), director Professor Elisabeth Noelle-Neumann, member of International Research Associates (INRA) founded by Elmo C. Wilson. Works for the federal government and for federal ministries, for CDU state governments and occasionally also for the CDU as a political party. It has close relationships with the magazine *Der Stern* (Noelle-Neumann, 1980b), the daily newspaper *Frankfurter Allgemeine Zeitung* and the business magazine *Capital*, but it also conducts regular surveys for other papers, magazines, television and radio. Allensbach is the institute with the greatest media: a German-language press release containing survey results is published three times a month, and an English-language press release is distributed worldwide once or twice a month. In addition, since 1947 survey results have been published in volumes summarising from three to six years: *Jahrbücher der öffentlichen Meinung* (Yearbooks of Public Opinion) since 1955, *Allensbacher Jahrbuch der Demoskopie* (Allensbach Yearbook of Survey Research) since 1976 (English edn, *The Germans*, 1967; 2nd vol., 1981). In conjunction with the Institut Infas (50/50 share) the Allensbach subsidiary company Teleskopie measures audience ratings for the two German television networks and on a daily basis in a total number of 1500 households.

Emnid Institut, Bielefeld (50 employees), director Walter Tacke, the German Gallup organisation. Subsidiary company of the market research institute Ifak in Wiesbaden. Emnid works for the federal government, for federal ministries, for the CDU. Emnid results are widely published in the media; surveys are frequently commissioned by *Der Spiegel* and the daily newspaper *Die Welt*. Emnid publishes monthly compilations of public opinion research results.

Institut für Angewandte Sozialforschung (Institute for Applied Social Research, Infas), Bonn-Bad Godesberg (63 employees), director Klaus Liepelt. Has worked for the federal government and the federal ministries since the 1969 change of government; also for SPD state governments, SPD-governed major cities and the SPD itself. Media contacts are maintained by means of press conferences at which completed research projects are presented. Measurement of TV audience ratings through the subsidiary company Teleskopie in conjunction with Allensbach.

Getas, Bremen (53 employees), directors Hans Jürgen Ohde and Barbara von Harder. Works for the CDU/CSU, developed from the Institut für Psychologische Studien (Institute for Psychological Studies) established in 1957.

Sinus, Sozialwissenschaftliches Institut (Social Research Institute) Nowak & Sörgel, Munich and Heidelberg (21 employees). From 1970 to 1978 Sörgel worked at Infratest, to which Sinus today still subcontracts fieldwork for major surveys. Works for the federal government, for federal ministries, for the SPD. Concluded research projects are presented at press conferences.

Forschungsgruppe Wahlen (Research Group Elections), Mannheim (12 employees), members of the board Manfred Berger, Wolfgang G. Gibowski and Dr Dieter Roth. Works mainly for the second German television network. Fieldwork is subcontracted to Infratest. The results are presented monthly on the television *Polit-Barometer*. The three directors have also established the Institut für Praxisorientierte Sozialforschung (Institute for Practice-Oriented Social Research, Ipos) as a non-profit institute.

The relationship between public opinion research institutes and the media is ambivalent. The publisher of *Der Spiegel*, Rudolf Augstein, described this aptly in his speech at the twenty-fifth anniversary of the Allensbach Institute: 'Well, as you know, we have come to terms with the voracious little brother' (Augstein, 1974; Noelle-Neumann, 1980b). You can hardly read newspapers or magazines, or watch television, or listen to the radio, at least in the Federal Republic of Germany, without learning daily about survey research results.

Since 1945 a picture of the current state of Germany has been continually provided by opinion polling and survey research. Journalists, but also industry, the political parties, the churches, the unions and even scientists and students working on dissertations deem it a natural privilege to obtain access to any desired information on the general population or certain subgroups, including the trends of the past decades. This is also assisted by the archival and publication policies of the Allensbach Institute. (The original card sets of the OMGUS surveys were lost, and the Emnid Institute did not keep its cards.) The more than 2500 surveys the Allensbach Institute has conducted are available either on tape or on punch cards. A visible card index allows the 140 000-odd questions posed once or several times to be found within minutes, along with each question's date, survey number, original questionnaire and code plan with marginals. A complete copy of the Allensbach Archives is stored at the official Archives of the Federal Republic of Germany in Koblenz, with a thirty-year blocking period. The Allensbach Institute established its own publishing company for book publications in the early 1950s. Staff members of the institute teach or taught at seven universities apart from their occupation at the Allensbach Institute.

The climate of official opinion towards political survey research is benevolent. The federal government sent Vice-Chancellor Blücher and a minister, Franz-Josef Strauss, to attend the first ESOMAR/WAPOR congress held in Germany (Constance, 1955). At the next ESOMAR/WAPOR congress held in Germany (1961), the Minister of Economic Affairs, Ludwig Erhard, gave the inaugural address. At the twenty-fifth anniversary of the Allensbach Institute the President of the Federal Constitutional Court, Ernst Benda, made a ceremonial speech in which he outlined why, from the viewpoint of the jurist, survey research strengthens democracy.

Former Chancellor Helmut Schmidt, however, told a journalist who interviewed him outside his vacation resort on the Brahmsee near Hamburg: 'This is the kind of scenery I like'; and all of a sudden, the journalist wrote, Helmut Schmidt added: 'But I don't like public opinion polls.'

BIBLIOGRAPHY AND REFERENCES

Augstein, Rudolf (1974), 'Demoskopie und Politik', speech given at the 25th anniversary of the Institut für Demoskopie Allensbach on 6 June 1972 in Bonn: reprinted in Elisabeth Noelle and Peter Erich Neumann (eds), *Jahrbuch der öffentlichen Meinung 1968–1973* (Allensbach/Bonn: Verlag für Demoskopie).
Conradt, David P. (1978), 'The 1976 campaign and election: an overview', in Karl H. Cerny (ed.), *Germany at the Polls, The Bundestag Election of 1976* (Washington, DC: American Enterprise Institute for Public Policy Research), pp. 29–56.

Gallup, George H. (1928), 'An objective method for determining reader-interest in the content of newspapers', dissertation, University of Iowa.

Grünewald, Arnim (1980), Keynote address on 'Opinion Polls', in ESOMAR: Seminar on Opinion Polls in conjunction with the World Association for Public Opinion Research, in Bonn-Bad Godesberg, 23–6 January (Amsterdam: ESOMAR), pp. 1–11.

Institut für Demoskopie Allensbach (1969), 'Wählermeinung – nicht geheim', a documentation of the second German television network (Allensbach/Bonn: Verlag für Demoskopie).

Institut für Demoskopie Allensbach (1978), 'Was heisst Meinungsforschung?', *Allensbacher Bericht*, no. 26.

Jahoda, Marie, Lazarsfeld, Paul F. and Zeisel, Hans (1933), *Die Arbeitslosen von Marienthal* (Leipzig: Verlag S. Hirzel). New edition by Verlag für Demoskopie, Allensbach/Bonn 1960, introduction by Paul F. Lazarsfeld, and appendix by Hans Zeisel, 'Zur Geschichte der Soziographie'.

Lazarsfeld, Paul F., Berelson, Bernard and Gaudet, Hazel (1944), *The People's Choice. How the Voter Makes Up his Mind in a Presidential Campaign* (New York: Duell, Sloan & Pearce, 2nd edn, 1948; 3rd edn, New York: Columbia University Press, 1968).

Merritt, Anna J. and Merritt, Richard L. (1970), *Public Opinion in Occupied Germany. The OMGUS Surveys 1945–1949* (Urbana, Ill.: University of Illinois Press).

Neumann, Erich Peter (1951), 'Politische und soziale Meinungsforschung in Deutschland', paper presented to a work session about Empirical Social Research in Weinheim/Bergstrasse, 14 December.

Noelle, Elisabeth (1940), *Meinungs- und Massenforschung in den USA. Umfragen über Politik und Presse* (Zeitung und Zeit, Neue Folge, Part A, vol. 16) (Frankfurt/Main: Verlag Moritz Diesterweg).

Noelle-Neumann, Elisabeth (1947a), 'Die Meinung der Studenten', in *Studentische Blätter*, July.

Noelle-Neumann, Elisabeth (1947b), 'Vom Zeitbild der Studenten. Bericht über eine Umfrage in Tübingen und Freiburg', in *Die Gegenwart*, vol. 2, nos 21/2, 30 November, pp. 15–18.

Noelle, Elisabeth (1963), *Umfragen in der Massengesellschaft. Einführung in die Methoden der Demoskopie* (Reinbek: Rowohlt Paperback Press, 1963, 7th edn, 1976 Ref.: vol. 177). Translations are available in French, Dutch, Czech, Spanish and Russian. A new edition is under way and will probably appear in 1983; likewise an English edition.

Noelle-Neumann, Elisabeth (1973), 'Return to the concept of powerful mass media', in *Studies of Broadcasting*, no. 9, March, pp. 67–112 (paper presented to the XXth International Congress of Psychology on 16 August 1976 in Tokyo).

Noelle-Neumann, Elisabeth (1974), 'Wahlentscheidung in der Fernseh-demokratie. Eine sozialpsychologische Interpretation der Bundestagswahl 1972', in *Auf der Suche nach dem mündigen Wähler. Die Wahlentscheidung 1972 and ihre Konsequenzen,* ed. Dieter Just and Lothar Romain (Bonn: Köllen) pp. 161–205. (Schriftenreihe der Bundeszentrale für politische Bildung, Heft 101); reprinted in: Noelle-Neumann, Elisabeth (1980), *Wahlentscheidung in Der Fernsehdemokratie* (Freiburg/Würzburg: Verlag Ploetz).

Noelle-Neumann, Elisabeth (1977), 'Das doppelte Meinungsklima. Der Einfluss des Fernsehens im Wahlkampf 1976', in *Politische Vierteljahresschrift*, vol. 18, nos 2/3, 1977. Wahlsoziologie heute. Analysen aus Anlass der Bundestagswahl 1976, pp. 408–51; reprinted in: Noelle-Neumann, Elisabeth (1980), *Wahlentscheidung in der Fernsehdemokratie* (Freiburg/Würzburg: Verlag Ploetz).

Noelle-Neumann, Elisabeth (1978a), 'The dual climate of opinion: the influence of television in the 1976 West German federal election', in *Elections and Parties. Sociopolitical Change and Participation in the West German Federal Election of 1976*, ed. M. Kaase and K. von Beyme (*German Political Studies*, vol. 3) (London/Beverly Hills: Sage) pp. 137–69.

Noelle-Neumann, Elisabeth (1978b), 'Kampf um die öffentliche Meinung', in *Entscheidung ohne Klarheit. Anmerkungen und Materialien zur Bundestagswahl 1976*, ed. Dieter Just and Peter Röhrig (Bonn: Köllen) pp. 125–56. (Schriftenreihe der Bundeszentrale für politische Bildung, Heft 127); reprinted in Noelle-Neumann, Elisabeth (1980), *Wahlentscheidung in der Fernsehdemokratie* (Freiburg/Würzburg: Verlag Ploetz).

Noelle-Neumann, Elisabeth (1980a), *Die Schweigespirale. Öffentliche Meinung—unsere soziale Haut* (Munich: Piper).

Noelle-Neumann, Elisabeth (1980b), 'The public opinion correspondent', *Public Opinion Quarterly*, vol. 44, pp. 585–97.

Noelle-Neumann, Elisabeth and Neumann, Erich Peter (eds), *Jahrbuch der öffentlichen Meinung* (Allensbach/Bonn: Verlag für Demoskopie): vol. I: Ergebnisse 1947–55; vol. II: Ergebnisse 1956–7; vol. III: Ergebnisse 1958–64; vol. IV: Ergebnisse 1965–67; vol. V: Ergebnisse 1968–73.

Noelle-Neumann, Elisabeth (ed.), *Allensbacher Jahrbuch der Demoskopie* (Vienna/Munich/Zurich/Innsbruck: Molden): vol. VI: Ergebnisse 1974–6; vol. VII: Ergebnisse 1976–7.

Noelle, Elisabeth, and Neumann, Erich Peter (eds) (1967), *The Germans. Public Opinion Polls 1947–1966* (Bonn: Verlag für Demoskopie).

Noelle-Neumann, Elisabeth (ed.) (1981), *The Germans. Public Opinion Polls 1967–1980* (Westport, Conn.: Greenwood Press).

Oberschall, Anthony R. (1962), 'Empirical social research in Germany 1848–1914', dissertation, Columbia University, Bureau of Applied Social Research.

Riegel, O. W. (1950), Report on a Survey of Public Opinion Research and Training in West Germany, June–September 1950, submitted to the Department of State, Washington, DC, 30 October.

Schmid, Carlo (1976), 'Ein Gruss an Elisabeth Noelle-Neumann zum 60. Geburtstag am 19 Dezember 1976', in *Publizistik*, no. 21, p. 467.

Schmidtchen, Gerhard (1959), *Die befragte Nation. Über den Einfluss der Meinungsforschung auf die Politik* (Freiburg: Verlag Rombach, 2nd edn 1961; revised paperback edn, Munich, 1965, Fischer Taschenbuch 689).

Stackelberg, Karl-Georg von (1975), *Souffleur auf politischer Bühne. Von der Macht der Meinungen und den Meinungen der Mächtigen* (Munich: Verlag Moderne Industrie).

Wendt, Friedrich (1960), 'Wann wird das Quotenverfahren begraben?', in *Allgemeines Statistisches Archiv*, vol. 1.

4 Political Opinion Polling in Great Britain

ROBERT M. WORCESTER

THE HISTORY OF POLITICAL POLLING IN GREAT BRITAIN

The Early Days: Founding Fathers

British Gallup, originally known as BIPO (British Institute of Public Opinion), was the first organisation of its kind in Britain, being founded in 1937 just two years after its American stepfather. It published its poll findings in the *News Chronicle* until that paper's demise in 1960 and has since then published regularly in the *Daily Telegraph*. Gallup polls were conducted monthly until the mid-1950s, and have been done weekly, although published only once a month, since then. Gallup has not only published its findings in the *News Chronicle* and *Daily Telegraph*, but also more extensively in its monthly *Gallup Political Index*, which has been running for nearly twenty years, and in the past two years in an annual paperback.

Its poll findings on all sorts of topics for the years 1937–75 are published in two fat, useful and frequently amusing volumes (Gallup, 1976). In the early days most questions were of the 'yes/no' variety, at first covering such topics as divorce, mercy killings, compulsory military training and recognition of Franco's junta in Spain. Among the first few questions reported are these and they do, indeed, make fascinating reading:

Q: 'If you had to choose between Fascism and Communism, which would you choose?'

	%
Fascism	49
Communism	51

(46 % expressed no opinion)

SOURCE: Gallup 1937

61

Q: 'Should Great Britain remain a member of the League of Nations?'

	%
Yes	84
No	16

(14 % expressed no opinion)

SOURCE: Gallup, 1937

and . . .

Q: 'Have you ever travelled to America?'

	%
Yes	8
No	92

SOURCE: Gallup, 1937

Interestingly, MORI asked a similar question in 1979 and found that the proportion of the British public who said they had visited the USA was still 8 per cent (MORI, 1980).

Some questions asked in 1938 have considerable relevance today: they include questions on the reunification of Ireland, devolution in Scotland and participation in football pools. Others began the series of political questions that continues today; first, in October 1938, on the public's satisfaction with Neville Chamberlain as Prime Minister (57 per cent satisfied, 43 per cent dissatisfied, 10 per cent no opinion).

The first voting intention question was introduced in February 1939, when 64 per cent answered that they would vote for the government 'if there were a general election tomorrow' and 36 per cent for the opposition (16 per cent no opinion). In March of that year the question was posed: 'If Mr Chamberlain retires, whom would you like to be Prime Minister?' Anthony Eden was outstandingly the popular choice with 38 per cent; Lord Halifax and Winston Churchill, the real choice when the crunch did come, got 7 per cent each. But a majority, 56 per cent, did favour Churchill being invited to join the Cabinet.

Gallup's first associate in Great Britain was Dr Henry Durant, who reminisced in 1979 about how he began polling in the first place:

I had taken my degree at LSE. As usual in the early 30s no job: I lectured, was registered for a PhD, was writing, earning money any way I could. Not Gallup himself, but an associate of his, Harry Field, came from the USA in 1936 looking for somebody to start up part-time Gallup work from home. He went to LSE Appointments Bureau, was given half-a-dozen names and he chose mine; just like that. For a lordly £150 per year I did postal surveys, till the *News Chronicle* became interested. They said, 'We want you to forecast the bye-election to show that the system works.' West Fulham: Edith Summerskill was Labour candidate. It was a Conservative seat and she upset the Conservative, as I had forecast, and by a miracle I got it on the nose within one per cent; beginner's luck. (Quoted in Chappell, 1979)

It was certainly to some degree luck, and also to some degree sampling skill, as was proved some years later:

When the General Election came, in May '45, Gallup showed that Attlee was going to win with the Labour Party. Nobody believed us, including all the *News Chronicle* people.

Gallup in the USA began as a means of journalism, as did its stepchild in Great Britain. As Dr Durant explained:

People constantly asked us to put questions on our regular surveys and at the beginning I was stupid enough to regard these as a nuisance: then I suddenly realised that this was a beautiful way of making money. It grew and soon had its own Omnibus survey: today it's one of the things that researchers live off.

The polls at the British general election of 1950 came close, even if two out of three called the wrong winner, and they seemed to overcome the scepticism towards the polls which had resulted from the Dewey–Truman fiasco in the USA in 1948 (Abrams, 1951). Three national morning newspapers took the mood of the electorate at different dates before election day. That election demonstrated that to poll *latest* meant to poll *closest* – something that tended to be overlooked two decades later (see Table 4.1).

During the 1950s politicians began to take political polls seriously. This was demonstrated by the statement by Morgan Phillips, general secretary of the Labour Party, who warned against 'a new technique of

TABLE 4.1 *General election 1950*

	Interviewing period			
	Daily Mail (15 Feb.) (%)	Daily Express (17–21 Feb.) (%)	News Chronicle (22 Feb.) (%)	Actual Result (23 Feb.) (%)
Con	45.5	44.5	43.5	43.0
Lab	42.5	44.0	45.0	46.8
Lib/Other	12.0	11.5	11.5	10.2
Lab Lead	−3.0	−0.5	+1.5	+3.8

propaganda . . . the publication of polls' (Butler, 1952). Nearly a quarter of a century later, the Labour Party was still critical of the polls (although graciously making a nod in MORI's direction), saying in its 1974 Report:

> Throughout the campaign the opinion polls indicated a heavy swing against Labour and, of course, proved once again to be totally incorrect. It would also seem that the opinion polls published in the press had a considerable effect in increasing the Liberal vote.
>
> Our own private [MORI] polls were accurate to a high degree and the findings of these polls, which were presented to the Campaign Committee each morning, were of great value. (Labour Party, 1974, p.3)

Three other polls appeared during the 1950s. The *Daily Express* conducted its own (and in 1955 got the Labour vote exactly right, to one decimal place), yet encumbered it in 1959 with the 'endorsement' that 'The *Daily Express* has no confidence in its own poll, although it is conducted with complete integrity and all possible efficiency' (Teer and Spence, 1973).

In 1951 Research Services Limited (RSL) published its first polls under its chairman, Dr Mark Abrams, who also during the 1950s and 1960s conducted private polls for the Labour Party. When Dr Abrams left RSL to become a civil servant, before the 1970 general election, there was a hiatus in RSL's political polling work until its re-entry into the field in 1979 (see section below on the role of the polls in the 1979 General Election).

JK1764 M4H 1993

HM261 .M4M 1992

HN90.P8 H47 1993

HM 261 C585 1991

HM261 . C93 1988

HM261.P565 1983

JK1764 M5 1999

HN90 .P8 P64 1999

P95.5 .P595 1998

HM261 M33 1992

HM261 .S53 1995

PN2080 B4747 1999

Hadleigh, Boze.
Conversations with my elders / Boze
Hadleigh. -- 1st ed. -- New York : St.
Martin's Press, c1986.
xiii, 209 p. ; 22 cm.
ISBN 0-312-00115-0

1. Gays--United States--Interviews.
2. Motion picture producers and
directors--United States--Interviews.
3. Motion picture actors and actresses
--United States--Interviews. I. Title

In 1957 R. M. P. Shields, now managing director of Associated Newspapers (AN), set up National Opinion Polls (NOP) as an AN subsidiary, which it continues to be to this day, still under Mr Shields's active chairmanship, but directed jointly by Frank Teer and John Barter between 1966 and 1972 and subsequently by John Barter. NOP publishes its polls in Associated Newspapers' *Daily Mail* and also publishes a bi-monthly *Review* of its poll findings.

NOP's first general election poll was in 1959, when it supplemented its resources with interviewers and tabulating machines made available by the Gallup Poll, much to the consternation of the *Observer*, which ran a headline 'Four polls from one source'. According to Butler and Rose (1960), the *Observer's* caveat did not seem to diminish the interest with which the polls were followed.

Election day was 8 October; from 21 September onwards polling results in sponsoring papers (no cross-reporting) began to encourage the Labour Party and to shake up the Tories. What had been a 6.8 per cent Tory lead slid down to around 2 per cent, and three days before polling Gallup reported a neck-and-neck race in the *News Chronicle*. In earlier elections the polls had tended to underestimate Labour's strength. Yet the popular belief that the Conservatives would win did not fluctuate greatly, with a steady three-to-one majority expecting this at every stage in the campaign. Business (City) opinion was more attuned then as now (see p. 101 below) to the poll reports. Stock prices fell on mornings when opinion polls showed a decline in the Tory lead.

Butler and Rose suggested that, while before 1959 polls had had an appreciable effect on the morale and expectations of politicians, they had made little impact on the electorate. However, in 1959 there were signs of a wider impact. Curiously, it was the detractors from the polls rather than their sponsors who ascribed great influence to them. Certainly, Butler and Rose concluded, Labour supporters were given heart by the appearance of the polls as they reported Labour gains. During this election there were 'one or two' voices raised in favour of the suppression or regulation of poll forecasts. But in the opinion of Butler and Rose:

It does not appear that people jump on the winning band-wagon – or even that they side with the underdog . . . it is also true that the turnout may be increased by signs that the rivals are neck-and-neck . . . the effect of the polls, like that of television, seems to be to stir up interest, and hence participation in the election.

They concluded:

> What is also needed is a higher degree of education about the limitations and possibilities of the polls and perhaps more information and humility from some of their sponsors. The first thing that has to be learnt is that their main value does not lie primarily in election prediction. The sampling of opinion can yield a vast amount of information of the greatest political and social importance – and such information, to be valuable, need not be nearly as precise as election forecasts must be. Through opinion polling, political parties and students of politics can find out in detail the views of different sections of the public, instead of simply guessing at them, or making inferences. Voting is only the end product of a series of influences. Polls will also be most valuable in discovering, not how people are going to vote, but why they vote as they do. Polls can reveal how well informed the public is about any issue and whether it has strong views; they can also reveal what people do and what media of communication they are exposed to. There has never been anything comparable to sample polls as a tool for advancing understanding of mass political behaviour.

Earlier, David Butler, in an article published in 1955, described election behaviour studies as of long duration, if shallow understanding. Before 1872, party agents knew who had voted and how, and

> Ever since the Reform Bill [1832], Tadpoles and Tapers have been speculating busily on what national 'cries' would go down best with the electorate, and what detailed techniques in constituency organisation would yield the biggest vote.

He went on to say, in his pessimistic article in the *British Journal of Sociology*:

> The academic study of elections is still young . . . . Before the Second World War no one in the universities had devoted detailed attention to the conduct of contemporary elections or to their results . . . . The real stimulus to research in voting behaviour was, of course, the advent of the sample survey . . . . Doubts have grown up about whether either the detailed investigation of the conduct of the campaign, or the elaborate sample survey, offer much prospect of yielding major new discoveries. Briefly, it can be argued that the

conduct of the campaign has remarkably little influence on the results of the election, while the practical limits of sample surveys make it unlikely that they have enormous further contributions to make to exposing either the facts of voting behaviour or the motives behind it.

In these early days of television the BBC, then a monopoly, did not report the election campaign at all, as a matter of policy. By 1959 the BBC had reversed this stance, recognising its responsibility for reporting such news as well as, to date, co-author another seven volumes in the Nuffield series of British General Election books (Butler and Rose, 1960; Butler and King, 1965, 1966; Butler and Pinto-Duschinsky, 1971; Butler and Kavanagh, 1974, 1975, 1980).

Another valuable commentary on polls and politics – of an international flavour – was offered by Durant (1962) in the *British Journal of Sociology*, showing how polls (starting with the National Peace Ballot of 1935 with over $11\frac{1}{2}$ million respondents) were taken in Britain to measure public attitudes to Britain's conduct of foreign affairs.

Sample overkill was not only a pre-war phenomenon. In 1957 the National Association of Local Government Officials surveyed more than 300 000 households, using 15 000 local council employees, on what people knew and thought of local government (*The Times*, 2 April 1957, pp. 12f.), and in 1958–9 Mr Colin Hurry spent some £450 000, partly financed by the then independent steel companies, to 'interview' some 1 948 314 electors in 129 marginal constituencies about their views on nationalisation. An editorial in the *Political Quarterly* in 1959 summed up the criticisms made of this method of attempting to influence public opinion:

> The wording as well as the sense of certain questions was . . . heavily loaded . . . . The questions were worded in such a way that they would almost certainly evoke prejudice against nationalisation in many of the persons asked to answer them . . . . The scheme aimed at influencing voters in every area where they might exert the maximum effect at the coming General Election. (Robson, 1959, p. 111)

The Middle Years: Coming of Age

During the 1960s polls in Britain began to come of age. Several new organisations entered the field, regular private polls were commissioned by the political parties, 'sensible' polling started to be used by pressure groups, and newspapers (and television) began to take the polls much more seriously.

Opinion Research Centre (ORC) was established by T. F. Thompson and Humphrey Taylor in 1965, with the Conservative Party as its first major client. Its main newspaper clients were the *Evening Standard* and the *Sunday Times*. Thompson had worked at Conservative Central Office, but both were critical of the attempts made by the party in the field of survey research in 1964.

The Tories had first employed survey research in 1958 in the Rochdale by-election, which may have been then, as now, in possible violation of the Representation of the People Act as an election expense, and in excess of the allowable expenditure. The Tories' advertising agency, CPV, employed research techniques in the 1959 elections, but these were largely ignored by Conservative Party leaders (CPV are reported to have spent less than £5000 on polls). In the early 1960s the Tories had some work done for them by NOP (Taylor was then an NOP employee), and in 1963 it conducted a 10 000-case study the major emphasis of which was to identify Conservative defectors and measure attitudes towards the two major parties and their leaders. Reports show that presentation of these findings confused rather than clarified the situation at Tory Central Office. This was in large part due to the leadership struggle which occupied Tory attention for the best part of 1963. From May 1963 to October 1964 the Conservatives reportedly spent about £10 000 on survey research (Teer and Spence, 1973).

Dr Mark Abrams, chairman of RSL, began work for the Labour Party in early 1956, when the late Hugh Gaitskell was leader, and continued work for Labour under Harold Wilson until the end of the decade. Dr Abrams was widely recognised as a committed social democrat, and acceptance of his work in Labour Party circles suffered as a result. His first work was on party policy (a forbidden area of inquiry in the 1970s), and, to a lesser extent, on the party's image. Only 400 electors were interviewed, and the results were regarded as preliminary. A study was, however, conducted the following year (on education), with Gaitskell's support. Further research was proposed in 1957, but Nye Bevan, as deputy leader and party treasurer, opposed the plan (as party treasurer Norman Atkinson did in 1979), and then Gaitskell dropped the idea. Abrams reflected on Labour's failure to employ survey research in an article in 1964:

Perhaps the most important reason why the Labour Party failed, in the 1950s, to engage in public opinion surveys was that the exercise could have led nowhere. The Party simply had no machinery that could have taken survey findings and used them to help shape effective political propaganda. It made sense for the Conservatives to commission research, because under the unchallenged and unchallengeable authority of the Party's informal liaison committee there was built a communications machine that digested survey findings. Nothing comparable existed in the Labour Party.

In the 1960s Nye Bevan's death removed an intractable opponent of opinion polls; Morgan Phillips retired in 1961, and a new general secretary – and publicity officer – were appointed at Labour Party headquarters. These changes led to Mark Abrams's first sizeable commissions in 1962. Teer and Spence (1973) argue that:

The message of this and subsequent surveys were [sic] clear. For the first time they were communicated to those who could benefit, not only the publicity group but also party officials and MPs. The first study was made up of interviews with 1,250 electors in marginal constituencies. The aim was to define the target voter in terms which the publicity group could use and MPs and officials could understand. And it was also to determine which issues were particularly pressing. The findings knocked on the head the original assumption made by Wilson in his 1955 report on party organisation that at least half the population were solidly Labour. They showed that the loyal supporters of the two major parties accounted for only about two-thirds of the electorate, that class, though important in defining which party a person supported, did not do so at all perfectly, that the uncommitted or floating voters were not drawn from any one particular section of the community, and that the vast majority of the voters were *not* ideological sophisticates and were not even particularly interested in politics. There were differences in the support given to certain 'policies' by Labour and Conservative backers but on many points where the Labour Party did have a particular policy Labour and Conservative voters thought very similarly. The uncommitted voters differed from these in that they were not particularly keen on either party. The objectives for the advertisers were relatively clear. They were to concentrate on the uncommitted voters, particularly in marginal seats, aiming not only at the young but also at the old, at those with children of school age and at the lower executive grades, most of whom were not very interested in politics and policies. The survey did not discover new policies, and was not intended to do so.

The survey research was continued in 1963 and 1964. Panels of the uncommitted voters were sent questionnaires at regular intervals and though several panels were kept going at the same time to keep a check on the findings, and though response rates did fall, continuing checks on those who did not reply showed that they were not dissimilar to those who replied. The panel findings were used to monitor advertising and to examine any vital changes in the priorities of the voters. In 1963, for instance, surveys found that Mr Wilson's popularity was greater than Mr Macmillan's, as a result of which the propagandists turned the spotlights on Mr Wilson.

Dr Abrams' reports were available and were reported to the whole campaign committee, but remained confidential to the campaign committee. One or two leaks apparently did occur, for instance in May 1964 the *Daily Mail* reported: 'Labour's investigations into public opinion show that the Tory campaign on defence is beginning to have an effect – and that the time has come to retaliate.' There are, however, those who believe this 'leak' was inspired by those in Conservative Central Office where emphasis on defence and foreign affairs was made in the Conservative publicity campaign of the time. Survey research was maintained even during the campaign itself in 1964 to monitor public opinion of party political broadcasts, and the overall result was clear. As Rose concluded: 'The 1964 Labour publicity group demonstrated by its use of market research, by its concentration upon the electoral audience and by the consistency with which it emphasised a few messages, that a considerable, even though imperfect, degree of rationality could be achieved in efforts to influence voters.

In 1968 Marplan began publishing quarterly political surveys for *The Times*, and for regional newspapers. There were also brief appearances by Conrad Jameson and Associates (for the Labour Party), A. J. Allen and Associates (for the *Guardian* and *The Economist*) and one or two others, none of whom had a continuing presence, except for Louis Harris Research Ltd ('Harris') which was an offshoot of the American firm in joint venture with Opinion Research Centre and Beaverbrook Newspapers. (It now exclusively owns ORC, and Beaverbrook Newspapers – now the Express Group – no longer has an interest and no longer uses ORC to do its polling.)

There were two general elections in the middle years, in 1964 and in 1966. During the period continuous polling was conducted by both Gallup and NOP, but at the 1964 election they were joined by the *Daily*

Express poll (still not taken very seriously by either the paper or the public) and RSL for the *Observer*. The election was close, the polls' record being, on the whole, not bad (see Table 4.2).

TABLE 4.2 General election 1964

	Observer (11 Oct.) (%)	Daily Mail (15 Oct.) (%)	Daily Telegraph (15 Oct.) (%)	Daily Express (15 Oct.) (%)	Actual result (15 Oct.) (%)
			Publication of Poll		
Con	45.0	44.3	42.5	44.5	42.9
Lab	46.0	47.4	46.0	43.7	44.8
Lib/Other	9.0	8.3	11.5	11.8	12.3
Lab Lead	+1.0	+3.1	+3.5	−0.8	+1.9

In 1964, as before and certainly since, company share prices on the Stock Exchange seemed to reflect poll stories, and were the subject of hostile comment. Other publicity given to poll findings (especially in by-elections) led to calls for banning them. In Orpington in 1962 the Liberal victory was widely thought to have been helped by publication of an NOP poll which indicated the likely possibility of toppling the Tory candidate if enough traditional Labour voters cast a 'tactical' vote for the Liberal. Resulting criticism seemed to enhance polls' reputation rather than detract from it. Butler and King, in their 1964 election book, argued:

> Polling is after all only a systematic expansion of reporting. In a free society people must be allowed to enquire into and report on public opinion. A ban on the publication of polls would lead to a black market in rumour about the findings of private polls. The major remedy to any supposed evil caused by pre-election polls lies in lively and expert criticism of the polls' findings and in the growth of public understanding about the strengths and limitations of the polls. There is, in fact, no evidence whatever that opinion polls have ever induced bandwagon voting.

Between September 17th and September 23rd the Gallup poll found that 38 % of people claimed that they knew what at least one poll was showing. Gallup, which then showed Labour ahead, was thought by 15 % to be doing so and by 11 % to be showing the Conservatives in the lead; NOP which then showed the Conservatives ahead was thought by 15 % to be doing so and by 7 % to be showing Labour in the lead; the *Daily Express*, which then showed the Conservatives ahead, was thought by 11 % to be doing so and by 6 % to be showing Labour in the lead. This extraordinary level of inaccuracy in ordinary people's recall encourages scepticism about the potential of polls to create bandwagon effects.

According to the chronicler of British elections, David Butler, and his colleague of the 1960s, Anthony King:

> Opinion polls reached a new level of political importance in the 1964 Parliament. Everyone watching to see when Mr Wilson would decide to call an election knew that Mr Wilson was watching the polls. (Butler and King, 1966)

Some commentators also credited the polls with a critical influence on Sir Alec Douglas-Home's decision to give up the Conservative leadership (reportedly not true according to T. F. Thompson, who was 'tactical adviser' to Sir Alec Douglas-Home at the time). The influence of the polls was not dimmed by their vagaries, according to Butler and King, even though NOP came a 20+ per cent cropper on a by-election in January 1965, predicting a 20 per cent win for Patrick Gordon Walker who, on the day, lost Leyton by half a percentage point.

During the period there were also inexplicable differences between NOP and Gallup, but perhaps the most important impact was being made in Conservative Central Office, by Humphrey Taylor, and in Transport House (the Labour Party HQ), by Mark Abrams. A ringing endorsement of Taylor's work (he was working virtually full-time on Tory work during the period) was made by one younger Central Office official, who said:

> When the old-timers talked nonsense before, all you could do was say 'Rubbish' and they'd just say 'Rubbish' back. Now you can produce some evidence. (Butler and King, 1966)

It was important, too, that both Taylor and Abrams became known, principally through the *Sunday Times*, for their private polling for the parties.

By the 1966 election the *Daily Telegraph*, *Daily Mail*, *Daily Express* and *Observer* had been joined by the *Guardian*, *Financial Times*, *The Economist* and *Sunday Times* in publishing polls. The fact that the two most highly regarded polls agreed in showing Labour 10 per cent or more ahead almost throughout the campaign took much of the steam out of the contest. This led to calls to ban polls, to which the defeated Heath responded sharply: 'Ban polls? Of course not. You can't do that in a free society': Wilson, in an early parliamentary reply as Prime Minister, flatly refused to consider any restriction on election polls (ibid.).

TABLE 4.3 *General election 1966*

	Publication of poll				
	Research Services (27 March) (%)	*Daily Express (31 March) (%)*	*NOP (31 March) (%)*	*Gallup (31 March) (%)*	*Actual Results (31 March) (%)*
Con	41.6	37.4	41.6	40.0	41.4
Lab	49.7	54.1	50.6	51.0	48.7
Lib/Other	8.7	8.5	7.8	9.0	9.9
Lab lead	+8.1	+16.7	+9.0	+11.0	+7.3

So, while the final polls were within a reasonable distance of the result, apart from the *Express*, Research Services came out marginally closest, despite finishing fieldwork a week before polling day (see Table 4.3). NOP, alone among the polls, re-interviewed at the end of the campaign a sample of the people interviewed earlier, thus introducing a panel technique into its prediction. Butler and King (1966) concluded with a suggestion for the press and a warning for politicians:

It is to be hoped that the press will now exploit the pollsters' techniques to throw light on opinion and attitudes in more sophisticated ways than hitherto. The Conservative party has, belatedly, found it worthwhile to invest considerable resources in the collection and analysis of survey data about the British public.

If such research is not to be abused, it is desirable that the sort of information which parties may have at their disposal should also be gathered independently – and published.

Politicians, and everyone else, can easily be misled by the apparent findings of polls. The intelligent statesman will neither ignore them nor be intimidated by them. In the short run public opinion sets limits to the politically possible and it is useful to know these limits. But public opinion can be fickle. As Winston Churchill showed before the war, there need be nothing suicidal in defying the opinion of the majority. It is worth remembering that democratic politicians have always conducted affairs with an eye on public opinion. They now have more accurate tools for measuring what public opinion really is. What they will need is education in how to use these tools – and how not to use them.

The publication of *Political Change in Britain* by David Butler and Donald Stokes (1969), which analysed results from a panel study conducted in 1963, 1964 and 1966, had an important impact on politicians, journalists, political scientists and pollsters. Unfortunately, the much improved understanding of British electoral behaviour did not help the polls when the June 1970 general election came along.

General Election June 1970: Great Britain's 1948

During the 1970 election campaign there were five polls being published – the same number as in 1966 – but they were read by an enormously increased audience as exclusive publication was abandoned. Earlier, newspapers had jealously guarded the copyright they had on their polls. The result was that in 1970, when the polls got it so badly wrong, they were very much in the public eye.

For the first time, polls dominated campaign reporting; eight of the twenty-three issues of *The Times* published between 18 May and 18 June headlined poll results as the main front page story. The Harris Poll, the following September, found that 62 per cent of the country remembered seeing polls (of those, 71 per cent recalled seeing them on television). In the 'sunshine' election, when the only surprise was the winner, polls dominated the election news.

ORC polled for the *Evening Standard* and the *Sunday Times*, Harris, the ORC stablemate, for the *Daily Express*, Gallup for the *Telegraph*, NOP for the *Daily Mail* and Marplan for *The Times*. Marplan was then a subsidiary of McCann-Erickson Advertising Agency. ORC also continued its work for the Tories, together with a long-term panel study, with fieldwork done by the British Market Research Bureau (BMRB). Mark Abrams's departure to the civil service meant that the *Observer* dropped Research Services and ran no poll and the Labour Party began to use MORI, which was set up in 1969. MORI is the acronym for Market & Opinion Research International (the author is its managing director).

During the years between 1966 and 1970 public opinion, previously extraordinarily stable, began to swing more wildly. Labour, the 1966 victor, enjoyed a 20 per cent lead in May 1966 but just two years later was 20 per cent behind. Four years later, in May 1970 when the election was called, Labour was ahead again. In the midst of this, and following the polls' rather mediocre record in 1966, the Speaker's Conference on Electoral Law reported in June 1967 and recommended a seventy-two-hour pre-election ban on the publication of poll findings. This recommendation was scorned by the press and leading politicians alike, and was not acted upon.

The press reports of the polls during the period seldom gave interviewing dates, hardly ever reported 'don't know's or refusals, seldom offered breakdowns of top-line figures and showed little interest in issues. Sampling error was seldom mentioned, and headlines frequently screamed out shifts of electoral support based on statistically insignificant changes.

At the beginning of the 1970 campaign, however, led by Humphrey Taylor (*The Economist*, 13 January 1979) of ORC, the pollsters banded together (in self-defence) and published a Code of Practice which ensured that the worst excesses of the papers would be curbed (see the appendix to this chapter). The effect of the publication of the code was to give the pollsters a weapon in their battles with their clients; for the most part poll reports thereafter reported at least fieldwork dates, sample sizes and number of sampling points.

In the event, after a notably wild month when NOP's trend-lines crossed Marplan's, ORC's crossed Harris's, and Gallup trends crossed themselves (one a national electorate series and the other taken in the marginals), they all got it wrong in straight poll figures; ORC adjusted its final figures by turn-out to be on the right side – just – of a Tory victory (see Table 4.4). All published on election day, except Marplan who published a day earlier. ORC's forecast was based on a recall on 257 respondents interviewed earlier (recalls now being common practice), and corrected for differential turnout, as shown in Table 4.5. Only one

TABLE 4.4 *General Election 1970*

	ORC (%)	Harris (%)	NOP (%)	Gallup (%)	Marplan (%)	Actual result (%)
Con	46.5	46	44.0	42	41.5	46.2
Lab	45.5	48	48.1	49	50.1	43.8
Lib/Other	8.0	6	7.9	9	8.4	10.0
Lab lead	−1.0	+2	+4.1	+7	+9.6	−2.4

voter ORC re-interviewed had switched from Conservative to Labour while fourteen switched from Labour to Conservative; and so on this thin reed ORC's reputation rested.

TABLE 4.5 *ORC's Final Prediction 1970*

	Survey 13–15 June (1583) (%)	Re-interviews 16–17 June (257)(%)	Re-interviews adjusted for turnout (%)
Con	42.0	45.5	46.5
Lab	46.5	45.5	45.5
Lib/Other	11.5	9.0	8.0
Lab lead	+4.5	0	−1.0

Interestingly, in 1970 three polls had been conducted by random methods, two (ORC and Gallup) by quota. The mean error of random samples on the Conservative lead was 7.6, by quota samples 5.4. NOP, Gallup and Marplan did not adjust their figures in any way (other than to reallocate 'don't know's), ORC adjusted for differential turn-out, changing level pegging for a 1 per cent Tory lead, while Harris merged a 4 per cent national Labour lead with a 1 per cent Conservative lead in a special sample of marginals and found a 3 per cent Labour lead. Harris then adjusted 1 per cent for differential turn-out and ended up with a 2 per cent Labour forecast.

Why did the polls get it wrong? Late shifts and inaccurate quota sampling seemed to answer a similar question in the USA in 1948. Certainly the method of sampling did not appear to be the answer, and late shift evidence was suggestive rather than conclusive. Hypotheses were many, and included differential voting by non-contacts, organised deception on the part of Tory supporters, an anti-poll bandwagon, collusion on the part of the pollsters, selective turn-out, and others. Post-mortems by the polls and academic examinations are for the most part inconclusive, but tend to support the late swing hypothesis. (See Teer and Spence, 1973; Butler and Pinto-Dushinsky, 1971; Hodder Williams, 1970; Abrams, 1970; Market Research Society, 1972; Rose, 1970.)

Public polls were in the limelight; private polls went underground. In the late 1960s and in early 1970 Mark Abrams conducted the last of his work for the Labour Party, on a budget of £15 000, on a variety of subjects including party activists, youth, party advertising and other topics. His last poll, reported only to the party leader, suggested Labour might well lose an early election. His findings were held close to the chest by top party brass, only three copies being given over to the party. It was then, in late 1969, that the party's publicity advisers recommended that MORI be asked to do Labour's private polls. Like everyone else, MORI was instructed to plan for an autumn election and was startled by (and unready for) the May election call. Only two studies were conducted. The first was a 2000-case random survey to identify changers and potential changers, and important issues. It identified working-class women, especially those living in the midlands and the north, as the potential risk group, and prices as Labour's Achilles' heel. The party, for the most part unconcerned as a result of Wilson's popularity lead and the fine weather which promised a high turn-out, none the less commissioned a second, quickie poll on standards of living, Wilson's (and Heath's) television performance and canvassing. Several aides, including Ron Hayward, later general secretary, sensed the message, especially that the public were fed up with the 'slanging' that the politicians were seen to be doing. Hayward did not attend the top strategy meetings, but he was sufficiently concerned to take the findings to Number 10 to see Wilson privately. His worries were dismissed by the leader, however. Less than £10 000 was spent altogether, and there is no evidence that MORI polls had any impact on Labour's election strategy in 1970 other than to tone down the more strident attacks by Labour speakers.

The Conservatives, meanwhile, had mounted an elaborate and consistent programme of private polls. Starting in 1966, the Tories spent approximately £30 000 a year with ORC (and on a BMRB panel). There were continuous panel operations (starting with the 4500 electors interviewed in 1965), re-interviewing 700 or so every seven months to detect and determine causes of changes in voting intentions. One startling finding was that at least 30 per cent of the electorate had changed their voting intention in some way between 1964 and 1966, and tended to be the C2s (skilled working class), under-35s and women. This finding affected party policy, election strategy and advertising. It also brought a sense of proportion to Tory leaders, reminding them in the mid-term period, when record anti-government swings both in the polls and in by-elections were running their way, that the tide of public opinion went down as well as up.

The ORC work also included monthly studies on specific topics, issues, newspaper readership, critical seats and so on. The findings from these were fed into Tory policy study groups as well as into Central Office and to the leadership. The sale of council houses which proved to be such a winner for the Tories in 1979 was first discovered almost by accident in an ORC poll for the Greater London Council (GLC) election in 1967 and first applied nationally – if gingerly – in 1970. Other work included polls the day after party broadcasts, publicity tests, slogan and semantic studies, speech impact studies and, of considerable importance, by-election studies.

The election campaign saw three sets of daily 'quickie' polls (with 500 respondents) on the previous night's television, on issues and on the impact of the mass media. These were telephoned back and ready by, respectively, lunch-time for the party's television advisers, tea-time for the Research Department's issues team and early evening for the Central Office publicity people.

The contrast between the parties' polling operations has been likened to operating blind (Labour) and with 20:20 eyesight (Tories). In Transport House polling figures were jealously guarded and available to a few; at Central Office they had a distribution list of over fifty and were regularly presented to the party leadership.

February 1974

A silent commentary on the record of the polls in the 1970 election is that for the first time since 1955 they did not receive a chapter to themselves in the Nuffield book. Despite this, the polls were as much quoted in the press as they had been in 1970 – and perhaps even more on television – and both major parties mounted substantial private polling programmes.

Six polling organisations conducted major national polls for the press. All contracts continued except that *The Times* dropped Marplan in favour of ORC and the *Observer* re-entered the polling business with Business Decisions, then part-owned by Gallup. From the outset the polls presented a confused picture. Gallup, ORC and Harris all published Conservative leads on St Valentine's Day (14 February), two weeks before election day, of 1.5, 2 and 11 per cent (*sic*) respectively. Earlier, Marplan (for London Weekend Television's *Weekend World*) had shown a 6 per cent Tory lead while Business Decisions' (*Observer*) poll showed a 7.7 per cent Conservative lead on 10 February. The polls plainly had an impact on the Liberals, according to Butler and Kavanagh (1974). After an early slump every poll showed a trend to the Liberals, and added impetus to the Liberal spirit. It was an unpopular election – the result of a confrontation between the miners (who had great sympathy among the public) and Edward Heath (who had respect but little sympathy). Heath's pollster, still the now-familiar Humphrey Taylor, urged a quick, sharp election in January. His advice was considered, but Heath soldiered on while Labour frantically prepared its attack. The effect of the month's delay was to throw away the key advantage of surprise that a British Prime Minister enjoys of an almost sole right to determine when an election shall be (only in practice subject to a five-year limit on the life of a Parliament or on a vote of no confidence in the House of Commons). The major piece of advice which Taylor gave his client once the election started was that he should avoid the bread-and-butter issues, and play to the hilt the government's role as a saviour from national chaos – advice that Heath also rejected.

The Tory government was generally agreed to have won the first week's campaign on the theme of 'Who runs Britain?', but by the second week Labour's concerted attack on the government's handling of the economy began to turn the tide (Crewe *et al.*, 1976). One hopeful Conservative Party official propounded a 'V-shaped theory of voting behaviour': 'The Government always wins the first week. The Opposition always gains in the second week. The big question is how near the Government comes to regaining the peak of the first week.' It failed.

On the day the published polls came close, but were too Tory. The Conservatives won the popular vote, by 0.8 per cent, but Labour, with more MPs elected, won the election (see Table 4.6). The two employing the largest sample sizes, random sampling and re-interviewing, Harris and NOP, were the furthest adrift. The closest published poll, Gallup, used a quota sample of 1013 and a re-interview of 868 respondents.

TABLE 4.6 *General election, February 1974*

	ORC (%)	Harris (%)	NOP (%)	Gallup (%)	Marplan (%)	Actual Result (%)
Con	39.7	40.2	39.5	39.5	36.5	38.8
Lab	36.7	35.2	35.5	37.5	34.5	38.0
Lib/Other	28.3	24.6	25.6	25.0	29.0	23.2
Lab. lead	−3.0	−5.0	−4.0	−2.0	−2.0	−0.8

The ORC–Harris people were quick to shout *mea culpa*. ORC's private polls had indicated the Tories would coast in. Louis Harris was in Britain and both on television and in the *Daily Express* said: 'We . . . could not have been more mistaken.' Taylor told *The Times*:

'We very much regret that we misled a great many people into believing the Conservatives would win by a comfortable majority', and T. F. Thompson, ORC chairman, said: 'Once again the opinion polls as a whole appear to have misled commentators, the public and the politicians themselves.' Yet all the polls said was that the Tories would get more votes than Labour – and they did.

All the polls overestimated the Liberals: they did not contest 106 of the 623 British seats, and the pollsters failed to take this into account. All the polls underestimated Labour – all but Marplan adjusted for differential turn-out and in each instance this increased the Tory lead erroneously (Worcester, 1975). And the difficulty of translating votes, which is what the polls measure, into seats in the House of Commons was crucial this time. Rose, in *Britain at the Polls* (1974), discussed this problem at length. He concluded his treatise on the polls and the February 1974 election with the following thoughtful remarks:

> The 1974 election demonstrated that newspapers are not interested in using the polls to do anything more than give a forecast about which party is winning or will win the election. The *Daily Mail* and the *Daily Express* spent more money on high quality samples than any other paper, they neglected to publicise in detail what their money bought, or even to give briefly the technical facts documenting the quality of their samples. After the election, both polls issued on their own account well-documented studies reporting more details of their pre-election polls than their client newspapers wished to print. The serious papers, with smaller type and much more lineage, gave more space to reporting the opinions of voters; but first priority was always given to opinions that would tend to corroborate or qualify the replies about voting intentions – for example, attitudes about party leaders or about which party would handle best the most important questions of the day.
>
> The single-mindedness of the press is striking because the British press was burnt in 1970 by publicising election forecasts that were wrong by any standard. This single-mindedness is also surprising because the 1974 election occurred at a time when the issues facing the country were very serious and popular attitudes uncertain. Yet no paper during the campaign used opinion poll data to explore in depth the reaction of the British people to a domestic crisis as grave as any in a generation.
>
> The chief conclusion that this writer would draw from the performance of the polls (and the press) is that there is need for

fundamental rethinking about polls by those who sponsor them. Each newspaper editor currently sponsoring a poll should ask himself a simple question: Why am I doing this? If it is 'to get tomorrow's news today', he should realise that the risks of getting the story wrong are real, especially at a time when the party system and the electoral system are not working as predictably as in the quarter-century since 1945.

Ironically, the press could provide more political information for its readers if it returned to the original concept of the polls as a device for assessing *opinion*, rather than for forecasting *behaviour*. An error margin of 3 or 5 percentage points is of little consequence if one wishes to ascertain how the country divides on matters of major policy, or abortion. It is technically simple (and economically attractive) to take the results of a single poll and use them in several different stories reporting popular attitudes about issues of the day. In fact, before the surge of interest in forecasting polls, the now defunct *News Chronicle* published brief stories several times a week giving Gallup Poll reports of popular opinions about issues without regard to voting intentions.

This was the first general election campaign in which both major parties had invested in extensive pre-election and daily election polls. It was the first time polls 'seem now to be a permanent part of the parties' campaign armoury' (Rose, 1974). It was the first time both parties' pollsters sat at the 'top table' and it was the first extensive use of multivariate analysis of large-scale panel data.

ORC had been conducting regular polls on issues, target voters and the like, but had neither the budget nor the attention it had enjoyed while the Conservatives were out of office in the 1966–70 period. The nature of British politics is such that political leaders in power focus, naturally enough, on the running of the government, while, again naturally enough, the focus of the 'outs' is on getting back. This tends both to loosen party purse strings and to 'concentrate the mind wonderfully' on anything which may assist in winning back the reins of government.

This no doubt was a factor in the Labour Party's decision in July 1972 to employ MORI on a regular basis, both to advise and interpret published polls and to carry out extensive qualitative and quantitative research on behalf of the party. In addition to a large-scale panel study, several by-election studies and run-up tracking studies, MORI published a monthly *Public Opinion Digest* from late 1972 until the autumn of 1974, initially supplying fifty copies to the Campaign Committee and senior Transport House staff and eventually 2000 copies to all local constituency parties, all Labour MPs and parliamentary candidates, all professional staff and others.

The private research carried out during this period and during the election was closely guarded, although presented internally to such groups, in addition to the Campaign Committee, as the regional organisers, research department staff, the national executive of Young Socialists and party advertising advisers.

In the autumn of 1973 a small team consisting of Percy Clark, publicity director of the party, Dennis Lyons (the late Lord Lyons), Peter Davis (later Lord Lovell-Davis) and Dr Bernard Donoughue, a lecturer at the London School of Economics, joined together (assisted by Adrian Shaw, one of Wilson's staff aides) to work with MORI on the formulation of questions for a series of semi-monthly 2000-case tracking studies to consider poll findings and advise Wilson on pre-campaign tactics. This group met weekly, and its work enabled the party to be up to date on public attitudes to issues as it had never been before. It also worked out a planned programme of research for the election period.

The false election period in January 1974 intensified the group's efforts and when the election call came a final panel recall was initiated, a series of daily 'quickie' surveys was launched and a special sounding was taken in Scotland (MORI liaised with a separate Scottish advisory group on this work). The findings from these studies (and those of the October 1974 election) were lodged by direction of the National Executive Committee of the Labour Party (overriding some MORI misgivings) at the Social Science Research Council (SSRC) Archives at the University of Essex, but embargoed until after the 'next' (May 1979) election.

Former Prime Minister (Sir) Harold Wilson commented on MORI's work for the Labour Party in his presidential address to the Market Research Society's 1978 conference:

It is no secret that Bob Worcester and MORI produced daily polls for me in the most speculative of all elections, the 'confrontation' election of 1974, when even the most experienced politician could not forecast whether it would be confined to a single issue – where we might have lost or whether my effort to widen it would succeed. At the end of the day, we had a plurality of five seats, with, for the first time, the arrival of considerable numbers of MPs from new parties. What Bob Worcester's polls were so useful for, and it was to this that they were directed, was the highlighting of *issues*. A political leader in a general election, apart from being chronically overworked and unable to study even the daily press very carefully, is like a warrior or a pilot operating in almost total fog.

What we got – and I have no doubt our opponents had the same – were authoritative estimates on public opinion on which were the most important issues. Was it simply 'who runs the country – the Government or the miners'? Or was the Common Market a big issue? What about the cost of living – or housing? Were pensions a big issue? How were different groups of the nation, constituency, regions, age groups going to vote on some of these big issues? What difference would nationalisation make? What were the Liberals doing and where?

This was more important by far than daily estimates of the total final vote. On this latter question, I am an agnostic, though not an atheist. I could be convinced, but on the identification of issues I believe market research has a valuable role to play provided that, as in any other campaign, intelligence is the servant and never the master of those conducting the campaign. So much depends on hunch and long years of training – and knowing people and their areas.

And of course, as political market research has become more sophisticated, those responsible are more able not only to recognise the limitations of their research, but also to make allowance for the underlying factors. (Wilson, 1978)

The daily polls were based on 540 interviews using a tightly controlled interlocking (eighteen-cell) quota sample in fifty-four randomly selected constituencies throughout Great Britain. Their questionnaire coverage was mixed, voting intention being used mainly for cross-analysis (the figures themselves were given only to Wilson and Party Secretary Ron Hayward after early – and damaging – leaks occurred). The question-naires were short, usually about ten questions. Key topics were issues, salience and party preference, canvassing, television broadcast recall and assessment, 'slanging', 'promises the country cannot afford', national press readership (for cross-analysis purposes) and other items. A pattern of questions was worked out in advance, with some questions asked daily, some every other day and many less frequently. Space was left for last-minute additions. These polls were used by the party to keep its campaign on track and were used principally (as were the Tories') in matters of tactics and presentation of policy.

A last-minute addition to the polling programme was a 1000-case Scottish sample, as the rise in the support for the Scottish National Party (SNP) placed a number of Scottish Labour seats in jeopardy. The strategy had to be 'hold Scotland and Wales, and get gains in England'. The results of the Scottish surveys determined shifts in the party's stance, helped shape Wilson's key Glasgow speech, and were thought by some to be an important factor in Labour's relative success in Scotland.

The greatest impact on the party's campaign came from a multivariate analysis of the data from the recall of the panel. Nearly a thousand respondents were recalled the first week of the campaign, and individuals' shifts were identified. A 'semantic differential' party image profile technique was combined with issue salience and party preference analysis in a factor-cluster analysis cross-tabulation. This enabled MORI to identify a target group of 10 per cent of voters who could be persuaded to vote Labour. The survey found these voters were most concerned with the issues of wages and salaries, housing, poverty and unemployment. Their 'ideal image factors' were a party which 'represented all classes', was 'moderate' in tone and which 'kept its promises'. These findings were presented to the Campaign Committee the Saturday before polling, were reflected in the leader's press conference that morning and in his speech that evening, and became the party's communications strategy during the final crucial few days.

The quota, small-sample 'quickies' proved highly sensitive to short-term shifts, giving Wilson advance notice of likely public poll findings published later and, in the end, were highly accurate in forecasting the outcome.

October 1974

Polls won back their own chapter in the October 1974 Nuffield election study, despite the egg on their collective faces. Every single prediction in June 1970 had been too Labour, every single prediction in February 1974 was too favourable to the Conservatives. The pollsters were on the defensive.

Client–poll liaisons were largely unchanged. As in February, ORC was used by *The Times*, the London *Evening Standard* and the Conservative Party. Marplan (whose 1970 forecast in *The Times* was the worst general election forecast ever recorded in Britain) was working for the 'popular' Murdoch-owned newspapers (the *Sun* and the Sunday *News of the World*). Gallup polled for the *Telegraph*, Harris for the *Daily Express* and NOP for the *Daily Mail*, although it produced no final predictive poll. Harris had also replaced Marplan for *Weekend World* on independent television. Business Decisions carried on for the

Observer and ORC conducted a limited panel operation for the *Sunday Times*. During the three-week pre-election period the published polls carried out some 40 000 interviews with well over 10 000 more conducted privately.

Every poll apart from one (NOP, 16 September) showed Labour comfortably ahead. They were also published in a more clustered way than ever before. Of the twenty-five polls that were published, twenty appeared on a Thursday or a Sunday, none on a Monday or Tuesday and only one on a Friday or Saturday. The last week there were no polls on the Monday and Tuesday before polling despite numerous City rumours to the contrary. Then when the *Daily Mail* published an NOP poll on Wednesday 9 October, showing a 14.5 per cent Labour lead (fieldwork 2–5 October), followed on election day, Thursday, by Marplan with 10.5 per cent Labour, Harris 8.4 per cent Labour, ORC 7.4 per cent Labour, and Gallup 5.5 per cent, only the fact that they had got it so wrong before kept interest alive. In the event, they were mostly wrong again, this time too Labour, and pro-government (see Table 4.7). NOP and the *Daily Mail* stated that their eve-of-poll result was not intended as a forecast. It was, however, widely considered to be such. It showed a 12.5 per cent Labour lead. NOP and Harris employed random sampling (combined sample of over 4000) and overestimated Labour's lead by 7 per cent; Gallup, ORC and Marplan used quota samples (re-interviewed) and were out 7.8 per cent on the Labour share. All used late fieldwork, re-interviews, adjustment for turn-out (except Gallup), but all (except Gallup) were outside the usual ±2 per cent margin usually quoted as sampling tolerance. Other theories having fallen by the wayside, there followed the observation that the October 1974 election was the fourth in a row in which every single poll overestimated the support for the party that was in the lead. This led to the speculation of the 'underdog' effect, replacing the 'bandwagon' effect that had held sway earlier. (Of course the May 1979 results negated that theory, with

TABLE 4.7 *General Election, October 1974*

	ORC (%)	Harris (%)	Gallup (%)	Marplan (%)	Actual Result (%)
Con	34.4	34.6	36.0	33.3	36.7
Lab	41.8	43.0	41.5	43.8	40.2
Lib/Other	23.8	22.4	22.5	22.9	23.1
Lab lead	+7.4	+8.4	+5.5	+10.5	+3.5

three under- and two overestimating the Tory share and all within ±2 per cent.) Turn-out adjustments this time (they usually favour the Tories) improved predictions: ORC reduced a 10 per cent Labour lead to 7.4 per cent, Harris reduced an 11 per cent Labour lead to 8.4 per cent. Marplan did not ask a question about likelihood of voting in its survey for the *Sun*.

According to Butler and Kavanagh (1975), the two main parties' private polls' programmes were similar. ORC augmented its February research design by adding advertising effectiveness studies and especially focusing on the possibility of a Liberal breakthrough. Labour had MORI continue its fortnightly 2000-case tracking studies in the summer, and two 1000-case studies of substantial length mounted in Scotland, some motivational research and another recall on the 1973 panel. Its election period effort was expanded from the February model, with all broadcasts, including the Liberals', being measured.

The value of private polls is often challenged by some party officials, mostly on the grounds that they duplicate much that is available from published sources. Yet that they offer quick, focused and confidential assessment of specific campaign problems was certainly proved in this election. On Friday 27 September, when Mrs Thatcher, then a shadow minister, announced a policy of $9\frac{1}{2}$ per cent mortgages and guaranteed to implement the Tory mortgage promise 'by Christmas', her promise received widespread coverage on television and in the weekend's newspapers. This worried the Labour Party, and tentative plans were made to counter the offer. A MORI survey on the Sunday, however, found that 63 per cent of the public felt the Conservatives were 'making promises the country cannot afford', compared with 45 per cent who had thought so on the previous Thursday, the day before Mrs Thatcher's undertaking. This settled the issue for Labour; Conservative private polls later showed that less than half the electorate believed the $9\frac{1}{2}$ per cent pledge.

Shifting electoral intentions, obscured by independent surveys, continued to be identified by panel studies. In October 1974 Harris found 23 per cent of its panel changed their intentions between dissolution and election day, while 33 per cent of the smaller ORC/*Sunday Times* panel reported that they had changed their minds, less than the 43 per cent found in February but much more than the 20 per cent recorded in comparable studies a decade earlier.

Further, recall studies conducted by NOP after each 1974 campaign showed that while two-thirds of the electorate claimed to have made up their minds before the election was called, there was still a victory to be fought for, and an election to be won, or lost, during the three-week campaign.

THE ROLE OF THE POLLS IN THE 1979 BRITISH GENERAL ELECTION

The long period between October 1974 and April 1979 when Parliament forced an election on a reluctant Prime Minister was enlivened by Britain's first national referendum (on joining the European Economic Community), a devolution referendum in Scotland, the resignation of Wilson and the election of Callaghan as Leader of the Parliamentary Labour Party and thereby Prime Minister, and the reportedly 'accidental' election of Mrs Thatcher to replace Edward Heath as Tory leader. It was also a period of minority government, when the Liberals (formally) and other parties (in practice) kept a cautious Labour Party in power.

The EEC referendum, in June 1975, gave the polls their first chance to measure their skills against an outcome in Britain that did not have to be recalculated as seats in the House of Commons. On the whole, they came out very well although, once again, the random sample (Harris) performed worse, not better, than the quota ones, and larger sample sizes did not necessarily mean better (see Table 4.8). Four of the results were as close as anyone can get, but as Butler and Kitzinger (1976) observed: 'The error in the forecast of ORC (13 % in terms of the gap between victor and vanquished) was greater than in any final poll in any British general election since 1945.'

TABLE 4.8 *EEC Referendum, 1975*

	Gallup (%)	ORC (%)	Harris (%)	Marplan (%)	NOP (%)	MORI (%)	Actual Result (%)
Yes	68	73.7	72	68	68	67	67
No	32	26.3	28	32	32	33	33
Yes lead	36	47.4	44	36	36	34	34

When the election finally did come it was long expected, and most polling contracts had long been settled. Gallup had continued its every-third-Thursday-in-the-*Telegraph* time-series, and swung into the election without a pause. NOP, owned by the *Daily Mail* Group, had published sporadically only under a somewhat strained relationship with the *Mail's* editor, and Marplan continued with the *Sun*, now Britain's best-selling newspaper, having edged out the *Daily Mirror* as 'King of the Pops'. The main change was that following Humphrey Taylor's move to the USA to work with Louis Harris, first the *Sunday Times* and then the *Express* Group (the London *Evening Standard* and *Daily Express*) approached MORI in 1977. ORC continued to do the Tories' private polling, however, and Labour continued to employ MORI. Research Services returned to political polling (under new people and after a decade) for the *Observer*.

The use sponsors make of polls is neatly, if perhaps too simply, summed up by Butler and Kavanagh (1980): 'In a general election the press sponsors public opinion polls which are concerned with predicting the result; the parties sponsor private opinion polls which are concerned with analysing reactions to the campaign.' There were more published polls than ever before. The reason for this was that the campaign was a long one, partially to give the public their Easter long weekend but also to slow the pace of the campaign. Again, some 50 000 electors were questioned by the major polling organisations.

From the outset the Conservatives led by a substantial margin, but nothing like the 21 per cent recorded by RSL in the *Observer* on the first Sunday of the campaign. Their first poll departed from the usual practice of asking those who refuse or say don't know how they'll vote, 'Which party are you more inclined to support?' or 'Which party do you lean towards?' or a similar follow-up. In later surveys they revised their questioning procedure, although this did not bring their polls into line with the others. Most commentators quickly cautioned against reading much into the RSL findings, although they were duly included in the 'poll of polls' calculated by several newspapers.

Leaving RSL aside, the message of the polls throughout the campaign was clear: fifteen out of fifteen polls taken between the call of the election and 25 April, i.e. over the first three weeks of the campaign, had the Tories at 48 ± 2 per cent and Labour at 40 ± 2 per cent. The fourth week of the campaign, sensing a handsome Tory victory, the public narrowed the gap, first in MORI's poll in Saturday's *Daily Express* reporting a 3 per cent Tory lead, then in the NOP 0.7 per cent Labour lead on television the Monday evening before polling day and published in the *Daily Mail* on the Tuesday. Asked that day by a journalist if I was a 'bandwagon' or a 'boomerang' man, I said: 'In this election I'd say I'm a "boomerang-backlash-bandwagon" man.' By that I meant that the public were then boomeranging against the thought of an 80–100 seat

Tory majority, but would backlash when they thought Labour might win after all, and in the final day or two of the campaign would bandwagon as the momentum of the backlash built up. In the event, I think that is exactly what happened.

On the day, the polls proved to be nearly all within a whisker of the actual result (see Table 4.9). Gallup, closest in both 1974 elections, was furthest out, yet still in terms of average error well within the normal sampling limits of ± 2 per cent given its substantial sample, although considerably overestimating the Labour share. The polls with the latest fieldwork, NOP and MORI, neatly bracketed the gap, within a single percentage point, and both the Labour and the Liberal share of vote.

In contradiction to the earlier Butler–Kavanagh quotation, the *Sunday Times*, on strike during the campaign, none the less commissioned MORI to conduct the most extensive evaluative survey research programme yet sponsored by a newspaper. In 1977, when the *Sunday Times* political team and MORI agreed the *Sunday Times* panel outline, it was determined that the study's purpose was to be explanatory rather than predictive, and that its objective would be to explain, throughout the campaign and following its conclusion on election day, *why* what happened did happen and *who* among the electorate was affected by the campaign itself.

Two reasons were behind this decision: one, the fact that there was substantial evidence to indicate that in the last three general elections preceding this one the election was won and/or lost in the last week of the campaign and therefore that the publication of data necessarily collected nearly a week before election day precluded a predictive effort; second, that the approach of the *Sunday Times* itself is one of 'insight' and analysis, and thus a panel study, with its unique ability to examine with absolute precision whether an individual's voting intention had indeed changed between week one in the election and, say, week three, because MORI were recalling on the same people throughout *and immediately following the campaign*, would provide a sounder analytical tool.

Of course, any panel study introduces bias into the attitudes and behaviour of its members. Also it is recognised that the nature of a recall survey means that some of its original members are unable to be contacted in later weeks due to illness, holidays, lack of patience. In this instance, a reasonable recall rate was achieved (as indicated in Table 4.10) and in each case the recall sample was weighted in the computer analysis to ensure that a differential recall achievement (say, between young people and OAPs) did not affect the analysis.

TABLE 4.9 *General election 1979*

Poll	Gallup	MORI	Marplan	NOP	MORI	Actual Result
Newspaper	Telegraph	Express	Sun	Mail	Ev. Std	
Sample size	2348	974	1973	1069	1089	
Fieldwork	30 April–1 May	30 April–1 May	1 May	1–2 May	2 May	3 May
Method	Quota	Recall	Quota	Quota	Quota	
Weighting	Yes	Yes	Yes	Yes	No	
	%	%	%	%	%	
Con	43.0	44.4	45.0	46.0	45.0	44.9
Lab	41.0	38.8	38.5	39.0	37.0	37.7
Lib	13.5	13.5	13.5	12.5	15.0	14.1
Other	2.5	3.3	3.0	2.5	3.0	3.3
Con lead	2.0	5.6	6.5	7.0	8.0	7.2
Error on gap	–5.2	–1.6	–0.7	–0.2	+0.8	
Average error	1.65	0.55	0.45	1.20	0.50	
Maximum error	3.4	1.1	0.8	1.3	0.9	

TABLE 4.10 Sunday Times Panel *General Election 1979*

| | Week | | | |
	I	II	III	IV
Date	4–6 April	17–19 April	24–26 April	4–5 May
Sample size	1087	928	894	883
Percentage of original	100%	85%	82%	81%

SOURCE: MORI
    Sunday Times Panel

The Findings

On 3 May 1979, at the general election, 92 per cent of the panel members voted, according to the results of the recall survey conducted on the Friday and Saturday, 4–5 May, following election day. As the actual turnout was only 76 per cent (because of the inaccuracy of the register, see p. 99 below, the comparable figure might be of the order of 83 per cent), it is likely that the experience of being interviewed repeatedly throughout the campaign had the effect of heightening interest in the campaign and increasing turn-out. It did not, however, much affect voting behaviour, other than slightly to overstate the Conservative and Labour Party shares and understate the Liberal vote somewhat. One interesting finding of the MORI/*Sunday Times* panel study is that two-thirds (65 per cent) of those who said at the outset of the campaign that they were 'absolutely certain they would *not* vote' did, on the day, vote. Another is that nearly a quarter (24 per cent) of the electorate changed their minds (at least once) from the beginning of the campaign to the end.

The published polls had shown that there was very little change during the first three weeks of the campaign, followed by a narrowing of the Tory lead in the fourth week, and then a widening back again in the final few days of the campaign. This pattern was followed among the panellists as well and at the end of the day the Labour Party won the campaign (barely) even though it lost the election.

That Labour won the campaign is shown in Table 4.11. Labour won over 5 per cent of Tories, and lost 3 per cent in return, and during the campaign three-quarters of the 'don't know's made up their minds, and 33 per cent went into the Labour camp while 26 per cent went to the Tories.

TABLE 4.11 *General Election 1979, change matrix*
(4–6 April to 4–5 May)

	Electorate (%)
From Conservative	8.5
To Conservative	4.5
Net change	−4.0
From Labour	6.5
To Labour	6.5
Net change	0
Labour gain	+4

SOURCE: MORI
Sunday Times Panel

There is a stark lesson to be learned from the reasons panellists gave for their election vote. Seven alternatives were presented to each panel member who was asked to tell our interviewer which of the reasons given were among those determining his or her vote (only 6 per cent said there were 'other reasons'). The top marks went to 'Believe the party I voted for will be best at looking after the interests of people like me', selected by 58 per cent overall, and 61 per cent of both Conservative and Labour voters. Otherwise, policies (62 per cent) topped the Tories' choice, and habit (49 per cent) led Labour voters' list.

More Labour voters than Tories (33 to 25 per cent) gave 'Liked its leader(s)' as an important reason for their choice; more Tory voters than Labour (31 to 25 per cent) gave 'Disliked the other party's policies' as an important reason for them. Only 16 per cent indicated the local candidate played a role in their decisions.

Prices (55 per cent) were only marginally ahead of strikes and industrial relations (52 per cent) among the issues our panellists gave as important in helping them to decide for whom to vote, and law and order was also a key issue for Tory voters (58 per cent) as was taxation (53 per cent). Among Labour voters other important issues were unemployment (41 per cent) and the national health service (26 per cent).

On issues, the Labour Party seemed to be winning the campaign (having started behind) until a week before election day. In the final week, however, much of the ground it had gained was lost back to the Tories; only on the issue of jobs and unemployment did the Labour

Party end up having won more voters than it lost over the campaign. In fact, the Labour Party lost a net 9 per cent of the electorate during the final week of the campaign on both strikes and taxes, and 4 per cent on prices and 3 per cent on jobs. The figures suggest that the Tories finished strongly.

A number of changes characterised the private polling, although MORI was serving in its fourth general election and ORC in its fifth. The change of Labour leadership meant Callaghan was no longer party treasurer, and his replacement, Norman Atkinson, was implacably opposed to polls. This, and the general increase in strength of the left wing, always cynical about the value of polls which frequently showed the public less than enthusiastic about the left's policy proposals, meant a tough fight for money for private polls, especially in the light of the extreme financial straits of the party. Also MORI was now publishing other polls in the press, and was no longer the 'exclusive property' of Transport House. While this should not have mattered, it did. These and other factors led to a relative reduction in budget for MORI's election polling, e.g. cutting the number of daily polls from seventeen in the October 1974 23-day election period to ten in the longer (36-day) 1979 campaign. There were no Scottish election polls for the party – which was doing well there anyway – and there was no extra analysis budget. When Wilson resigned MORI lost a keen student of its work.

On the Tory side, the move of Taylor to the USA meant a new face at the table and while his replacement, John Hanvey, was well enough regarded as a technician, he had less of the political and personal flair of his predecessor. He too had a less enthusiastic client in Mrs Thatcher than Taylor had had in Heath.

According to Atkinson, the Labour Party spent £87 000 on polls in 1978 and 1979, and Butler and Kavanagh estimate the Conservatives spent more with ORC during the election itself than Labour did with MORI. ORC's work included four major 'state of battle' surveys, six mid-week 'quickies', eleven post-tests and party election broadcasts, a special survey of Liberals and three sets of Scottish surveys. Also, the Tories retained Saatchi & Saatchi as their advertising agency for the 1979 election, and Saatchi conducted its own qualitative research to assist in the development of its advertising efforts.

Instant history makes difficult objective analysis, especially if the historian was an active and involved participant. So I shall leave the last word on private polling to a new Labour MP, who was formerly a politics lecturer and Nuffield Fellow, Austin Mitchell:

More modern parties see the need for objective information of the type forthcoming from surveys of opinion. In 1978 such surveys provided early warnings of the changing predilections of the skilled worker, of the growing feeling for a 1978 election, of Labour's weak points. They can also provide much information about specific groups, and reactions to policies, individual issues and even the party generally. Yet polling needs to be done regularly to warn of trends and to allow the party to develop the skills and the habits of dealing with the information. This does not mean adopting the Tory approach of formulating policies just because they are popular, though in a democracy popularity has to be a major argument in favour of a policy and certainly not one against it. Rather the information is used as a chart of the territory through which the party has to treck. Polls bring knowledge of which subjects to tackle head on, which chords to strike, which issues to push home and which to avoid, which policies will sell and which won't. Labour is as much in the merchandising business as the makers [of] biological Ariel. There is little point in confusing bad merchandising with high principle. (Mitchell, 1979, p. 19)

The Performance of the Polls

Over the eleven general elections since the Second World War, and over the period of election polling, polls have performed, on average, about as well as one would expect. At times they have been better, at times much worse, than the ± 2 per cent sampling tolerance level (the 95 per cent confidence interval for 2000-case samples) or ± 3 per cent for 1000 respondents.

Journalists tend to regard 'getting it right' as picking the next occupant of Number 10. On that basis, every forecast from 1945 to 1966 was 'right' and yet in 1951 all three polls picked the Tories to win, and they did, yet Labour won the most votes. Since 1966 there have been eighteen election forecasts, and half (nine) backed the wrong winner: five of them in February 1974 for the wrong reason, picking the Conservatives, who won the most votes, instead of Labour, who won the most seats (Rose, 1976).

A better test of the accuracy of the polls is how close they were to the actual gap between the parties; the best test is how close they were, on average, to the share of votes for each party. The House of Commons is made up of elected representatives from the four constituent parts of the United Kingdom of Great Britain and Northern Ireland. Nearly all poll figures exclude Northern Ireland, as its political system of election is different, its party make-up is different, and the nature of its people's electoral behaviour is different in kind, not just degree. Taking just the British figures, the record of the polls is as shown in Table 4.12. The margin of error on the gap should be double that of share, according to sampling theory, and indeed, it is, according to the empirical evidence of thirty-seven election forecasts over thirty-four years. Length of experience has not seemed to matter: Gallup was almost as accurate in 1945 and 1950 as in recent years; its two worst efforts were 1970 and 1979. The two newest polls which participated in the 1979 election came closest. Random sampling has, on average, produced worse results than quota samples, and larger sample size has not led to more accurate forecasts. The early 'bandwagon' theory has been destroyed, and the later 'underdog' hypothesis was brought into question by the polls' results in 1979.

TABLE 4.12 *Accuracy of the Polls, 1945–79*

Year	Mean error gap (%)	Average error per party (%)	Number of polls
1945	3.5	1.6	1
1950	3.2	1.5	2
1951	6.0	2.6	3
1955	1.1	0.7	2
1959	1.0	1.1	3
1964	1.8	1.3	4
1966	3.9	1.7	4
1970	6.6	2.6	5
1974 Feb.	2.4	1.6	5
1974 Oct.	4.2	1.3	4
1979	1.7	0.9	4
Average	3.1	1.5	37

SOURCE: Updated from Rose (1976, p. 313) to include 1979 figures.

These thirty-seven polls have on average marginally underestimated the Tory share of the popular vote (−0.3 per cent) and marginally overestimated the Labour share (+0.8 per cent). As polls do not measure postal voters and these are generally agreed to favour the Tories perhaps by as much as 3 : 1, and have only recently been adjusted for turn-out – again generally favourable to the Conservatives – the direction of these averages is not surprising. Looking at it another way, about a quarter of the polls since 1945 have been able to estimate the

Labour and Conservative share of the vote to within ±1 per cent, and over 60 per cent have forecast to within ±2 per cent.

Adjustments for turn-out made a winner out of ORC in 1970, and worsened its forecast – and those of others who employed such adjustments – in February 1974. Weighting data internally was employed in 1979 by the poll furthest out (Gallup) and by NOP and Marplan but not by MORI (MORI's final (*Evening Standard*) poll: its final *Daily Express* poll was a recall on electors interviewed ten days previously, weighted back to the earlier sample's voting intention figures). The effect of the weighting was in some cases considerable and in others negligible (see Table 4.13).

Marplan (Clemens, 1979) weighted in two stages, first interlocking sex, region and class and then

> the data was re-examined and there was found to be more people in the sample who claimed to vote Conservative in the last election than who claimed to vote Labour. In order to enable comparison with the earlier polls the data was then weighted to the profile of the claimed past voting behaviour reported in their first two surveys.

Marplan's weighting factors were as large as 1.2 and 0.7.

Gallup (Wybrow, 1979) weighted by region by marginality of constituency at the last general election. NOP (Barter, 1979) found

> the proportion working full time and the percentage of Trade Unionists were both about 3% short of expected figures. The differences between the voting intention of Unionist and non-Unionist observed in the previous poll (carried out 48 hours earlier) were used to calculate weights which were applied to the survey. This resulted in a reduction of the Conservative lead by about 3%.

NOP did not keep a precise record of its weighting. None of the newspaper reports of these polls explained the effect of the weighting or even that weighting had been used.

RSL (Cornish, 1979) employed a weighting procedure in its first election poll in 1979 which reduced the Conservative lead to 21 per cent. The raw data produced a 22.5 per cent Tory lead! The procedure it used on this occasion was based on

> the assumption that the Liberal and other voters at the 1974 election would have been drawn in the ratio of 3.3:1 from people now claiming

TABLE 4.13 *Weighting effect, 1979*

	Unweighted	Gallup (%) Weighted	Difference	Unweighted	Marplan (%) Weighted	Difference
Con	40.3	40.8	+0.5	41.0	38.9	−2.1
Lab	38.9	38.8	−0.1	31.4	33.5	+2.1
Lib	12.0	12.9	+0.9	13.2	11.8	−1.4
Nationalist	2.9	1.4	−1.5	} 2.3	2.6	+0.3
Other	1.1	1.1	0			
Would not vote	} 5.1	5.2	+0.1	3.4	3.4	0
Refused/DK				8.6	9.8	+1.2
Con lead	1.4	2.0	+0.6	9.6	5.4	−4.2

to have voted Conservative and Labour. Consequently to restore our results to this assumed distribution we weighted claimed Conservative voters in 1974 × 0.952, and claimed Labour voters × 1.054. The 3.3 : 1 ratio was based on the finding that Liberal and other claimed voters in 1974 divided in these proportions in their 1979 voting intention.

RSL did not weight its three subsequent election surveys. Its weighting procedure was not described in the *Observer* articles.

DIRECTIONS FOR THE FUTURE

Polling Methodology

Polling techniques have evolved in Britain to the point where polls commissioned one evening can be conducted nationally the next day with representative samples of over 1000 respondents using tightly interlocking quota controls in a face-to-face personal interview of some dozen or so questions and reported back the same afternoon.

The 1979 election saw the first use of telephone surveys in election polls in Britain, by Marplan. As telephone penetration in Britain is only about 75 per cent, many are still sceptical of the value of such surveys, especially for voting intention measurement. An unpublished analysis by NOP (1980) comparing the voting intention of respondents with telephones with those without indicates a Tory bias of between 11 and 13 per cent; normal weighting procedures using an 84-cell interlocking matrix of sex, age, social class and region reduced this bias to about 6 per cent, but could never really control for it effectively. It makes many attitudinal measures suspect to some degree as well. As telephone ownership continues to increase, such bias will gradually diminish, of course.

As indicated above, turn-out measures are sometimes helpful, sometimes not. Normally Conservatives are more likely to have a higher propensity to vote, but in the winter election of 1974 Labour supporters were more keen to get the Conservatives out than the Tories were to keep Heath in office. Conventional wisdom holds that since Labour voters are less committed to go to the polls than Conservatives, they will be more likely to stay at home when it rains. Also, most observers generally assume that overall turn-out will fall if the weather is bad. Neither of these assumptions held true in either 1974 election, so adjustments in forecast polls to take these factors into account would have worsened the error in 1974. In 1979, however, the Tory lead was indeed greater in the 15 per cent of the country that had rain, by a substantial factor.

The examination of panel data, where respondents have been interviewed repeatedly, has shown a biasing effect, but mainly one of increasing interest in the outcome, thereby increasing turn-out.

Most pollsters in Britain have now turned from random to quota sampling. Empirical evidence has shown that by itself random sampling has not improved election forecasts. There are a number of hypotheses for this, despite the fact that the mandatory voter registration system has given British researchers an excellent, annually updated, sampling frame. Each autumn the postman delivers a voter registration form to every household in the country. If the form is not filled in and returned smartly, a none-too-gentle reminder is subsequently pushed through the letterbox announcing that the fine for not registering is £50. Even so, the register is never completely accurate. Deaths occur between completion of the forms in mid-October and publication of the registers in mid-February. There is emigration overseas. There is some legitimate duplication. There are many movers who for the most part cannot economically be followed up by the pollster (although most have a postal vote, another source of error), and there is, inevitably, human error in the electoral roll compilation. It has been estimated by Butler and O'Muircheartaigh (1979) that in mid-year – say, June – the register is only 92.5 per cent effective. Recent years have seen a substantial increase in the number of working women, making electoral register contacts that much more difficult during the day; people generally, and the young especially, are less easy to contact; and studies have shown that refusal rates, although still not a big factor, have risen in recent years. The repeated recalls required for respectably high completion rates on random surveys cost time and money. In the heat of a general election both are at a premium. The ability to poll late carries with it a significant advantage. And the interlocking quota controls (frequently sex by age by social class with an override on working women and retired people), while often increasing costs to the level of random surveys, can be done faster, and that factor (and the relative failure of random samples in recent years to prove to be more accurate) has led to the now nearly universal use of quota samples.

Computers have added greatly to the ability of pollsters to analyse data and draw conclusions. Data can be weighted using complex multicellular calculations, all interrelated. Cross-tabulation, automatic mean-score calculations, standard deviation and other statistical tests can be accomplished easily and quickly. And some use has been made of fairly complex multivariate analysis schemes, even in the pressure of a three-week pre-election period. In the 1980s the use of interactive microprocessor devices for interviewers as well as tabulation will be used. Prestel, the British Telecom computer-television link, is now up and running, and while there are only some 12000 sets currently on-line, British Telecom has projected a 40 per cent saturation by the end of the decade. While this will still be too low for consumer interviewing, it will certainly facilitate obtaining data from individual interviewers' input through the sets in their own living rooms direct to the computer, so the analyst at his office can see trends developing, cross-tabbed by demographic, behavioural and attitudinal characteristics on his set (and protected by the system from snoopers), calling for a print-out whenever wanted for a conference with editor or party leader.

Banning the Polls

In Great Britain Parliament rules supreme. There are no written constitutional safeguards to freedom of the press. If Parliament were to ban publication of *The Times* tomorrow, *The Times* would cease publication. It is only the unwritten constitution that has endured for centuries that keeps Britain's press free, and the excesses of a parliamentary dictatorship in check. Parliament has been described as a 'democratic dictatorship' in that once a government is elected with a sizeable majority it can, so long as it keeps its own back-benchers in line, pass any legislation it wishes.

Thus, when the Speaker's Conference recommended in 1967 that polls be banned in the immediate period before polling day it had to be taken very seriously indeed. When an MP (a former academic) introduced a Private Member's Bill in the mid-1970s, it had to be cause for considerable concern, despite the fact that parliamentary advice was that 'it was not going anywhere'. One senior Labour NEC member expressed to me his desire to ban opinion polls for the fortnight before the 1979 election, explaining 'it is sometimes necessary to be anti-democratic in order to save democracy. . . . Of course we would still continue to do our private polls', he said.

In a free society polls cannot effectively be banned: if they were, the political parties would do even more polling than they do now – and leak it even more widely than they do now; second, stockbrokers, jobbers and other City 'gents' would do private polls and leak them (or make them up as they do now); third, foreign media would commission private polls in Britain and publish them overseas, and of course the results would be transmitted and reported subsequently in this country.

The 1979 general election was the fourth since I have been here in which on the Monday and Tuesday before polling day the City has been swept by rumours that one or another of the major polls is coming out the following morning showing a sharp swing to Labour. In 1979 it was MORI, with a 3 per cent Labour lead, in the *Express*. When it did not appear, it was 'being suppressed' and would appear in the next day's *Express*. The poll never existed, as we and the *Daily Express* told approximately 140 callers. Gallup, I later learned, was also plagued with calls from brokers and jobbers, some of whom were furious because Gallup and MORI would not give them the figures from our (non-existent) polls.

According to the *Financial Times*, these rumours wiped hundreds of millions of pounds off share prices. One paper especially well-read in the City, the *Evening Standard*, carried a City pages headline 'Should we ban opinion polls?', stating: 'banning the polls would certainly make life easier for the fund managers and brokers . . . a moratorium on polls before polling day would avoid the kind of panic we saw yesterday' (McGrandle, 1979, p. 46). In the concluding paragraphs, the *Standard*'s City Editor said that it wasn't 'practical' to ban polls and that the City would just have to live with them. In the meantime, though, it cannot have helped our popularity, especially among those described in the 'City View' column in election-eve's *Daily Express*: 'Men have faced death with more dignity than displayed yesterday by some of those who thought their wallets were being threatened.'

What, then, is the public's view of the polls? In a study conducted in 1978 by the Market Research Society, 84 per cent of the sample said they had noticed the results of opinion polls in newspapers. Two questions were then put to those who were aware of the polls; the results make rather distressing reading (see Table 4.14). And when pressed, only a third of the public give polls credit for generally 'getting it right' (Table 4.15).

Finally, disturbed by these and other (anecdotal) signs of the times such as snide comments by journalists and editors, editorial cartoons, politicians' (of all parties) calls for banning of polls, we at MORI decided to test public opinion on the issue during the 1979 election (see Table 4.16).

As of today, we have a majority with us. Pollsters of all people should know that public opinion can change. We will continue to monitor public opinion on this vital issue in the years to come.

TABLE 4.14

Q: 'What do you think of public opinion polls?' (open-ended)

	%
Pointless/take no notice of them	33
Not very accurate/vary	19
Give an idea of what's going on	11
Polls influence voting intentions	9
People don't tell the truth	9
Sample size not large enough	5
People change their minds	5
Don't influence me	5
(Other answers/don't know omitted)	

SOURCE: MRS 1978

TABLE 4.15

Q: 'Do you think the opinion polls are normally right or wrong?'

	%
Right	32
Wrong	46
Other answers	15
Don't know/not stated	7

SOURCE: MRS 1978

TABLE 4.16

Q: 'Do you think that the publication of opinion polls should be banned during an election or not?'

	%
Yes	32
No	56
Don't know	12

SOURCE: MORI 1979

The Polls and the Media

Four in five adults in Britain read at least one national newspaper daily, and many read more than one. Every town and village has its local newsagent, most of whom employ paperboys who deliver the morning paper well before breakfast. In all, there are some eight or nine national dailies to choose from, covering the political, social and economic spectrum of opinion and taste, and another three or four in Scotland. The market is highly competitive and financial pressures are significant (several run at losses of substantial magnitude).

Opinion polls are an expensive form of journalism, yet nearly every national and Scottish newspaper sponsors its own poll at election times (and several between elections as well). All newspapers report all the others' polls, sometimes at considerable length, as do the television news programmes. Yet a love–hate relationship exists between the polls and the press.

This relationship is based on the need of newspapers for something better than what one editor once described to me as 'sniffing the London air'. Polls provide instant expertise, polls *make* news, and polls provide a natural whipping boy if something goes wrong as it did in 1970 and again in February 1974. Ivor Crewe (1982) recently put four propositions about the way polls are reported in Britain:

1. However static public opinion actually is, the polls provide the media with a basis for giving the impression of flux, change and excitement. The more polls there are . . . the more true this is.
2. However improbable a poll's finding is, the media will publish or broadcast it . . . the more improbable a poll's finding is the more likely the media will give it prominence.
3. However clear the election outcome and the election trend, polls allow the media to hedge their bets.
4. The duller an election is, the greater the use of and prominence given to the polls.

There is truth as well as poetry in these propositions, and there is a sound – if short-term – rationale for them. Sampling fluctuations will inevitably suggest change at first; it was not until half-a-dozen results were in in May 1979 that a static pattern became apparent, especially when the early RSL finding defied all attempts to fit it to a pattern. Improbable results make news: they may foretell a trend or shift in public opinion; they may suggest reaction to a promise, a broadcast or speech, a policy; they may even be right. The seventh poll saying nothing is changing is not news; the eighth suggesting change certainly is. Polls enable analytical assessments to be made. How will women, young people, or one-eyed jacks vote – or not vote? Will the marginals topple/prop up the government? Will people vote for issues, or for a leader? Polls provide grist for the journalist's mill; how fine he grinds it is part of the problem.

Pollsters in Great Britain take considerable pains to see that their clients get it right, do not overclaim on marginal shifts, insist on fieldwork dates, sample sizes, etc., but in the end have little control over headlines, story placement, length of coverage and less, much less, control over secondary coverage in other papers or on radio and television. Newspapers here have conducted their own straw polls and run them without benefit of any statistical pretension, have bought bogus or biased polls and run them without disclaimer (rarely, I'm happy to say), and one television programme headlined, four weeks before election day, 'Tories to win with overall majority of 60 + '.

Other problems that beset pollsters in dealing with the press include: sub-editing after they have agreed stories with the reporter by sub-editors who do not understand (or care?) about the accuracy of the copy; well-meaning academics or other third parties who 'interpret', sometimes unknowledgeably, opinion poll results; inevitably short lead times and tight deadlines; space pressures; competitive 'scoops'; 'polls of polls', averaging polls taken over the past week or so to suggest greater statistical reliability (theoretically so, but not if one poll is inaccurate as was the case in 1979, and not if there has been a sharp swing of public opinion); and, perhaps my favourite, publication of the amateur poll, as seen in the *Daily Express* on 9 April 1979 – described as 'an *Express* poll', it was taken among 500 coloured immigrants by amateur pollsters among an undefined sample during an undefined period, reporting to the first decimal place the answers to such questions as: 'Will you live in Britain forever?'

Television has by its nature even more difficulty in reporting poll results, no matter how hard it tries. It is even shorter on copy deadlines and time to include the essential information of when the poll was conducted and other details. Perhaps the most creative use of polls in the May 1979 election was the *Granada 500* produced by David Kemp and described by Bob Self (1982). This series of programmes commissioned a survey of a bellwether constituency in the heart of its coverage area to identify issues of concern to the electorate (which determined later programme content), establish an initial panel study data base, and recruit a representative sample of people to attend and take part in the programme series during the election campaign. Panellists were re-interviewed on several occasions, including the weekend following the elections.

One of the worst examples in the same election was on BBC's *Nationwide* when commentators were asked to discuss poll findings illustrated by a large graphic display showing three polls' figures, two reallocating 'don't know's, one not. The interviewer neither understood nor was willing to listen to the arithmetic explanation of why their comparison was nonsense.

That polls make television news is shown by McKee (1982), who reported that Independent Television News (ITN) ran a poll story two nights out of three in its late news during the 1979 campaign compared with just under 60 per cent in 1974. ITN also used poll data to determine programme focus on issues. Further, it asked the public how they thought television should cover the campaign and how election news – including polling results – could be improved. The first way it tried to improve poll data presentation was to put it into as clear a framework as it could, relating it to the campaign, clearly sourcing it as to both polling organisation and sponsoring newspaper, and blending in other information beyond voting intention, such as issues, leadership ratings, regional polls, etc. The second initiative it took was to wrap up the week's polling coverage on Sunday night to point out trends and implications. It also ran an extended feature on how a polling organisation works (as the BBC had done earlier).

Some see the solution to the poll–paper conflict at the sponsor level in having the copy written by the polling organisation and commented on by journalists or even academics. This is better than the editorial licence taken by some papers when political reporters are saddled with poll stories they are neither interested in nor understand, but leads, in my view, to dull and unrelated journalism. My own preference is for interested and knowledgeable journalists to develop a poll speciality and yet be able to bring in reaction, comment, analysis of impact and the like beyond what is possible or proper for a pollster.

Same-Day Polls

The development of 'same-day' polls, as they are described in Great Britain, or 'exit' polls, as I believe they are referred to in the USA, has led to considerable criticism on both sides of the Atlantic. Some have been outrageously wrong: in the October 1974 election, BBC analysts calculated a forecast of a 150-seat Labour victory based on incomplete returns by the Louis Harris Organisation who conducted polling station interviews in eighty-five English and fifty Scottish constituencies in an election that turned out to be a Labour win by a three-seat margin (a calculation which was done without the knowledge of Taylor, head of the Harris Organisation, who was categorically assured beforehand that its data would not be used to make this kind of prediction).

The difficulties in getting it right on the night are compounded for the polling organisation by differential turn-out, the reluctance of coloured voters to tell white interviewers how they voted, a comparative differential reluctance on the part of Conservatives to tell anyone how they had cast their ballots, the effect of snow or rain, the sampling of polling stations, the fact that polls are open in Britain from 7.00 a.m. to 10.00 p.m., and the effect of postal votes. Nevertheless, McKee (1982) believes that ITN (whose same day polls are conducted by ORC) has the system about right, and evidence is that its same day polls are as accurate as many eve-of-election polls conducted in the more traditional way.

It is argued that the result forecast ('the horse-race') is of little value in the hour between the time the polls close and first declarations (usually received shortly after 11.00 p.m.). Newsmen say that the nation is waiting, the pundits are discussing the day, the turn-out, the weather, and that the result of the same-day poll becomes an ingredient in the news mix. Opponents say that the record is spotty and adds little to knowledge or understanding. The alternative argument of the proponents is that in addition to the forecast of the outcome, same-day polls enable election analysts to determine the relevance of issues on voting behaviour, and other electoral factors which help to explain the outcome. How much this improves the same information from polls conducted the day before is hard to see, given the relative accuracy of the two methodologies.

CONCLUSION

Finally, do polls influence voting behaviour? I believe they do. For many years pollsters and psephologists in both Great Britain and the USA showed that the public took notice of the polls and that their voting behaviour was affected thereby. NBC tested (in California in the 1964 presidential election) the effect of knowledge of computer-based forecasts of early (East Coast) returns on voting behaviour. Comparisons of behaviour between matched groups who saw the forecasts and those who did not showed only slight differences.

Butler and Kavanagh (1980) concluded after the 1979 general election in Britain that 'there is some circumstantial evidence that polls may affect voting behaviour' but 'there is clearly no general or consistent effect of the polls on voting behaviour'. The best evidence is from the study conducted for the BBC in May 1979 by Gallup (Table 4.17) which shows no support whatsoever for the bandwagon theory; indeed, it suggests some degree of measurable support for the 'underdog' theory. It shows that 3 per cent of the electorate admitted to being influenced by reports of polls (67 per cent had heard poll results), and the losers (Labour and Liberals) were over twice as likely to record this influence as those who voted for the winning Conservative Party. This would suggest that the polls could have affected the votes of some 700 000 electors in the May 1979 general election out of the 31 million who cast votes, more than voted postally.

TABLE 4.17 *The effect of polls*

Q: 'When you finally decide (d) which way to vote, were you influenced at all by what the opinion polls were saying?'	
	Yes (%)
All	3.0
Con	2.0
Lab	5.0
Lib	4.5

SOURCE: Gallup
BBC/Essex Survey

It is said that polls influence voting behaviour; I believe they do, as I have said. It is also true in my judgement that newspapers and television influence elections. I have even heard it alleged that politicians have been known to affect the outcome, but on the last point I remain (in Sir Harold Wilson's words) agnostic, though not an atheist.

REFERENCES

Abrams, M. (1951), *Social Surveys and Social Action* (London: Heinemann).
Abrams, M. (1964), 'Opinion polls and party propaganda', *Public Opinion Quarterly*, vol. 28, no. 1, pp. 13–19.
Abrams, M. (1970), 'The opinion polls and the 1970 British election', *Public Opinion Quarterly*, vol. 34, no. 3, pp. 317–24.
Barter, J. (1979), letter to author, 13 November.
Butler, D. (1952), *The British General Election of 1951* (London: Macmillan).

108 *Political Opinion Polling in Great Britain*

Butler, D. (1955), 'Voting behaviour and its study in Britain', *British Journal of Sociology*, vol. 6, pp. 93–103.

Butler, D. and Kavanagh, D. (1974), *The British General Election of February 1974* (London: Macmillan).

Butler, D. and Kavanagh, D. (1975), *The British General Election of October 1974* (London: Macmillan).

Butler, D. and Kavanagh, D. (1980), *The British General Election of 1979* (London: Macmillan).

Butler, D. and King, A. (1965), *The British General Election of 1964* (London: Macmillan).

Butler, D. and King, A. (1966), *The British General Election of 1966* (London: Macmillan).

Butler, D. and Kitzinger, U. (1976), *1975 Referendum* (London: Macmillan).

Butler, D. and O'Muircheartaigh, C. (1979), 'What is 40%? A note on the eligible electorate', unpublished paper, 13 February.

Butler, D. and Pinto-Duschinsky, M. (1971), *The British General Election of 1970* (London: Macmillan).

Butler, D. and Rose, R. (1960), *The British General Election of 1959* (London: Macmillan).

Butler, D. and Stokes, D. (1969), *Political Change in Britain* (London: Macmillan; 2nd edn, 1974).

Chappell, B. (1979), 'Founding fathers: Henry Durant', *Market Research Society Newsletter*, nos 157–8 (April–May).

Clemens, J. (1979), letter to author, 27 November.

Cornish, J. (1979), letter to author, 31 October.

Crewe, I. (1982), 'The polls and the media in the 1979 general election', in Worcester and Harrop (eds), op. cit., pp. 115–25.

Crewe, I., Särlvik, B. and Alt, J. (1976), 'The how and why of voting in February 1974', in R. Rose (ed.), *Studies in British Politics* (London: Macmillan) pp. 239–53.

Durant, H. (1962), 'Public opinion, polls and foreign policy', *British Journal of Sociology*, vol. 13, pp. 331–49.

The Economist (1979), 'Poll watcher wanted', p. 19, 13 January.

Gallup, G. (ed.) (1976), *The Gallup International Public Opinion Polls, Great Britain, 1937–75* (New York: Random House).

Hodder-Williams, R. (1970), *Public Opinion Polls and British Politics* (London: Routledge & Kegan Paul).

Kavanagh, D. (1980), 'Political parties and private polls', in D. Butler, H. Penniman and A. Ranney (eds), *Democracy at the Polls* (Washington, DC: AEI) p. 212.

Labour Party (1974), *Report of the National Executive Committee of the Labour Party*.

McGrandle, L. (1979), 'Should we ban opinion polls?', *Evening Standard*, 2 May.

McKee, P. (1982), 'Opinion polls. How television used them', in Worcester and Harrop (eds), op. cit., pp. 132–40.

Market Research Society Committee on the Performance of the Polls (1972), *Public Opinion Polling on the 1970 Election* (London: Market Research Society).

Mitchell, A. (1979), *Can Labour Win Again?*, Tract No. 463 (London: Fabian Society).

MORI Survey (1980), 'Why the British are still a world apart', *Now!*, 1 February, pp. 20–5.

NOP (John O'Brien) (1980), 'Telephone interviewing', unpublished paper, May.

Robson, W. (1959), 'The survey on nationalisation', *Political Quarterly*, vol. 30, no. 2 (April–June).

Rose, R. (1970), *The Polls and the 1970 General Election*, Occasional Paper No. 7 (Strathclyde: University of Strathclyde Survey Research Centre).

Rose, R. (1974), 'The polls and election forecasting in February 1974' and 'The polls and public opinion in October 1974', in H. Penniman (ed.), *Britain at the Polls* (Washington, DC: AEI), pp. 109–30, 223–39.

Rose, R. (1976), 'Opinion polls and election results', in R. Rose (ed.), *Studies in British Politics*, 3rd edn (London: Macmillan), pp. 305–22.

Self, B. (1982), 'The *Granada 500*', in Worcester and Harrop (eds), op. cit., pp. 78–87.

Teer, F., and Spence, J. (1973), *Political Opinion Polls* (London: Hutchinson).

Wilson, Sir H. (1978), 'Market research in the private and public sectors', *Journal of the Market Research Society*, vol. 20, no. 3 (July), pp. 111–26.

Worcester, R. (1975), 'Winning in the rain', *New Society*, vol. 31, no. 643 (13 February), p. 394.

Worcester, R., and Harrop, M. (eds) (1982), *Political Communications* (London: Allen & Unwin).

Wybrow, R. (1979), letter to author, 5 November.

APPENDIX: THE POLLSTERS' CODE

1 Every substantial published report of poll findings should give:

   a) the sampling method used
   b) the sample size
   c) the dates of fieldwork.

2 Where, in reply to questions on voting intention, there are sharp changes in the number of those who say they would not vote or who are undecided, these facts should be published.

3 The polls will, on request, make available to a reasonable number of journalists, academics, students, other polling organisations and the political parties, the following additional information:

   a) the numbers and type of sample areas
   b) other details of sample design, such as stratification, clustering and success rates
   c) composition of sample
   d) the questionnaire used
   e) description of the method used to collect the information (e.g. personal interview, postal questionnaire).

4 Where the polling organisation retains the copyright of poll findings which have not been published by their newspaper clients, they will continue to make these findings available through other media, after ascertaining that the newspaper does not wish to use them.
5 It is the responsibility of signatories to ensure that the published reports of surveys by their newspaper or television clients do not misrepresent or distort the data.
6 Wherever a published report of a poll includes a table of figures, it shall also include the question asked.
7 In the event that a client releases data from a survey which was not originally intended for publication the Code of Conduct will apply to it as if it had originally been commissioned for publication.

Note: The last three clauses were added in January 1974.

5 Political Opinion Polling in the Republic of Ireland

JOHN F. MEAGHER

THE HISTORY OF POLITICAL POLLING IN IRELAND

The Republic of Ireland was something of a latecomer to market research and consequently to political opinion polling. Conventional, quantitative, *ad hoc* market research, based on statistical sample surveys, did not emerge as a feature of the Irish business scene until the early 1960s. This was in marked contrast to the situation in the neighbouring United Kingdom which, like the USA, had seen the setting up of *ad hoc* market research and opinion polling organisations prior to the outbreak of the Second World War. However, the climate in Ireland in the 1930s was not conducive to business generally, never mind the new business sciences. At that stage Eamonn De Valera, the then Taoiseach (Prime Minister) was engaged in his 'Economic War' with Britain; this was to have a generally depressing effect on the economic climate in Ireland which was to last through the 1940s and 1950s. Ireland benefited from the worldwide economic lift-off which characterised the early 1960s. The two polling organisations which between them conduct virtually all published political opinion polling work in the Republic of Ireland were set up at that time: the Market Research Bureau of Ireland (MRBI) was established in 1962, and Irish Marketing Surveys (IMS) was set up a year later in 1963. While the balance of that decade was to see both of these companies grow from small beginnings to become substantial market research organisations, there was very little political opinion polling undertaken prior to 1970.

Nevertheless, some political work was carried out and published in the 1960s. The first such survey with which I am familiar is one which was commissioned by the *Irish Press* in July 1961. This dealt with political attitudes to the question of the accession of Ireland to the EEC.

The first detailed survey of political party support was conducted by British Gallup (which at that time had an office in Dublin) prior to the June election of that year. The main findings of that survey were made public after the election and have provided a useful basis for comparison with more recent surveys in terms of changes in the demographic profiles of the various parties.

Apart from these two surveys, there was very little other work published in the 1960s which touched on the political arena, but IMS did conduct and made public a survey in 1964 which dealt with a highly political topic, namely, the attitudes then prevailing to the Irish language. It showed that while the language itself was held in considerable affection, the majority felt that Irish as a compulsory subject for university entrance should be phased out. Many defenders of the language attacked the survey in an emotional fashion, largely, it seemed, because they found the results of it to be unpalatable. This negative reaction had the effect of dampening IMS's enthusiasm for 'political' research. It made it consider seriously whether, commercially, it was prudent for it to be seen as controversial at a time when the company was trying to establish itself as a bona fide market research company. It was to be six years before IMS was again involved in any published surveys dealing with political issues.

In the 1970s the situation changed fairly dramatically and IMS, in particular, was involved in a number of surveys. In 1970, working for *This Week* magazine, IMS assessed public reaction to the dismissal by the then Taoiseach, Jack Lynch, of two Cabinet ministers (one of whom, Charles Haughey, himself became Taoiseach in December 1979). Also in 1970 IMS, for the same magazine, conducted a survey on the public attitude to divorce being permitted, and contraceptives being generally accessible to the Irish public. (At the time the survey was done, it was against the law for contraceptives to be sold in Ireland and divorce, as it is generally understood, is not available in Ireland.) Working for the same client, an attitude survey was undertaken among the population of the Republic of Ireland to the Northern Ireland problem, which was then just a little over one year old.

In May 1972 an opinion poll was commissioned from IMS by the largest circulation morning newspaper, the *Irish Independent*. (It was a particularly important event as it was to encourage IMS actively to engage in the business of political opinion polling.) This dealt with the voting intentions in the forthcoming referendum on entry to the EEC. The survey indicated that a massive majority of those who intended to vote in the referendum were in favour of entry. At the time of the poll (approximately three weeks before polling date) none of the political commentators had put forward the notion that the majority would be as sizeable as the poll suggested. Reaction to the poll amongst some politicians was grudging (and this rejection of opinion polling as a useful indicator of the electorate's feeling was to remain a feature of the Irish scene for some time). The then Deputy Leader of the Irish Labour Party, James Tully, whose party opposed Irish entry, dismissed the findings, saying: 'Mr Harold Wilson has bitter memories of a job done by experts on opinion polls before the last British election.'[1]

Prediction in a referendum is rather simpler than is the case in proportional representation elections. The actual result of the referendum largely vindicated the forecast in the *Irish Independent* poll. The poll had suggested that 77 per cent would vote in favour of accession. This compared with 83 per cent voting 'yes' three weeks after the poll and following a campaign in which the two major parties both advocated accession.

Northern Ireland was to arise frequently as a topic for exploration in terms of the attitudes held to various possible 'solutions'. One very worthwhile project conducted in 1973 for the *Sunday Independent*, in conjunction with the *Belfast Telegraph* and the *Sunday Times*, was a three-part survey conducted simultaneously in Northern Ireland, Great Britain and the Republic of Ireland, thus representing the fullest possible picture of the views of all who could be said to have a stake in Northern Ireland's future.

In 1978, the BBC's *Panorama* programme commissioned a survey on Northern Ireland; in particular, it dealt with prevailing attitudes in the Republic of Ireland to the IRA. In August 1979 Radio Telefís Eireann (RTE) commissioned a survey on border security in the immediate aftermath of the assassination of Lord Mountbatten. IMS also returned a number of times to the question of prevailing attitudes to divorce and contraception.

IMS was not the only research company active in publishing data of a political nature in the 1970s. MRBI, working for *Magill*, an Irish current affairs monthly, from 1977 to 1979, surveyed the questions of Irish unity, female status, government and ministers' performance, national economic issues and assessments of political issues and personalities. It also conducted a survey with significant political overtones – the question of the use of nuclear power as an energy source – for RTE in 1978.

In the run-up to the European election in 1979, MRBI also conducted a series of surveys for two of the political parties, Fine Gael and Labour, and subsequently, with its clients' permission, made its findings public. Its report serves as a very useful case history of the use by political parties of survey research in the planning of a political campaign.[2]

VOTING INTENTIONS

So far in this chapter the reference has been to surveys or issues that have, or have had, a political relevance. The major point to be addressed is, of course, political opinion polling, in the sense in which it is used to take the electorate's pulse at any point in time to indicate likely party support in the event of an election.

The business of assessing people's voting intentions, or, if you like, coming to a conclusion about which party is likely to win a general election, is compounded by the proportional representation system which obtains in Ireland. Because there is no constant relation between the number or percentage of first preference votes and the number or percentage of seats in the Dáil, the predictive value of pre-election surveys is a limited one. (This is quite separate from the general argument about whether opinion polls can be validly used to predict the outcome of an election which is going to take place at a point in time later than the survey itself.)

It is necessary here to say a word or two about the proportional representation system which exists in Ireland, as opposed to the first-past-the-post system used in Britain. It is in fact derived from the idea of an English barrister by the name of Hare who put forward the fundamental principles in 1850, and was praised by John Stuart Mill at the time for his innovative ideas.[3]

1. *Multi-seat constituencies:* In the Irish context, this has led to the development of three-, four- and five-member constituencies, primarily dependent on the size of the total constituency's population.
2. *A single or transferable vote:* The voter votes by order of preference on the ballot paper, 1, 2, 3, etc., as between all the candidates, irrespective of party. Should a candidate be eliminated, the vote can be transferred; or it can be transferred as part of a surplus if the candidate is elected, provided always that the voter has indicated a lower preference on the ballot paper.
3. *An electoral quota:* The quota which is normally affiliated to the Hare system is the 'droop quota' and is worked out by the following formula:

$$\text{Quota} = \frac{\text{Total valid poll}}{\text{Number of seats} + 1} + 1$$

Thus, if the total valid poll is 100 000 and the number of seats to be filled is four, then the quota is 20 001 votes (the extra vote is to remove the unlikely possibility of five candidates each getting a quota).

The proportional representation system poses inherent dangers for pollsters attempting to judge the likely outcome of a general election. A survey in which respondents answer the question 'To which party would you give your first preference vote?' can take little account of how transfers may work and the effect this will have on the number or percentage of any individual party's members who may get elected.

As already stated, there is no constant relation between the percentage of first preference votes and the number or percentage of seats in the Dáil. This point is illustrated by Figure 5.1. As can be seen from this chart, the Fianna Fáil party was elected to power in 1943 with only 41.9 per cent of the popular vote, whereas in 1973 it lost the election with 46.2 per cent. Indeed, in the 1973 election Fianna Fáil's vote rose from the 45.7 per cent figure seen in 1969, and yet it failed to form a government, despite the fact that it had formed a government with as little as 43.8 per cent of the first preference votes twelve years earlier, in 1961.

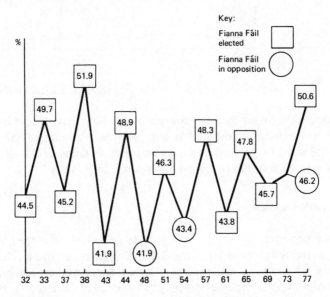

FIGURE 5.1 *The percentage of first preference votes for Fianna Fáil at general elections 1932–77*

Professor Basil Chubb has included a useful table in his chapter dealing with Ireland in *Political Parties in the European Community*.[4] As can be seen (Table 5.1) the 41.9 per cent of first preference votes Fianna Fáil got in 1943 gave it 48.6 per cent of the seats and the election, while the 46.2 per cent of first preference votes in 1973 yielded only 47.9 per cent of seats and not enough to form a government.

TABLE 5.1 *The translation of First Preference Votes into Seats in the Dáil*

Election	First preference votes (%)	Seats won (%)	Into office/opposition
1932	44.5	47.1	Office
1933	49.7	50.3	Office
1937	45.2	50.0	Office
1943	41.9	48.6	Office
1944	48.9	55.1	Office
1948	41.9	46.3	Opposition
1951	46.3	46.9	Office
1954	43.4	44.2	Opposition
1957	48.3	53.1	Office
1961	43.8	48.9	Office
1965	47.8	50.0	Office
1969	45.7	52.0	Office
1973	46.2	47.9	Opposition
1977	50.6	56.8	Office

POLITICAL OPINION POLLS AND GENERAL ELECTIONS

The publishing in the media of answers to questions seeking to elicit first preference voting intentions has only become a feature of the Irish political scene in the most recent general election (June 1977) but some work was done in the two previous general elections.

The 1969 Election

As was mentioned earlier, prior to the 1969 general election the Labour Party in Ireland commissioned the Gallup Poll, who then had an office in Dublin, to conduct a detailed study. This was for its own use and private consumption, but the results were published after the election. It has been reviewed extensively by Professor John Whyte[5] and provides a very useful base against which to measure changes in the demographic make-up of the three main political parties. However, the main point to be made here is that there were no political opinion surveys *published* prior to the 1969 election.

The 1973 Election

In the run-up to the 1973 election IMS was commissioned by the *Irish Independent* to conduct a survey to examine the attitudes of the electorate to a number of issues which were thought likely to have a bearing on the outcome of the election. Due to the proven difficulty of correlating first preference voting intentions with likely percentage of seats in the Dáil, and the relative state of the art at the time, first preference voting intentions were not sought. The survey did suggest that the opposition National Coalition's campaign, which centred on prices and health charges, found a readier response with the electorate than did the Fianna Fáil government's emphasis on Northern Ireland and internal security. It was the bread-and-butter issues which were to dominate and it was discovered that all elements of the general public, but particularly housewives, were greatly concerned with the issue of rising prices. On the day of the election the *Irish Independent* ran a headline 'Prices may sink Lynch' (who was then Taoiseach) over a story detailing the main findings of the poll.[6] The underlying theme of that story was that the Lynch government was likely to fall in what was thought likely to be a close election; this proved to be the case.

The 1977 Election

After the 1973 election it was clear that general interest in opinion surveys was on the increase and IMS, off its own bat, commenced its collection of data on its political monitor in 1974. This was facilitated by the fact that the company conducted a national omnibus survey; initially this was fielded on a quarterly basis, but subsequently, monthly. The questions included on this survey, and which have been asked on a regular basis since then, are:

Q.1: If there was a general election tomorrow, which party would you give your first preference vote to?

Q.2: Are you satisfied or dissatisfied with the way the government is running the country?

Q.3: Are you satisfied or dissatisfied with —— as Taoiseach?

Q.4: Are you satisfied or dissatisfied with the way —— is doing his job as leader of Fianna Fáil/Fine Gael/Labour Party [depending on which party or parties are in government or opposition].

The results of the data collected on the political monitor survey were made public in RTE's *The Politics Programme* on 10 December 1976. Figure 5.2 details the results which were published. The figure excludes 'don't know's and those who claim they would not vote if there were a general election in the near future. It shows that over the period November 1974 to December 1976 there was a consistent Fianna Fáil lead over the Coalition with just two exceptions. All political commentators at the time of the publication took the view that the Coalition was well placed to win the next general election, in the main because it had redrawn the boundaries of some constituencies allegedly in its favour. This manoeuvre, conducted by the then Minister for the Environment, James Tully, was thought to ensure a Coalition victory. Indeed, Mr Tully had himself declared in the Dáil: 'I cannot improve on it [the electoral amendment] in any way. I think it's great. Fantastic.'[7]

The media generally were very sceptical. On the day after the television programme, the *Irish Press* had the following to say in the course of its lead story commenting on the findings: 'Politicians are not

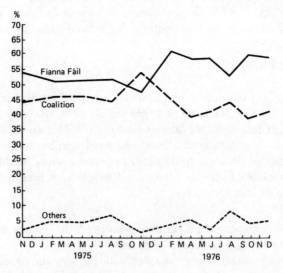

FIGURE 5.2   *Voting intentions (excluding 'don't know's) November 1974–December 1976*

likely to be influenced by the findings, however . . . the need to treat the findings with considerable reservations is further indicated.'[8] The viewpoint was echoed in the *Irish Independent*: 'Lynch win is poll forecast . . . however, the poll, conducted by Irish Marketing Surveys Limited for the RTE show *The Politics Programme* must be treated with scepticism . . . this seems unbelievable.'[9]

Political commentators amplified their adverse comments by quoting the reactions of certain politicians. On the evening of 11 December 1976 the *Evening Herald* devoted considerable space to the comments of the then General Secretary of the Labour Party, Mr Brendan Halligan: 'He described the figures published today as ludicrous.'[10]

Despite this fairly hostile reception, IMS continued to collect political data on its regular omnibus surveys. RTE also published the results of the February 1977 data which revealed a picture summarised in Figure 5.3.

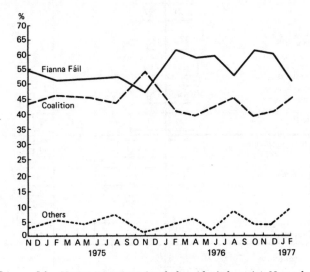

FIGURE 5.3 *Voting intentions (excluding 'don't know's) November 1974–February 1977*

The February 1977 survey also sought respondents' views on the major political issues of the day. As had been the case in December 1976, the February 1977 results exposed an inherent threat to the retention of the Coalition government in its perceived handling of several issues. Most noticeably, the majority of the electorate thought the government was handling badly the issues of unemployment, prices and jobs for school leavers. A significant number of the electorate also thought Fianna Fáil would handle all these issues better than the existing government (see Figure 5.4).

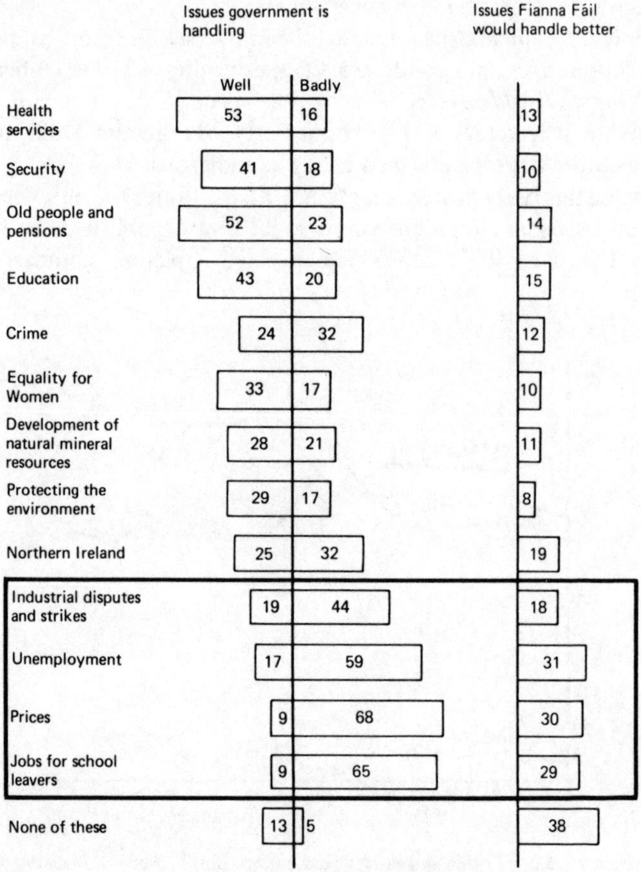

	Issues government is handling		Issues Fianna Fáil would handle better
	Well	Badly	
Health services	53	16	13
Security	41	18	10
Old people and pensions	52	23	14
Education	43	20	15
Crime	24	32	12
Equality for Women	33	17	10
Development of natural mineral resources	28	21	11
Protecting the environment	29	17	8
Northern Ireland	25	32	19
Industrial disputes and strikes	19	44	18
Unemployment	17	59	31
Prices	9	68	30
Jobs for school leavers	9	65	29
None of these	13	5	38

FIGURE 5.4   *An assessment of the government's performance, February 1977*

Although the results of the IMS political monitor had been made public on *The Politics Programme* up to and including the February 1977 data, an agreement was reached with RTE not to publish in the run-up to the election. Immediately after the election, however, IMS published the data which had been collected on the political monitor from February up to the election itself.[11] This is reproduced in Figure 5.5, together with the actual election result.

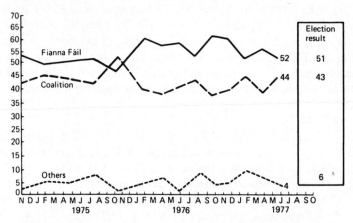

FIGURE 5.5   *Voting intentions (excluding 'don't know's)* vs *June 1977 election result*

The national press had assumed at the outset of the election campaign that a victory for the national Coalition was to be expected. By the middle of the campaign it was recognised that Fianna Fáil had made a major impact and that the sides were more evenly balanced than had been the case initially. However, on the eve of the election most political commentators once more forecast a return to power for the incumbent Coalition government. On the Sunday before the election (12 June 1977) Sean Duignan, the RTE political correspondent, on the radio news programme *This Week*, summed up a discussion with his political correspondent colleagues in the following manner: 'If Fianna Fáil win, it will be the greatest come-back since Lazarus.'

The accuracy of the survey result as compared to the actual election result was, to say the least, heartening from IMS's point of view. The election result was even more heartening for Fianna Fáil – it was returned to power with the highest number of seats ever gained in the history of the Dáil and with its second largest ever share of the popular vote.

As is often the case with opinion polling companies, IMS was simultaneously conducting private research for one of the political parties – Fianna Fáil –and had been doing so since early 1977. This research suggested that the party had a particularly good chance of winning the election. As the election approached, IMS made a private prediction to Fianna Fáil that it would obtain 51 per cent of the popular vote. Initial analysis of the data had indicated that it might expect to obtain 53 per cent of the vote if one simply re-percentaged all of those who expressed an opinion. However, careful analysis of the 'don't know's suggested that they were 2:1 in favour of existing government policy on all the major issues and therefore the projected Fianna Fáil figure came down to 51 per cent. Senator Eoin Ryan, the Fianna Fáil election campaign director, said in a newspaper interview given after the election:

> Our private research showed . . . that our vote would go up to 51 per cent this time. This, in the end, was remarkably accurate. We did not consider publishing this because we thought it might make our organisation a bit too complacent.
>
> The polls also showed us that the most important issues were prices and unemployment, particularly youth unemployment and we were told that the electorate believed that we could handle these problems better than the Coalition. The polls also enabled us to change the emphasis in our speeches and ads.[12]

Certain of the media were not as gracious in their assessment of the value of opinion polling. While discussing the fact that three Cabinet ministers had lost their seats in the election, John Whale, long an Ireland-watcher for the *Sunday Times*, said in that newspaper: 'A more generally welcome casualty was the polls. They backed a loser.'[13] This of course was simply not so and is one further depressing example of the ready tendency of some journalists to 'knock' opinion polls with little concern for the facts; perhaps this is because they see their private preserves being trespassed upon.

IMS was not alone in 'getting it right'. MRBI, who had been conducting the privately commissioned work for the two Coalition political parties (Fine Gael and Labour), was getting much the same playback as IMS. This was confirmed in a letter to the *Irish Times* which Jack Jones, the managing director of MRBI, wrote on 22 June 1977.[14]

Michael Mills, the much-respected senior political correspondent with the *Sunday Press*, reported the Coalition was ahead of Fianna Fáil in its own polls. Mills ran this as the lead story in the *Sunday Press* on the Sunday prior to the election. Jack Jones's letter was written to set the record straight.[15] While MRBI had not undertaken any published work, its private research (for the Coalition) had accurately predicted a Fianna Fáil victory.

The other feature of note which took place in the period immediately prior to the election was the commissioning by the *Irish Times* of a series of opinion polls during the campaign. These were conducted by NOP; it did not publish the answers to the direct question of how people intended to vote but sought, among other things, an assessment of how the electorate was reacting to the issues in the campaign. It found that on economic matters Fianna Fáil was ahead, but on social issues, security and Northern Ireland the Coalition had a narrow lead. On being asked which politician would make the best Taoiseach, 53 per cent opted for Jack Lynch and only 29 per cent for Cosgrave (Fine Gael). The general findings of the NOP polls clearly pointed towards a Fianna Fáil win but, like the earlier IMS surveys, the inherent message was not fully appreciated.[16]

In the immediate aftermath of the election Dr Garret FitzGerald, who had been Foreign Minister in the Coalition government, himself an economist and statistician, had the following to say in an article in the *Irish Times*:

> The failure of most commentators and politicians to detect the change in mood, and to evaluate its political consequences, has been aggravated by what might perhaps be described somewhat paradoxically as the naive cynicism of most people in Ireland with regard to public opinion polls. Perhaps the result of this election will encourage all concerned to take these polls more seriously in the future.[17]

If the media had been incredulous and sceptical of IMS's earlier published work prior to the election, they were, generally speaking, more amicably disposed towards the work published after the pre-election polls had been proved 'right'. For example, in October 1977 IMS investigated reaction to the new government and when the results were published the newspaper coverage took them largely at their face value.[18, 19] The publication of opinion polls since that time has been by and large accompanied by cautious and careful commentary on the part of political commentators and the media in general.

The 1981 Election

Fianna Fáil had been returned to power in June 1977 with the largest ever majority (of seats) in the history of the state and despite the loss of two seats in twin by-elections in Cork in November 1979 it retained an overall majority of 16 in the 148-seat Dáil. An Irish government has a five-year mandate and consequently the initiative as to whether or not to hold an election prior to June of 1982 lay in the gift of the Taoiseach, Charles Haughey. He had become Taoiseach in December 1979 in a bitterly contested leadership battle following Jack Lynch's resignation. Since his departure from office, the former Taoiseach had stated that he had always intended to resign about midway through his term (to give his successor an opportunity to govern before facing an election); he has since confirmed that he had settled on January 1980 to coincide with the termination of Ireland's presidency of the EEC Council of Ministers. However, Fianna Fáil's first preference support sank to an historic low in the Cork by-elections in Jack Lynch's home territory and this followed on the party's poor showing in the direct elections to the European Parliament (when Fianna Fáil succeeded in taking only 5 of the 15 seats). Jack Lynch returned from a visit to America in late November 1979 to find that the previous discontent evident among a large number of his own back-benchers had come to a head in his absence. He decided to resign more or less immediately, having been assured by George Colley, the Tanaiste (Deputy Prime Minister) and Minister for Finance – and Lynch's own choice as a successor – that he was set to win the leadership battle. Voting for the Fianna Fáil party leadership is confined to sitting TDs (Members of Parliament) of the party but in the event, Colley's confidence was ill-founded and his long-term rival, Charles Haughey, then Minister for Health and Social Welfare, won the day gaining 44 votes to Colley's 38.

While the pressure for Lynch's resignation was not by any means universal throughout Fianna Fáil, what had prompted the call for a new leader was the fear among the majority of the party's back-bench TDs (33 per cent of the Fianna Fáil deputies elected in 1977 were first-time elected members) that the party's fortunes were at an all-time low. This had in part been prompted by the factual evidence of the very poor performance both in the EEC elections and in the November by-elections in Cork. Those who felt that the party's prospects in the event of a national election were not good had that pessimistic view confirmed by a poll IMS conducted for the *Sunday Independent* in June 1979.[20] This showed a bleak picture for Fianna Fáil at that time (see Figure 5.6). (IMS had continued to ask the key political questions on its regular omnibus surveys and the results of the surveys conducted before and following the election in June 1977 were included in the publication of the data in the *Sunday Independent*.)

Early in 1980 IMS contracted with the *Irish Times* to conduct a series of surveys both to precede and to coincide with the next general election.

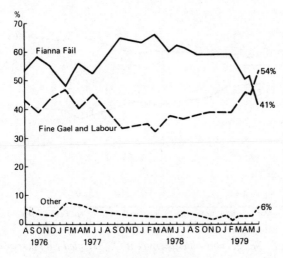

FIGURE 5.6 *Voting intentions (excluding don't know's) August 1976–June 1979*

These dealt with the traditional questions on first preference voting, satisfaction/dissatisfaction with government, Taoiseach and opposition leaders, and preference among the electors as between the two most likely contenders for the office of Taoiseach. The surveys were conducted in March, May, June, September and October 1980.[21] In early 1981 speculation was rife that there would be an election in that year. A further three surveys were conducted in the early part of 1981 (January, February and April).[22] In summary, these showed that there was little lift in the generally depressed level of satisfaction among the electorate with the government of the day. The results of the eight surveys are shown in Figure 5.7.

First preference voting intentions (shown in Figure 5.8 but extending over a longer period, that is, from May 1979 to April 1981) indicated that there was evident a new volatility in the Irish electorate; the very comfortable lead which Fianna Fáil had enjoyed for about two years prior to the 1977 election and extending right up to early 1979 had been clearly eroded – in fact, between May 1979 and April 1981 the lead expressed in terms of first preference voting intentions (excluding 'don't know's) had changed several times – a seemingly new phenomenon in Irish political life.

In April 1981 there was a consensus among the political cor-

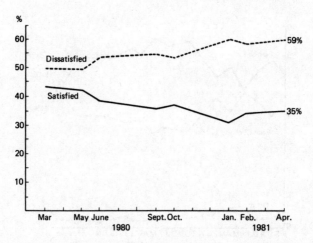

FIGURE 5.7   *Satisfaction with government (% satisfied with performance)*

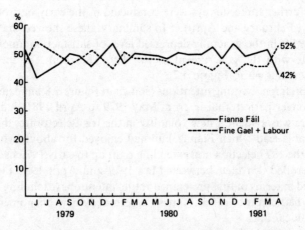

FIGURE 5.8   *Voting intentions (excluding 'don't know's) May 1979–April 1981*

respondents that a general election was in the offing. It was initially expected to be held in late May but in the event, Charles Haughey dissolved the Dáil on 21 May, calling an election for 11 June. It is generally believed that the delay in calling the election was occasioned by the increased tension throughout the country due to the pending death on hunger-strike of another IRA prisoner at the Maze Prison in Northern Ireland.

In all, five surveys of national voting intentions were commissioned by various media during the course of the three-week election campaign. MRBI conducted two of these – one for *Magill*[23] and a further one for the *Irish Independent*.[24] IMS conducted three surveys for the *Irish Times*.[25] Tables 5.2 and 5.3 give the results of these five surveys on the key question in regard to first preference voting intentions (in the sequence of the fieldwork dates).

In the final IMS survey published in the *Irish Times*[26] on the day preceding the election it was suggested that the gap separating the two main groupings (Fianna Fáil and the potential Coalition partners) was just one percentage point; all the other indicators contained in the poll pointed to a situation so finely balanced that, the article written by IMS led with: 'It make[s] it impossible to predict with any surety what will happen tomorrow.' In the event, the main contestants for power emerged with just one percentage point separating them.

The voting intention question in polls such as the *Irish Times*/IMS series measures first preference voting and in the election these came out as shown in Table 5.4. The final *Irish Times*/IMS poll is given in Table 5.5.

It was argued by IMS at the time that two interpretations were possible. On the one hand, if the 'don't know's were simply eliminated and the views of the committed voters re-percentaged, this would result in a one percentage point lead for Fianna Fáil (over the combined strength of Fine Gael and Labour). Conversely, the point was made that the 'don't know's did not mirror the committed voters in terms of pro-government and anti-government leanings. The article accompanying the poll went on:

> If one allows for the anti-Government leanings of the uncommitted voters, this will leave Fianna Fáil trailing Fine Gael/Labour by one percentage point. As has been the case in all of the *Irish Times*/IMS Polls (going back to March of last year), an analysis of the disposition of uncommitted voters suggests that this group traditionally harbours anti-Government sentiments to an above-average degree. Making

TABLE 5.2 *First preference voting intentions (excluding 'don't know's/refused)*

	IMS/Irish Times 27 May	MRBI/Magill 25–6 May	IMS/Irish Times 29 May	MRBI/Irish Independent 3–4 June	IMS/Irish Times 7–8 June
Fianna Fáil	52	49	49	45	48
Fine Gael	32 } 43	42 } 49	36 } 47	38 } 49	36 } 47
Labour	11	7	11	11	11
Other	5	2	4	6	5

TABLE 5.3 *First preference voting intentions (excluding 'don't know's/refused)*

	IMS/Irish Times 22 May	MRBI/Magill 25–6 May	IMS/Irish Times 29 May	MRBI/Irish Independent 3–4 June	IMS/Irish Times 7–8 June
Fianna Fáil	52	49	49	45	48
Fine Gael	32 } 43	42 } 49	36 } 47	38 } 49	36 } 47
Labour	11	7	11	11	11
Other	5	2	4	6	5

TABLE 5.4 *First preference votes, actual result (%)*

Fianna Fáil	45.41	
Fine Gael	36.57	Coalition 46.5
Labour	9.93	
Others	8.09	

TABLE 5.5 *Final* Irish Times/*IMS Poll (%)*

Fianna Fáil	44	
Fine Gael	33	Coalition 43
Labour	10	
Others	5	
'Don't know'	8	

allowances for this fact in allocating uncommitted votes leaves Fianna Fáil with 47 %, the combined strength of Fine Gael and Labour with 48 % and others with 5 %.

The effect of weighting the data to allow for anti-government leanings of the 'don't know's was illustrated in a chart which appeared in the *Irish Times* on the day before the election (see Figure 5.9). With the very

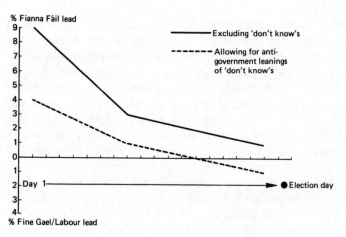

FIGURE 5.9 *Fianna Fáil vs Fine Gael/Labour*

considerable benefit of hindsight, one can now say that the weighting of the 'don't know's to take account of their inherent anti-government sentiments seems to be vindicated as an exercise in attempting accurately to read the runes. It would also appear that the one percentage point lead this exercise gave Fine Gael/Labour stabilised around day 18 of the 21-day election campaign. This weighting of the data by taking account of the disposition of the 'don't know's was not a new application. As has been already noted, IMS used just this method in the 1977 election in making a final and accurate prediction in the private work it conducted at that time for Fianna Fáil.

A further and important problem identified which made predictions perilous was the question of getting the support for 'others' right. This difficulty was first addressed in the *Irish Times* on 2 June and commented on further by IMS in the final pre-election piece (on 10 June):

> The problems of predicting the election outcome are compounded by the fact that opinion polls tend to understate the support for minor parties and independent candidates. In the present poll, we show a support level of 5 % for candidates other than those from Fianna Fáil, Fine Gael and Labour. In the 1977 General Election, this 'Other' grouping drew 7.3 % of first preference votes. The sheer number of 'Other' candidates in the field this time, coupled with the high profile of many of them, suggests that they could match or possibly exceed their 1977 showing. The final results will be effected by how substantially their votes dilute support for any of the three main parties.

With the final result of how first preferences were distributed, it can be seen how the votes of the three main parties were diluted. Of course, it cannot be said for certain that this erosion applied proportionately to the three main parties, but that is the assumption. The final *Irish Times*/IMS poll showed support for 'others' at 5 per cent. It was said at the time that this was likely to be an understatement, and it was. In the election, the 'other' candidates garnered 8.09 per cent of the first preferences. It is an interesting exercise to adjust the final poll data taking account of the real support for the 'other' candidates (Table 5.6).

The complexities of the single transferable vote, multi-seat constituency, proportional representation system are many, and the task of the opinion pollster in Ireland is rendered in no measure easier by having to ply his trade within it. It is all the more rewarding then to see the survey method apparently working well and the estimates it provides being proved reliable.

TABLE 5.6 *The effect of recalculation*

Irish Times/*IMS Poll, 8 June*

	Weighted to take account of anti-government leaning of 'don't know's (%)	Re-percentaged on basis of 8.09 % for 'Others' (%)	Actual result (%)
Coalition: (Combined Fine Gael/Labour)	48	46.44	46.50
Fianna Fáil	47	45.47	45.41
Other	5	8.09	8.09

NOTES

1 *Irish Independent*, 4 May 1972.
2 Market Research Bureau of Ireland, *European Election Research Programme – July 1978 – April 1979*.
3 Cornelius O'Leary, *Irish Elections 1918–1977* (Dublin: Gill & Macmillan, 1979) p. 2.
4 Basil Chubb, *Political Parties in the European Community* (London: Allen & Unwin/European Centre for Political Studies, 1979) p. 127.
5 John Whyte, in Richard Rose (ed.), *Ireland: Politics without Social Basis – Electoral Behaviour: A Comparative Handbook* (New York: The Free Press, 1973) pp. 619–51.
6 'Prices may sink Lynch', *Irish Independent*, 26 February 1973.
7 Mr James Tully on the Electoral (Amendment) No. 2 Bill 1973 (*Dáil Debates*, vol. 268, col. 2048).
8 Michael Mills, 'Fianna Fáil get big poll boost', *Irish Press*, 11 December 1976.
9 Chris Glennon, 'Lynch win is poll forecast', *Irish Independent*, 11 December 1976.
10 'Politicians slam survey findings', *Evening Herald*, 11 December 1976.
11 *Irish Marketing Surveys – Political Opinion*, June 1977.
12 Renagh Holohan, 'Private polls, promises and crafty planning', *Irish Times*, 23 June 1977.
13 John Whale, 'The Irish result', *Sunday Times*, 19 June 1977.
14 Letter to *Irish Times* from managing director of MRBI, 22 June 1977.
15 Michael Mills, 'Poll shows coalition recovery', *Sunday Press*, 12 June 1977.
16 *Irish Times* NOP polls, 2 June 1977, 8 June 1977 and 10 June 1977, respectively.

17 Dr Garret FitzGerald, 'The oil crises and the seeds of defeat', *Irish Times*, 21 June 1977.
18 Chris Glennon, 'Jack is doing well in No. 1 political job, 85% says', *Irish Independent*, 10 December 1977.
19 Michael Mills, '70% backing in poll, Lynch off to good start', *Irish Press*, 10 December 1977.
20 *Sunday Independent*/IMS polls, 17 April 1980, 29 May 1980 and 3 July 1980, respectively.
21 *Irish Times*, 17 April, 29 May, 3 July, 9 October, 31 October 1980.
22 *Irish Times*, 24 January, 13 February, 24 April 1981.
23 *Magill*, 31 May 1981.
24 *Irish Independent*, 8 June 1981.
25 *Irish Times*, 26 May, 2 June and 10 June 1981, respectively.
26 *Irish Times*, 10 June 1981.

6 Political Opinion Polling in Italy

PIERPAOLO LUZZATTO-FEGIZ

THE EARLY DAYS, PRE-WAR TO 1948

The Impracticability of Opinion Polls under Fascism

When George Gallup started his pre-electoral polls in 1936 in the USA, very few in Italy took notice of them. For those who did, it was obvious that such an operation would not be possible in fascist Italy, where the only admitted opinion was that of Mussolini. When *Fortune* magazine began publishing the results of Elmo Roper's surveys on the attitude of Americans towards Germany, Great Britain, the war and the possible involvement of the USA, the few who could afford *Fortune* and understand it perceived that such data were indeed very important; but the press did not report them and nobody discussed the method.

In 1942 I published an article in *Statistica* with the title 'Statistical sampling of public opinion'[1] in which Gallup's and Roper's methods were described and some results of *Fortune's* opinion polls given. I thought then that public opinion surveys would be made sooner or later in Italy also (that is, after the return of democracy) but it was only during the war and immediately afterwards that I began to think seriously of the creation of a Gallup-type organisation in Italy. When, two months after the fall of Mussolini, the Badoglio government asked for an armistice (on 8 September), the Germans immediately occupied Italy; and I repaired to the island of Lussino, home of my wife, where I had a summer house. In the following months the island changed hands several times: after the Italians came Royalist Yugoslavs, then Tito's partisans, then the Germans (and Mongols serving under them) and finally Tito's regular troops.

Between 1943 and 1945 I witnessed many atrocities of warfare and guerrilla war, saw bombardments and cruel reprisals, and gained the impression that normally decent people could become, in a climate of hatred and vendettas between and within races and clans, beasts capable of unbelievable cruelty.

After one of those episodes I decided suddenly to dedicate the rest of my life (if there was still life in store for me) to doing 'something' to help avoiding those errors which, made in peacetime, often lead to war. The systematic sounding of public opinion appeared to me one possible method of avoiding major mistakes by rulers. After returning to my activity as a university professor I discussed with friends in Rome and Trieste the possibility of establishing an organisation for the systematic study of public opinion in Italy. Talking to Bruno De Finetti, the noted mathematician, I heard that Giulio Vuccino, president of Watson Italy (subsequently IBM, Italy), was also studying the possibility of founding such an institute.

THE FOUNDATION OF DOXA

In October 1945 Vuccino and I met, and asked the co-operation of Achille Bossi, then governor of the Rotary Club of Italy (just reconstructed after being suppressed by Mussolini). Bossi and a group of Rotarians saw at once that an organisation for the polling of public opinion would be something in the true Rotarian spirit of 'service'; and so, on 15 January 1946, DOXA was born. The name had been suggested by Vuccino: it means, in ancient Greek, opinion (orthodox = of the right opinion). Modern Greeks smile at the name, because in modern Greek it means glory! The complete name of the Institute is: DOXA, Institute of Statistical Research and Public Opinion Analysis, Limited, and it is based in Milan. The original capital was 1 million lire, then about 1700 dollars.[2] The initial personnel consisted of three people: myself, Ernesto Norbedo and Ines Vattovaz (still my secretary). Within a few weeks two other girls joined the staff (and they remain today): Anna Negri, in charge of one punching and one sorting machine, and Fiorenza Ballerani.

While recruiting of interviewers and designing a national sample was still in progress, the newly born institute faced a big challenge: Italy's Constituent Assembly had called, in the spring of 1946, a referendum on the issue 'Monarchy or Republic?'. DOXA decided to poll a sample of about 6000 adult Italians, and carefully prepared a questionnaire based on many cafeteria-type questions, with precoded alternatives (see

Table 6.1). The tables are published, with a short comment, in a supplement of *Il Sole*, a respected economic daily in Milan.

TABLE 6.1 *Monarchy* vs *Republic* (%)

Q: Which of the following sentences comes closest to expressing your opinion on the choice between monarchy and republic? (April 1946)

	All	Men	Women
The accusations against the present dynasty are unjust	5	4	6
The king may have erred, but the monarchy must remain	27	22	35
The monarchy is obsolete, but this is not the time for a change	16	18	13
The republic may be a risk, but the monarchy must be abolished	16	18	13
Only the republic will enable this country to rise again	24	30	15
Don't know	12	8	18
	100	**100**	**100**

DOXA deliberately abstained from forecasting the outcome, leaving it to readers and commentators to interpret, as pro- or anti-monarchist, such answers as the following: 'The monarchy is obsolete, but this is not the time for a change.' The result of the referendum was: for the republic, 54.3 per cent of valid votes, against 45.7 per cent. (Blank and void ballot papers were 6.1 per cent of all votes cast.) The monarchists were more numerous in the South than in the North, as had been anticipated by the poll. Since DOXA had not indicated a winner, nobody argued whether it had been right or wrong. Table 6.1 permits one to conclude, however, that at least 32 per cent of those voting were decidedly in favour of the monarchy, and 40 per cent decidedly in favour of the republic. But what about the remaining 28 per cent?

Die-hard monarchists still affirm, after thirty-six years, that the DOXA poll, if rightly interpreted, showed a majority for the monarchy, and that this would have been the outcome of the referendum, if it had been honest. But those who wanted to oust the king (mostly left-wingers) had falsified results with the complicity of the Socialist Minister of the Interior, by handing voting certificates of absent or deceased persons to their faithful (who thus voted more than once). It is impossible to say now whether this accusation is well founded; but another DOXA poll showed, four years later, that most Italians were not deeply interested in the issue (Table 6.2): only 15 per cent said that the monarchy must absolutely *not* return, and 21 per cent that it should return; all the rest either expressed indifference (14 per cent) or gave vague answers.

TABLE 6.2 *Return of the Monarchy (%)*

Q: Which of the following sentences comes closest to your present opinion on the monarchy? (October 1950)

	All	Men	Women
For no reason should the monarchy return	15	22	8
It's preferable that the monarchy does not return	16	16	16
The issue is not important	14	12	15
It's preferable that the monarchy returns	19	16	23
The monarchy must return, but not the Savoia	2	3	2
The monarchy must return, *with* the Savoia	19	18	20
Other answer	3	3	2
Don't know	12	10	14
	100	**100**	**100**

MARKETING SURVEYS AS A MEANS TO FINANCE POLITICAL SURVEYS

The 'Monarchy or Republic' issue was soon forgotten, but the country faced other serious problems. One concerned the peace treaty. Italy, having lost the war, was being asked to sign a treaty that implied, among other things, the loss of all colonies, the forfeiture to France of two stretches of territory (Briga and Tenda) and to Yugoslavia of a large part of Venezia Giulia east of Trieste. In the DOXA poll taken in October 1946, two preliminary questions were meant to explore the degree of information of respondents. Answers showed that 43 per cent were informed exactly, 30 per cent approximately and 27 per cent not at all about the French border; 30 per cent almost exactly, 36 per cent approximately and 34 per cent not at all about the eastern border. The first of the main questions was: 'Of the three projected mutilations (Briga and Tenda; Venezia Giulia; Colonies), which seems to you the most painful?' Answers: Briga and Tenda, 14 per cent; Venezia Giulia, 54 per cent; Colonies, 6 per cent; 'Don't know', 26 per cent. Second question: 'If the treaty imposes on Italy the above mutilations, what should we do?' Answers: 'Sign', 17 per cent; 'Postpone the signature', 26 per cent; 'Refuse to sign', 36 per cent; 'Don't know', 21 per cent. If respondents are classified according to the political tendency of the newspaper read, we find that the answer 'Sign' was given by 41 per cent of readers of the Communist press, by 30 per cent for the Socialist papers, 20 per cent for the Christian Democratic press and 16 per cent of readers of independent newspapers. In October 1947, the Constituent Assembly approved the signing of the treaty with 64 per cent in favour, 17 per cent against and 19 per cent abstaining.

In its first year of life DOXA conducted also a poll on the relationship between Communists and Socialists – an issue of great importance then and still very important today, since it is almost impossible for a Cabinet to get the majority in the Chamber when the Christian Democrats (DC) have to confront not only the Communist (PCI) but also the Socialist Party (PSI). The question, asked of a sample of over 5000 adults in October 1946, was: 'With regard to the relationship between Communists and Socialists, which solution is best for the country?' The answers were: 'No change (i.e. a pact of co-operation like now)', 15 per cent; 'Two independent parties (no pact)', 48 per cent; 'Fusion in a single party', 14 per cent; other answers, 3 per cent; 'Don't know', 20 per cent. It will be shown later how the attitude of the public towards this problem changed in the course of over thirty-three years.

When the young institute tried to probe public attitudes towards national and international problems, it had to face a serious financial problem. No newspaper or magazine was willing to pay for surveys on political or social issues, so DOXA was confronted with the problem of getting a regular income. From the very beginning of their efforts the promoters of DOXA had declared that they wanted complete independence from political, religious and financial groups, and that in order to have the money needed to conduct political and social surveys – the main purpose of the institute, but one for which neither newspapers nor magazines seemed to have funds – they would conduct market research at the request of all those willing to pay. For several years it was hard to find enough clients and make ends meet, but as business people began realising the advantages of research, it was first possible to balance the budget and then – around 1950 – to make a profit.

In the spring of 1947 I attended, at the personal request of George Gallup, the first Gallup conference in Loxwood (England); and the same year the institute was accepted as member of the Gallup Group (later called the Gallup International Research Institutes, Inc.).

THE ELECTION OF 18 APRIL 1948

The first free election after the fall of fascism took place on 2 June 1946. It did not elect a parliament, but a 'Constituent Assembly' which had the task of writing the Constitutional Charter of the Italian Republic. The election of a regular parliament, composed of a Chamber of Deputies and a Senate according to the new Constitution, took place on 18 April 1948, after a very intense electoral campaign in which the pro-Western Christian Democrats opposed the Communists.

The vote was awaited anxiously by the whole nation and by the world, because it would decide whether Italy would align itself with the West or with the East. After the success of the anti-monarchists in the referendum of 1946, which had been considered a Communist victory, millions feared – or hoped for – a triumph of the leftist coalition, the Fronte Popolare. This time the public wanted from DOXA not only a poll on attitudes, as for the 1946 referendum, but also a forecast of the outcome. The institute could not avoid making predictions, or the results of its surveys would be ignored by the press. On 10 April 1948 the weekly *Oggi* published the results of a DOXA poll taken a few weeks earlier. It contained several statistical tables (two of which are shown at Tables 6.4 and 6.5) and concluded:

TABLE 6.3 *General election 1948*

	Christian Democrat (%)	Popular Front (%)	Difference (%)
DOXA forecast for Chamber of Deputies	45 ±3	27 ±3	18
Actual results	48.7	30.7	18
Difference	3.7	3.7	

Except in case of an exceptionally low turnout at the polls, it is most improbable that on April 18 the Popular Front will get a majority or a plurality. About 45 % of the votes (plus or minus 3 %) can be expected to go to the Christian Democrats, 27 % (plus or minus 3 %) to the

TABLE 6.4 *Election of 1948 (%)*

Q: In your opinion which party, or group of parties, will get the highest number of votes at the next election?

Democrazia Cristiana	66
Fronte Democratico Popolare	30
Other parties	4
All indicating a party	100

TABLE 6.5 *Election of 1948 (%)*

Q: In the interest of Italy which party or political group should, in your opinion, become stronger?

Fronte Democratico Popolare (extreme left)	19.7
Other left and centre-left	11.0
Democrazia Cristiana	38.4
Other centre, centre-right and right	12.0
Don't know	18.9
	100.0

Popular Front. The Socialists may get 10 %, the National Bloc 9 % and the other parties the rest.

In Table 6.3 the above forecast is compared with official results. DOXA had predicted a turnout between 83 per cent and 87 per cent; since the actual turnout was even larger (93 per cent) it favoured the two major groups. This explains in part the fact that DOXA underestimated the success of both DC and Front, while anticipating exactly the gap of eighteen percentage points between the winner and the loser.

After distributing the 'don't know's among the different parties according to results of other analyses, DOXA published in *Oggi* (10 April) the forecast shown in Table 6.6.

TABLE 6.6 *Election of 1948 (%)*

	DOXA	*Actual results*
Fronte Democratico Popolare (extreme left)	27 ± 3	30.7
Democrazia Cristiana	45 ± 3	48.7
Other parties	28 ± 2	20.6
	100	100.0

In the same year, 1948, DOXA carried out also other opinion polls on international and domestic problems: on the Marshall Plan, relations between America and Russia, the Atlantic Pact, the strength of political parties in Italy; also on strikes, unemployment, happiness, divorce, the choice of a profession, housing.

POLITICAL AND SOCIAL SURVEYS AFTER 1948

Up to 1950 the history of political opinion polling in Italy is the story of DOXA. In April 1950 Ernesto Norbedo left DOXA to found two new companies: Istituto Italiano dell'Opinione Pubblica – IIOP (for opinion surveys) and Società Italiana Ricerche di Mercato (SIRM) for market research. The two organisations underwent several changes and ceased their activities in the sixties. In 1965 Carlo Erminero and Giampaolo Fabris joined the newly founded Demoskopea, which had the purpose of conducting both opinion and marketing studies. This institute is still active, but chiefly in market and audience research. In 1977 Fabris, a professor of sociology, published a book which contains the results of political surveys conducted by Demoskopea between 1968 and 1976. Chapters of the book deal, among other things, with political preferences, the image of parties, communism, divorce, abortion and civil rights.[3]

In the following years several other organisations appeared on the scene, but they performed political and electoral studies only sporadically. One reason for this policy is the fact that, as noted above, in Italy newspapers and magazines are reluctant to pay for survey material, while generally willing to publish such data if they can get them for nothing. Since DOXA has always considered it one of its main obligations to conduct periodical surveys of political, economical and social content, it has been for the last thirty-four years practically the sole regular supplier of this kind of information. Therefore the political studies that will be mentioned in the following pages were conducted mostly, if not exclusively, by DOXA.

In addition to Demoskopea the following Italian organisations have conducted, on one or more occasions, surveys on political issues: CISER (Centro Italiano Studi e Ricerche), Claparède, Eurisko, LCM, Makno, Mercurio, Misura, Pragma. Table 6.7 reports the approximate number of political surveys published between 1946 and 1967. The table is far from complete, because it covers only twenty-one years, and considers only three of at least ten organisations that have conducted opinion

TABLE 6.7 *Political and socio-political surveys in Italy (published 1946–1967)*

	DOXA	IIOP	CISER	Total
1946–50	15	–	–	15
1951–55	18	4	–	22
1956–60	48	2	12	62
1961–67	23	–	37	60
1946–67	104	6	49	159

SOURCE: Gianfranco Poggi, 'Le preferenze politiche degli Italiani – Analisi di alcuni sondaggi pre-elettorali', in *Quaderni dell'Istituto di Studi e ricerche Carlo Cattaneo* (Bologna: Il Mulino, 1968).

polls in the last thirty-four years. But those omitted are institutes that either had a short life, or were never engaged in political surveys.

In addition to typically political and electoral problems, DOXA has always studied through opinion polls those social and economic problems in which the attitude of Parliament, of political parties, of the press and the public is influenced more by 'party lines' than by individual convictions and ideals. One such problem, only in appearance of an ethic and administrative character, but essentially political, concerned the abolition of brothels. In 1948 Senator Angela Merlini of the Socialist Party proposed a law abolishing all the establishments housing prostitutes. (They were at that time tolerated and regulated by law.) The major party, which called itself Christian, could not openly defend laws legalising prostitution; yet many Catholic politicians, doctors and scholars envisaged with alarm the dangers of a free market in this field. It was a typical issue to raise before the forum of public opinion, and the following figures show that, according to a DOXA poll of February 1949, the majority were against the closing of brothels. Asked whether they thought true or false the sentence: 'Under present circumstances brothels are still the lesser evil', 57 per cent of the whole sample answered 'True', 9 per cent 'False' and 34 per cent 'Don't know'. When respondents were classified according to the political tendency of the newspaper they usually read, the following numbers said that the above sentence was 'True': Communists, 61 per cent; Socialists, 62 per cent; Liberals, 76 per cent; Christian Democrats, 56 per cent ('False', 13 per cent; 'Don't know', 31 per cent); readers of independent papers: 62 per cent, 'True'; 7 per cent, 'False'; 31 per cent, 'Don't know'; non-readers: 46 per cent, 'True'; 9 per cent, 'False'; 45 per cent, 'Don't know'.

But this was a typical case in which politicians completely ignored

public opinion. The consequences are evident to all. In another DOXA poll, taken in 1959, DOXA asked: 'Is there more or less prostitution in this place (town, village . . .) now than two or three years ago?' Answers: 'Less', 4 per cent; 'More', 40 per cent; 'No change', 16 per cent; 'There is no prostitution here', 11 per cent; 'Don't know', 29 per cent.

The next question was: 'In your opinion, is there a direct relationship between the increase in prostitution and the closing of brothels following the Merlini law?' Answers (of 100 who had said 'Prostitution increased'): 'Yes', 74 per cent; 'No', 15 per cent; 'Don't know', 11 per cent.

POLITICAL PARTIES AND THE POPULARITY OF PREMIERS

The main purpose of the surveys on political preferences made in USA, in Great Britain and in other countries is to assess, every week or every month, the comparative strength of the different parties. In Italy, where in addition to nine parties represented in Parliament there are many local and regional groups, such regular polls are technically impossible. Therefore questions on political preferences are asked by institutes mainly in order to provide background data, i.e. criteria that permit classification of the people sampled according to their political views. On many issues of a political or socio-economic nature answers vary not only with sex, age, education, etc., but also – and sometimes chiefly – with the political preferences of respondents. Consequently when the results of a study are broken down by various demographic or social characteristics, there will also be, as a rule, tables in which answers to each question appear separately for Communists, Socialists, Liberals, Christian Democrats, etc.

Conversely, tables giving the number of interviewees opting for each party are seldom published (although produced routinely by computers), one reason being that over one-third of respondents cannot be allocated confidently to a specific political group. In order to classify interviewees according to their voting behaviour or political preferences one or more of the following questions are used:

- If there was an election tomorrow, for what party would you vote?
- Bearing in mind what is good for all Italians, which party would you like to become stronger?
- Which political party deserves most confidence? (If 'None'): Which one has less faults than the others?

Since the political picture changes frequently, owing to the birth of new parties, the death of others, and mergers, splits and changes of name, a long-term panorama of changes in political preferences is almost impossible. More concrete data can be gathered on the popularity of politicians, and particularly of prime ministers. From scores of polls regarding those men, Table 6.8 has been extracted. It shows, among other things, that the electors unable (or unwilling) to express an opinion on the current premier were quite few with Degasperi, but never went under 26 per cent after him; and that no Prime Minister, however popular, ever got more than 40 per cent of the electorate to express full, or almost full, approval of his performance. The simple explanation is that all those premiers were Christian Democrats, and since that party usually gets in elections around 38 per cent of the national vote, those who approve fully the Prime Minister are mostly Christian Democratic voters.

THE 'CENTRE-LEFT'

In the election of 1948 (see above) the Christian Democrats *almost* reached the majority (48 per cent). In the following thirty-two years they not only missed the 51 per cent goal, but never repeated their 1948 success. Of those who voted Christian Democrat in 1948 and in the following elections the hard core was composed of electors from traditionally Catholic regions, especially women, farmers and elderly people in the north-east and south. But many others voted for them, although they were far from friendly to the Catholic hierarchy, because they felt the other parties (especially Liberals and Republicans) too weak to guarantee an efficient defence against Communism. In the following thirty years the Christian Democrats, unable to reach the majority and to govern alone, were obliged to seek the help of other democratic parties in order to form viable governments (at the rate of about one Cabinet every ten months). The ideal solution was considered by non-Communists to be an alliance of Christian Democrats with the Democratic Socialists (of the Scandinavian type). But among the Italian Socialists there were always (and still are) two currents: one pro-Communist and another which declares itself decidedly pro-Western and anti-Communist. After several splits and mergers and new splits, the present situation in the Socialist field is this: there is a Social-Democratic Party (PSDI), anti-Communist and actually co-operating with the government (about 4 per cent of the electorate); and the Socialist Party

TABLE 6.8 *Popularity of Prime Ministers, 1947–80* (%)

Q: Which of the sentences on this card comes closest to your opinion on how, —— has handled (so far) his job as Prime Minister?

	Degasperi 1947	1952	Scelba 1954	Fanfani 1960	Moro 1967	Colombo 1972	Andreotti 1977
I approve him completely	10	8	9	10	11	7	4
On the whole he did pretty well	30	30	27	30	29	25	20
He has been mediocre but made no serious mistake	21	21	16	16	20	19	18
He made mistakes that could have been avoided	16	14	8	5	8	9	16
I disapprove him completely	12	13	12	7	6	5	14
Don't know	11	14	28	32	26	35	28
	100	100	100	100	100	100	100

(PSI) (10 per cent of the electorate), unofficially divided into a right wing wanting and a left wing refusing co-operation with the Christian Democrats. In order to follow those rather complicated developments DOXA repeatedly asked samples of electors about their attitude towards the participation of Socialists in government; and some of the results of those polls are presented in Table 6.9.

The term 'centro-sinistra' (centre-left), meaning all parliamentary combinations which include Democrazia Cristiana and leftist parties but exclude Communists, was used by DOXA as early as May 1947. The answers, as reported in *DOXA Bulletin*, are shown in Table 6.10. The figures can be synthesised thus: total favouring a homogeneous government, 63 per cent; favouring a coalition, 11.9 per cent; other solutions and 'don't know's, 25.1 per cent.

SOCIALISM *VS* RELIGION AND OTHER STUDIES

To many foreigners it seems odd that in a country where 99 per cent of the population is Catholic, the atheistic Communist and Socialist parties can collect almost half (and in many zones much more than half) of the votes. In order to help explain this fact, DOXA asked, in 1953, and then again in 1961, 1968, 1976, the following question: 'Can one be a good Socialist and a good Catholic?' The answers are given in Table 6.11.

The figures show that the number of 'Yes' answers increased constantly, while the 'No's decreased only to the 17–20 per cent limit. In any case the majority believe that there is no contradiction in the fact that one votes Socialist and at the same time goes regularly to Mass. The same question asked about communism showed a different picture: those who think that a good Communist can be also a good Catholic never exceeded 45 per cent. The percentage increased dramatically between 1961 and 1968, but then did not exceed the number of those who were of the opposed opinion. This is shown by the figures in Table 6.12.

Further studies show that this trend towards tolerance and compromise is one aspect of the Italian national character. Many Italians do not believe there is a conflict between the two faiths – the Christian and the Marxist – because they see chiefly the practical and ritual rather than the spiritual aspects of both allegiances.

The surveys mentioned so far are only a small fraction of the political and socio-political studies conducted in Italy. An extensive collection of results of DOXA surveys carried out between 1946 and 1965 is presented

TABLE 6.9 *Evolution of public attitude towards the 'centre-left' (according to DOXA polls, 1956–78)*

	Question	Results	%	1977	1978
1956 (April)	Would you favour a government including the Socialists of PSI (Nenni) in addition to present parties?	Yes No DK	27 44 29 **100**		
1960 (Oct.)	In your opinion would co-operation between Christian Democrats and Socialists (of PSI) do Italy more good than harm or more harm than good?	More good More harm Other answer DK	34 15 2 49 **100**		
1961 (Dec.)	Is the 'opening to the left' good or bad for Italy?	Certainly good Probably good Probably bad Certainly bad DK	31 31 12 14 12 **100**		
1970 (May)	During the last six years Italy has always had, with short interruptions, centre-left governments. Would you say that the centre-left has proved a good idea or a bad idea?	Good idea Bad idea Neither good nor bad DK	25 12 22 41 **100**		
1977 (Sept.)	On this card are shown several possible coalitions of political parties. Which of these is, in your opinion, more likely to form a stable government?	Centre Centre-left Lefts with Chr. Democrats Lefts without Chr. Democrats DK		20 15 26 19 20 **100**	22 19 24 18 17 **100**

TABLE 6.10 *Preference (%)*

Q: Which party or group of parties should be given the responsibility of forming a government capable of solving quickly Italy's serious economic problems?

– A government of the extreme left	17.1
– A government of the left	12.3
– A government of Christian Democrats	16.5
– A government of the right	17.1
A coalition:	
– of centre and left parties	4.6
– of centre parties only	3.5
– of centre and right parties	3.8
– a government of independents, technicians	9.7
Don't know	15.4
	100.0

TABLE 6.11 *Compatibility of Socialism and Catholicism*

	1953 %	1961 %	1968 %	1976 %
Yes	37	47	66	70
No	45	28	17	20
DK	18	25	17	10
	100	100	100	100

TABLE 6.12

Q: Can one be a good Communist and a good Catholic?

	1953 %	1961 %	1968 %	1976 %
Yes	21	19	36	45
No	67	60	47	45
DK	12	21	17	10
	100	100	100	100

in two volumes, published respectively in 1956 and 1966 and totalling 3092 pages, entitled *The Unknown Face of Italy*.[4] A similar collection for the years after 1965 does not yet exist, but many results and articles on political and social opinion polls can be found in magazines and journals.[5]

BOOKS, ARTICLES AND SECONDARY ANALYSES
BASED ON OPINION POLLS

As stated above, neither DOXA nor other Italian organisations have
ever succeeded in getting their releases published regularly, whether by a
chain of newspapers (as is the case of Gallup in the USA) or by one
publication entitled to exclusive rights (as in Great Britain and in other
countries).

However, when a summary of results is given without charge to an
Italian news agency it is usually diffused widely and then printed by
many newspapers and magazines, and broadcast by television and
radio. Sometimes those data get big headlines. Furthermore, when a
publication (usually a weekly magazine) buys exclusive rights to a
survey, it wants to get maximum publicity from this material, which
becomes usually the theme of a cover story. Consequently the irregu-
larity of the appearance in the press of news about opinion polls is partly
compensated for by the wide interest created at all levels by those stories.
Quite often poll data become subjects of articles and editorial columns,
and sometimes they are quoted in Parliament.

Among the surveys that originated articles, debates and further
studies, those dealing with the following subjects should be mentioned:
divorce, birth control, abortion, prices, unemployment, unions, strikes,
absenteeism, communism and socialism, NATO, USA and USSR, the
Common Market, corruption in public life, the powers of Regions, the
nationalisation of electric utilities. To list all books, scientific papers and
articles published in Italy and abroad that are based on sample surveys
would be an impossible task. In order to give an idea of the kind of
literature produced by political polls in the last twenty years I wish to
mention just a few publications.

In 1962 Mattéi Dogan, a French sociologist, published a paper on the
social stratification of voters according to electoral results. Using the
data of surveys by DOXA and the Istituto Italiano dell'Opinione
Pubblica and also official statistics, Dogan tried to estimate the
distribution, among the various political parties, of the votes of three
social classes: industrial workers, farmers and farm hands, and the
urban middle class. He also showed the influence of education on voting
behaviour in the different social classes.[6]

In 1963 Professor Joseph Lopreato of the University of Texas planned
a large study on class conflicts in Italy, and asked DOXA to conduct a
survey based on a questionnaire he had designed. The books and papers
based on the results of those surveys (and of course also on other
sources) are listed at the end of this chapter.[7]

In 1965 the Naples daily *Roma* published a 250-page book with the title *Report on Naples: Portrait of a City*.[8] It was based chiefly on sample surveys conducted by CISER and DOXA, and on figures provided by the National Statistical Institute.

Between 1968 and 1970 the Consiglio Nazionale della Ricerche (National Research Council) financed a study of the influence of school education on the careers and success of managers and upper cadres. The study was conducted by the Institute of Statistics of the Rome University, in co-operation with the Centre for Studies and Social Investments (CENSIS). DOXA carried out all the sample surveys on which the research was chiefly based.[9]

Electoral surveys made between 1958 and 1963 have been the subject of secondary analyses conducted by the Istituto di Studi e Ricerche 'Carlo Cattaneo' with the financial help of the Twentieth Century Fund of New York.[10]

In 1970 Shell of Italy sponsored a DOXA study on Italian youth and the results of the survey were published in a 309-page book which contains much information of political and sociological relevance.[11] Later (1973) the company published another, 491-page, book similarly based on a DOXA poll and concerning the life and problems of women.[12] Like the volume on Italian youth, the book contains much information on the attitude of the chosen group toward politics, religion, etc.

In 1970 the association of former political deportees (Associazione Nazionale ex Deportati Politici – ANED) asked DOXA to conduct a survey among a random sample of Italian survivors from the Nazi concentration camps. The results of the study were published in a book[13] which is composed of a statistical summary and hundreds of verbatim answers by interviewees. The statements are impressive, because respondents who returned from different German *Lagers*, who did not know each other, describe in practically identical terms the ferocious treatment to which the inmates of the camps were subjected.

Between 1976 and 1980 Eurisko, an institute founded in 1972 and specialising in psychological sample surveys, undertook a series of 'psychographic' studies in which, among other things, the political behaviour of people sampled was correlated to life-styles and to many social and psychological dimensions. The results of this research and especially of the poll taken in 1978 and 1979 on a sample of 5000 adults are presented in a book by Gabriele Calvi (professor at the University of Florence and one of the pioneers of the new psychographic science) who planned and directed the Eurisko study.[14] The study is interesting both for its results and for the method used. In order to form homogeneous classes of life-styles and alimentary styles, Calvi makes ample use of multivariate analysis, reaching several conclusions on the connection – or lack of connection – between scales of values and political behaviour. One of Calvi's theses is that in Italy the gap dividing the 'real country' from the political class must be imputed to politicians who substituted a system of fears ('all evils derive from the political adversary') for a system of ethical values.

CONCLUSION: THE IMPACT OF OPINION SURVEYS ON ITALIAN LIFE

Opinion polls in Italy cannot claim to have had a tangible influence on legislation, but it is probable that they have modified the behaviour of voters by increasing their level of information and their interest in political issues. One of the aims of organisations for the study of public opinion is to inform the public about prevailing attitudes and pre-ferences; in other words, to teach people to know themselves better. Now it seems that in Italy such a goal has been attained to a remarkable degree. This is proved not only by the interest with which news about polls is followed by readers of magazines and watchers of television, but also by the eagerness with which people answer to interviewers question-ing them. Thirty years ago many respondents were quite diffident when asked about their private lives or political preferences; now even in regions like Sicily, Sardinia and Calabria, where people are reluctant to answer when questioned by officials or neighbours, interviewers are well received; and if a well-known polling institute is named and the purpose of the survey explained, they give, on the whole, reliable answers. This is a matter of gratification for those who started public opinion polls thirty-six years ago and affirmed in their promotional pamphlets that they wanted 'to give a voice to all citizens, including the weakest and those living far from cities'; and that they hoped 'to contribute to the political education of Italians'.[15]

The popularity of public opinion institutes increased noticeably when the national broadcasting company introduced in its electoral program-mes the so-called 'projections', really a big show based on estimates of final results (that appear on television screens directly from the computer), and dramatised by debates, interviews, music and the appearance of celebrities. In Italy electors vote on Sunday and also on Monday morning; and in the last five years the networks broadcast, almost immediately after the closure of precincts, 'projections' of results, calculated by one or two institutes. These estimates are based initially on a few dozen representative precincts, but after a couple of hours, when less than 1 per cent of precincts have been sampled, the 'projections' differ only slightly (by about 0.2 per cent) from the official results that the Ministry of the Interior announces around midnight. For Italians this show has become a kind of national sport. After the 1976 election the Minister of the Interior, Cossiga, telephoned the president of DOXA to say: 'Thank you for helping us to keep order. There were no demonstrations in the streets yesterday: all Italians were glued to their TV sets as if for an important soccer match.'

NOTES

1 P. Luzzatto-Fegiz, 'Sondaggi statistici dell'opinione publica', *Statistica*, 1942.
2 The capital was increased several times, and is now 150 million lire.
3 Giampaolo Fabris, *Il comportamento politico degli Italiani* (Milan: Franco Angeli, 1977).
4 P. Luzzatto-Fegiz, *Il volto sconosciuto dell'Italia. Dieci anni di sondaggi DOXA: 1946–1965* (Milan: Giuffrè, 1956); *Il volto sconosciuto dell'Italia, Seconda serie, 1956–1965* (Milan: Giuffrè, 1966).
5 All results of DOXA polls on socio-political subjects appear in the following bi-monthly publication: *Bollettino della DOXA* (Milan: DOXA, Galleria S. Carlo 6).
6 Mattéi Dogan, 'La stratificazione sociale dei suffragi in Italia', in *Elezioni e comportamento politico in Italia* (Milan: Edizioni di Comunità, 1962).
7 Joseph Lopreato and L. E. Hazelrigg, 'Class, Conflict and Mobility: Theories and Studies of Class Structure' (San Francisco: Chandler, 1972); J. Lopreato, 'Upward social mobility and political orientation', *American Sociological Review*, 32 (1967); J. Lopreato and J. S. Chafetz, 'The Political Orientation of Skidders: A middle-range theory', *American Sociological Review*, 35 (1970).
8 Petronio Petrone (ed.), *Rapporto su Napoli – Ritratto di una città* (Naples: Quotidiano 'ROMA', 1965).
9 R. Cagiano, P. Luzzatto Fegiz (ed.), U. Paniccia, A. Ruberto, C. Scala, A. Valentini and A. Zuliani, 'Formazione scolastica, carriera ed affermazione dei dirigenti in Italia', 3 vols, 606 pp., mimeo. (Milan: DOXA, 1971).
10 Gianfranco Poggi, 'Le preferenze politiche degli Italiani', in *Quaderni dell'Istituto di studi e ricerche 'Carlo Cattaneo'* (Bologna: Il Mulino, 1968).
11 Shell-DOXA, *Questi, i giovani*, Inchiesta Shell No. 9 (Geneva: Shell, 1970).
12 Shell-DOXA, *La donna oggi in Italia*, Inchiesta Shell No. 10 (Geneva: Shell, 1973).
13 DOXA, *Un mondo fuori dal mondo. Indagine DOXA fra i reduci dai campi nazisti* (Florence: La Nuova Italia Editrice, 1971).
14 Gabriele Calvi, *La classe fortezza. Scelte degli elettori e responsabilità della classe politica in Italia* (Milan: Franco Angeli, Editore, 1980).
15 Preface to *Il volto sconosciuto dell'Italia*, see note 4.

7 Political Opinion Polling in Japan

SIGEKI NISIHIRA

The present-day *Mainichi Shimbun*, a Japanese newspaper, took the first nationwide opinion poll in Japan in May 1940, when it questioned the public on middle school entrance examinations. In November the same newspaper followed with a nationwide poll on election procedures. These were perhaps the only opinion polls of the pre-war period. The sampling technique used in those polls was imprecise by today's standards.

The importance of public opinion has been known for a long time. *Yoron*, the modern Japanese word for public opinion, originated in China, where it was first used during the reign of Wu Ti (140–87 BC) in the Han dynasty. In Japan the word *yoron* began to appear in written records around the seventeenth century, and from about the time of the Meiji Restoration, in 1867, public opinion began to play an important role in Japanese politics and society. Public opinion at first referred only to the opinions of select groups of people, such as samurai, politicians and journalists. Only after the Second World War did *yoron* begin to refer to opinions shared by the general public.

After the Second World War the Supreme Command for the Allied Powers (SCAP) set up a Public Opinion and Sociological Research Division within its Civil Information and Education Section to spread both sociological research in general and public opinion polling specifically in Japan. In the autumn of 1945, two months after the end of the war, the *Mainichi* conducted a survey on gubernatorial election procedures, the first nationwide opinion poll of the postwar period. In 1947 a survey of Japanese literacy was conducted with the encouragement of SCAP. This survey did not inquire about people's opinions, but it enabled the Japanese to learn the new techniques of sampling, polling and data analysis, and thus determined the subsequent development of opinion polling in Japan.

OPINION POLLING IN GENERAL

Today Japan takes as many opinion polls as the USA and countries in
Europe, if not more. Every year the Public Relations Office of the Prime
Minister's Secretariat surveys opinion polls taken during the year. This
survey inquires about the opinion polls that government agencies and
local public organisations, universities and other research institutions,
mass media and private enterprises have taken on individuals' opinions,
awareness, desires, interests, judgements and attitudes. (It does not,
however, cover market surveys.) In 1980, for example, the Public
Relations Office mailed questionnaires to 1734 organisations and got
replies from 1428 – an 82 per cent return. Those that did not respond
were mostly organisations that had little to do with opinion polls. Table
7.1 gives the results.

TABLE 7.1 *Number of Public Opinion Polls, 1963–78*

	1963	1968	1980
All polls	504	496	902
Nationwide polls	104	94	147
Interview method	256	189	285
Random samples	398	327	713
By type of polling institution			
National government		84 (31)	64 (36)
Local governments		168 (0)	523 (0)
Mass media		151 (34)	160 (77)
Other institutions		93 (29)	155 (34)
Average response rate		86.6%	79.6%

Note: Figures in parentheses are for nationwide polls.

About 500 opinion polls have been taken every year since 1963, and in
recent years more than 900 annually. These figures include administrative research studies for government departments on such subjects as
postal delivery and railway traffic services. Approximately 100 are
nationwide opinion polls in the strictest sense.

By type of polling institution, the national government accounted for
84 (16 per cent) of the total number of polls taken in 1968, compared
with 64 (7 per cent) in 1980. On average, the government conducts about
40 nationwide polls each year. Polls by newspapers have amounted to
about 150 per year over the last ten years. Those of local public bodies
have increased over threefold, from 168 to 523. The recent increase in the

number of opinion polls is thus due to a rapid rise in the number of polls by local governments.

Towns and villages perhaps conduct more opinion polls in Japan than anywhere else in the world. Although these include interesting questions based on local conditions, they are sometimes crudely conceived.

Newspapers conduct more than half the 100-plus nationwide polls, and the government conducts between 30 and 40, as noted above. These polls are sometimes difficult to categorise by subject matter, particularly since a single poll may take up several subjects at once. In 1978, of the 464 polls that local public bodies took, 206 (44 per cent) dealt with local administration, self-government and community interests. Of the 136 mass media polls, 57 (42 per cent) dealt with political and other current issues. The 56 polls that the government undertook covered everything from pollution to life attitudes, politics, work, youth, education and social security, depending on the ministries conducting them.

TECHNICAL POLLING PROBLEMS

As indicated in Table 7.1, nearly all Japanese opinion polls use the random sampling method; the quota system is seldom used. This is because polls using the quota system failed to predict the winner in the US presidential election of 1948, soon after Japan began to take opinion polls regularly. Another reason is that random sampling frames have always been readily obtainable. From prior to the Second World War the Japanese were registering for rice rations. This was later replaced by resident registration. Under this system people must register their residence. Violations are punishable by law. Not only that, people have to register to draw social security, enter their children in school, register their seal (symbol) impressions, vote, and so on. Random samples are thus readily obtainable from resident registration records. However, the registration form varies from municipality to municipality, sometimes creating sampling problems.

Municipalities compile voter lists, which are revised on a certain day each year to reflect changes that have occurred in the resident register during the year. In addition, when there is an election, voter lists are corrected for residents' movements up to a certain date, and, if necessary, municipal officials check whether residents are actually living where they are registered. Thus when researchers conduct surveys on people over 20 years of age and entitled to vote, they often use the voter lists to select their samples.

Researchers can therefore rigorously select individuals by means of random sampling methods. But investigators must go in person to municipal offices (of which there were 3256 in 1980) to make use of either the resident register or the voter list. Therefore, most nationwide polls use the stratified multi-stage sampling method. In this method the nation's municipalities are first stratified according to population size, industrial composition, locality, and so on, as given in the *National Census Reports* (the national census is carried out every five years). Then in the first-stage sampling, one municipality is selected from each stratum, the probability of a municipality being selected being proportional to its population size. In the second-stage sampling, one voting district is selected from among the voting districts of each municipality selected in the first stage, the probability of a voting district being selected being proportional to its population size. In the third stage, systematic sampling methods are used to select individuals from the voter lists of the voting districts selected in the second stage.

The size of the sample varies according to the size of the area polled and the extent of analysis desired. In 1980, for example, 473 (52 per cent) of all polls had a sample size ranging from 1000 to 2999 persons, and 39 polls sampled more than 10 000 persons. The sample size of nationwide polls normally ranges from 2000 to 3000 persons.

Interviews are widely used as a means of gathering information from respondents. In 1963, for instance, about half of all polls used the interview method. The number of polls using this method, however, is declining, as evidenced by the fact that 284 (only one-third) of the total number of opinion polls conducted in 1980 used this method (see Table 7.1). In the same year there were 275 polls conducted by mail, about the same proportion as those using interviews, and about one-quarter (243) used the self-administration method, where respondents are asked to fill out questionnaires on their own. The self-administration method is used mainly for municipal polls, while nationwide public opinion polls still normally rely on face-to-face interviewing.

The number of respondents that cannot be interviewed for interview polls is increasing: on average 14.4 per cent of respondents for polls taken in 1970 could not be interviewed; in 1980 the proportion increased to 20.4 per cent (see Table 7.1).

In a poll that my colleagues and I have carried out every five years since 1953, the portion of respondents we failed to interview gradually rose from 17 per cent for the first poll to 27 per cent in 1978. For this poll we ask college professors we know well to select students in their seminars or whom they know personally to serve as interviewers. We then give these students special instructions ourselves to make them the best interviewers possible. Our experience has shown that about one-quarter of all unpollable respondents have either died or moved but remained on voter lists. Another third were away or in hospital. The remaining 40 per cent might have been polled had the interviewer been a little more persistent and made repeated return calls. Thus we normally distrust polls that claim a response rate of over 85 per cent. Respondents that are hard to poll tend to be male, young and live in large cities. However, hard-to-poll respondents affect poll results by at most plus or minus 2 per cent. Moreover, though some interviewers turn in false questionnaires, several experiments have shown that their overall effect on the results is negligible.

NEWSPAPER POLLS AND VOTER POLLS

Newspapers in Japan differ from newspapers in Europe and America in several ways. The big three Japanese newspapers, the *Asahi Shimbun*, the *Mainichi Shimbun* and the *Yomiuri Shimbun*, all print their newspapers simultaneously in six or seven locations scattered across the country and deliver them to subscribers' doors. They not only enjoy large circulations but are excellent newspapers. Like the news agencies, they all have bureaux and correspondents in various news centres, facilitating their editorial activities. Since their correspondents cover the news themselves, they use reports coming out of the news agencies only as a check on their own stories. Though Japan has about fifteen major poll-takers that can poll the entire nation, the big three do not rely on them to conduct public opinion polls. Rather their polls are planned by the public opinion poll section of the main editorial office, who then have their bureaux throughout the country carry out the poll. Newspaper companies conduct these public opinion polls by interviewing about 3000 people at each of 200 to 250 spots across the country. The *Asahi*, the *Mainichi* and the Japan Broadcasting Corporation conduct polls on political and social issues several times a year. The *Yomiuri* has been conducting public opinion polls once every month since 1978. The *Mainichi* has conducted a survey of what people read every autumn since 1947, and since 1950 it has been polling the public on family planning every other year (except for the third poll, which was taken in 1955).

In addition to periodic public opinion polls, the three big newspapers, the Japan Broadcasting Corporation, and sometimes Kyodo News Service, separately conduct large public opinion polls before every

House of Representatives general election and House of Councillors election and key gubernatorial elections. Though in House of Representatives general elections there are 129 electoral districts with three to five seats each and one electoral district with one seat, each voter votes for only one candidate. In each district the candidate with the largest number of votes is elected, then the one with the second largest number of votes, and so on, until all contested seats are filled. Each of the five companies engaged in pre-election polling must predict the outcome by sampling 600 to 1200 voters in each electoral district, bringing the total number of people each company must poll to anywhere from 70 000 to 90 000, or 400 000 for the five companies combined. This means that one voter in 200 is polled.

Pre-election polls, however, are taken within a very short period of time, making it difficult to interview all the scheduled subjects. Even if pollsters manage to get an interview, many respondents refuse to indicate their party or candidate preference. This is particularly true of supporters of the Japan Communist Party and the Kōmeitō, affiliated with the Sōka Gakkai, an active Buddhist sect. Candidates of these parties always get more votes than opinion polls predict. Thus polling companies must make predictions by comparing past poll data with actual election results.

Table 7.2 shows the *Asahi*'s and *Mainichi*'s predictions for each party's portion of the popular vote in recent House of Representatives general elections, compared with actual results. Predictions for each party's share of the popular vote erred on the average less than 1 per cent; the largest error was 2.5 per cent, an amazingly high degree of accuracy.

Newspapers take pre-election polls to predict the number of seats each party will capture, and particularly whether the ruling Liberal Democratic Party will retain a majority in the Diet. As Table 7.3 shows, the newspapers have generally been accurate in their predictions at party performance. Errors of over ten seats normally arouse public criticism. Despite their ability to make fairly accurate predictions of each party's share of the popular vote, the newspapers frequently err considerably in predicting the number of seats each party will capture. The reason for this is that elections in Japan are carried out according to a system of electoral districts, each with three to five contested seats. The Liberal Democratic Party's candidates thus frequently end up taking votes from each other and undermining other Liberal Democratic Party candidates' chances of winning, and similarly for opposition party candidates. In the June 1980 general election, for example, the difference

TABLE 7.2 *Actual and predicted share of the popular vote in House of Representatives elections (%)*

		LDP	JSP	Kōmeitō	DSP	JCP	NLC	Other parties and independents	Total
1972	Election results	46.9	21.9	8.5	7.0	10.5	—	5.2	100.0
	Mainichi	47.1	21.4	8.4	7.0	9.9	—	6.2	100.0
	Asahi	47.4	21.3	8.5	7.5	9.7	—	5.6	100.0
1976	Election results	41.8	20.7	10.9	6.3	10.4	4.1	5.8	100.0
	Mainichi	41.0	21.4	10.4	5.6	12.3	3.8	5.5	100.0
	Asahi	42.7	20.3	11.6	6.0	10.6	3.1	5.7	100.0
1979	Election results	44.6	19.7	9.8	6.8	10.4	3.0	5.7	100.0
	Mainichi	47.1	18.6	9.3	7.1	9.5	3.1	5.3	100.0
	Asahi	45.2	19.2	9.6	6.6	10.2	3.5	5.7	100.0
1980	Election results	47.9	19.3	9.0	6.6	9.8	3.0	4.4	100.0
	Mainichi	47.5	19.2	10.1	6.8	9.9	2.4	4.1	100.0
	Asahi	46.7	19.3	9.8	6.6	10.6	2.6	4.4	100.0

Note: LDP = Liberal Democratic Party; JSP = Japan Socialist Party; DSP = Democratic Socialist Party; JCP = Japan Communist Party; NLC = New Liberal Club.

TABLE 7.3 *Actual and predicted number of seats won in House of Representatives elections* (%)

		LDP	JSP	Kōmeitō	DSP	JCP	NLC	Other parties and independents	Total
1963	Election results	283	144	—	23	5	—	12	467
	Mainichi	+8	+9	—	−9	−3	—	−5	±17
	Asahi	+7	+9	—	−8	−2	—	−6	±16
1967	Election results	277	140	25	30	5	—	9	486
	Mainichi	−4	+13	−3	−2	0	—	−4	±13
	Asahi	−6	+1	−4	−3	+4	—	+8	±13
1969	Election results	288	90	47	31	14	—	16	486
	Mainichi	−12	+33	−4	−1	−5	—	−11	±33
	Asahi	−13	+28	−8	−1	−2	—	−4	±28
1972	Election results	271	118	29	19	38	—	16	491
	Mainichi	+10	0	+5	+8	−15	—	−8	±23
	Asahi	+8	−8	+6	+7	−12	—	−1	±21
1976	Election results	249	123	55	29	17	17	21	511
	Mainichi	+4	+8	−12	−8	+22	−7	−7	±34
	Asahi	+7	−8	−11	−2	+19	−5	0	±26
	Yomiuri	+3	+13	−21	−4	+15	−5	−1	±31
1979	Election results	248	107	57	35	39	4	21	511
	Mainichi	+21	+5	−6	−4	−13	+1	−4	±27
	Asahi	+22	−5	−11	−4	−10	+7	+1	±30
	Yomiuri	+26	+9	−17	−5	−15	+4	−2	±39
1980	Election results	284	107	33	32	29	12	14	511
	Mainichi	−18	0	+18	+4	+3	−6	−1	±25
	Asahi	−12	−2	+11	+4	−1	−2	+2	±17

Note: In 1963, for example, the *Mainichi* predicted that the Liberal Democratic Party would gain 290 seats, 8 more than the number of seats it actually won.

between the lowest winner and highest loser was less than 1 per cent of the popular vote in 50 out of 130 districts.

A close look at Table 7.3 reveals that the *Asahi, Mainichi* and *Yomiuri* erred in a similar direction. In 1980, for example, all three newspapers underestimated the number of seats that the Liberal Democratic Party would capture and overestimated the number that Kōmeitō and the Communists would gain. If these errors are the result of systematic flaws in the newspapers' polling methods, there is a good chance that statisticians will be able to improve future predictions. Perhaps statisticians erred because they tried to make the most of past experience and assumed that past voting behaviour would be repeated in the forthcoming election. In reality, however, voting behaviour changes with every election. This problem is not limited to election predictions; it is the fate of all statistical predictions.

For House of Councillors elections there are national and local constituencies. Each of Japan's forty-seven prefectures constitutes a local constituency, with one to four seats. Voters cast one vote in the national and one vote in a local constituency.

Predictions for House of Councillors elections are generally very accurate, as can be seen from Table 7.4, which shows each party's actual and predicted share of the popular vote, and Table 7.5, which shows the actual and predicted number of seats that each party captured in House of Councillors elections.

The Election of Public Officials Law, Article 138, Clause 3, states that it is unlawful to announce the proceedings or results of 'straw votes' that predict the most likely winners in an election. Poll-takers interpret this as allowing them to announce the results of their polls so long as they do not specifically mention individual candidates' share of the popular vote or their ranking.

Table 7.6 shows that the *Mainichi* was correct about 90 per cent of the time in predicting whether a candidate would be elected to the House of Representatives. Successes for 'could go either way' include candidates who barely won or just lost.

Longitudinal Surveys

As mentioned above, the *Mainichi* has been conducting two surveys for the past thirty years or so. In addition, I and my colleagues at the Institute of Statistical Mathematics, a national research organisation, have been researching the Japanese national character every five years since 1953; we conducted the sixth poll in 1978. In this research we

TABLE 7.4 *Actual and predicted share of the popular vote in House of Councillors elections (%)*

		LDP	JSP	Kōmeitō	DSP	JCP	NLC	Other parties and independents	Total
Local constituencies	1974								
	Election results	39.5	26.0	12.6	4.4	12.0	—	5.5	100.0
	Mainichi	39.4	24.7	13.7	3.8	12.5	—	5.9	100.0
	Asahi	39.0	24.8	13.6	4.7	12.4	—	5.5	100.0
	1977								
	Election results	39.5	25.9	6.2	4.5	9.9	5.7	8.3	100.0
	Mainichi	39.4	26.8	5.6	3.9	9.9	5.7	8.7	100.0
	Asahi	37.5	26.9	5.9	4.6	10.9	5.4	8.8	100.0
	1980								
	Election results	43.3	22.4	5.0	5.2	11.7	0.6	11.8	100.0
	Mainichi	46.4	21.3	5.5	5.1	10.8	0.0	10.9	100.0
	Asahi	43.3	22.0	6.0	4.7	12.3	0.4	11.3	100.0
National constituency	1974								
	Election results	44.3	15.2	12.1	5.9	9.4	—	13.1	100.0
	Mainichi	46.4	15.2	14.3	5.6	8.5	—	10.0	100.0
	Asahi	44.6	13.5	12.3	5.6	9.4	—	14.6	100.0
	1977								
	Election results	35.8	17.4	14.2	6.7	8.4	3.9	13.6	100.0
	Mainichi	35.4	16.6	12.6	7.4	8.4	7.0	12.6	100.0
	Asahi	31.4	18.9	14.8	6.9	9.5	4.2	14.3	100.0
	1980								
	Election results	42.5	13.1	11.9	6.0	7.3	0.6	18.6	100.0
	Mainichi	43.9	13.2	13.8	6.9	7.3	0.1	14.8	100.0
	Asahi	40.2	14.8	13.7	6.4	7.9	0.6	16.4	100.0

TABLE 7.5 *Actual and predicted number of seats won in House of Councillors elections*

		LDP	JSP	Kōmeitō	DSP	JCP	NLC	Other parties and independents	Total
1968	Election results	48	16	4	3	1	—	3	75
	Mainichi	0	+4	−1	−1	−1	—	−1	±4
	Asahi	−2	+5	−1	−2	0	—	0	±5
1971	Election results	42	28	2	2	1	—	1	76
	Mainichi	+6	−8	0	0	+1	—	+1	±8
	Asahi	+3	−3	0	−1	0	—	+1	±4
1974	Election results	43	18	5	1	5	—	4	76
	Mainichi	+8	−4	−2	1	−1	—	−1	±8
	Asahi	+4	−1	+1	0	−2	—	−2	±5
	Yomiuri	+6	−2	−2	0	−1	—	−1	±6
1977	Election results	45	17	2	5	2	2	3	76
	Mainichi	0	+1	0	−2	−1	+1	+1	±3
	Asahi	−2	+2	+1	−2	0	+1	0	±4
	Yomiuri	+4	−1	+1	−4	+2	−2	0	±7
1980	Election results	48	13	3	2	4	0	6	76
	Mainichi	0	0	+1	0	0	0	−1	±1
	Asahi	+1	−1	+1	0	−1	0	0	±2

Local constituencies

1968	Election results	21	12	9	4	3	—	2	51
	Mainichi	0	+1	0	0	0	—	-1	±1
	Asahi	+2	0	0	-1	0	—	-1	±2
1971	Election results	21	11	8	4	5	—	1	50
	Mainichi	+2	-2	0	0	0	—	0	±2
	Asahi	+2	-2	0	0	0	—	0	±2
1974	Election results	19	10	9	4	8	—	4	54
	Mainichi	+2	-1	0	0	-1	—	0	±2
National	*Asahi*	+4	-2	0	-1	-1	—	0	±4
constituency	*Yomiuri*	+5	0	-1	-1	-2	—	-1	±5
1977	Election results	18	10	3	9	4	1	5	50
	Mainichi	-1	-1	+1	0	0	+2	-1	±3
	Asahi	-1	0	+2	0	0	0	-1	±2
	Yomiuri	-1	+1	+6	-5	0	+1	-2	±8
1980	Election results	21	9	9	4	3	0	4	50
	Mainichi	-2	+1	0	-2	+2	0	+1	±4
	Asahi	0	0	0	-1	+1	0	0	±1

TABLE 7.6 *The Mainichi's success rates for predicting how candidates fare in House of Councillors elections*

Predictions	Actual results for 1976 (no. of candidates)			Success rates (%)					
	Elected	Defeated	Total	1976	1972	1969	1967	1963	
Certain to be elected	235	15	250	94	96	97	97	96	
Likely to be elected	107	26	133	80	93	81	85	85	
Could go either way	150	94	244	89	82	84	82	91	
Certain to be defeated	19	253	272	93	92	94	96	96	
	511	388	899	90	89	90	91	93	

examine how people think in their daily lives by presenting common hypothetical situations that people can readily imagine. In addition to conducting this poll and examining its results every five years, we also carry out supplementary surveys from time to time. Our institute also conducts polls comparing Japanese with Japanese Americans in Hawaii, non-Japanese Americans in Hawaii and Americans in general on the US mainland.

Our national character studies have apparently stimulated social-psychological studies throughout Japan, as evidenced by similar surveys that the Japan Broadcasting Corporation and government agencies conduct. Our work has also stimulated comparative surveys with foreign countries, which are now in vogue. The Youth Bureau of the Prime Minister's Office, for example, conducted a comparative study of youth in eleven countries in 1972 and 1977.

Newspapers' and government agencies' polls usually deal only with controversial issues. Our institute has been conducting a poll on social and political issues in Tokyo every spring and autumn since 1954. This poll studies changes and continuity in public opinion on non-controversial matters.

PUBLIC OPINION POLLS AND THE JAPANESE

Public opinion polls, as noted earlier, are very popular in Japan. One reason is that public opinion polls were considered necessary for democracy to take root in postwar Japan.

Another important reason is that the Japanese look at the results of opinion polls as an important source of information about how other people think, something the Japanese by nature are concerned about. The essence of democracy is that people can freely express their opinions even though they differ from those of others. In this the Japanese are weak. They do not always understand the importance of freely exchanging ideas. This is why they focus their attention on the process of adopting ideas, a visible aspect of democracy, while ignoring its essence. And they consider public opinion polls as part of the adoption process. But even when the Japanese have adopted an idea, they do not necessarily put it into practice.

Not only are the Japanese more interested in knowing what others think than in expressing their own ideas, they also tend to want to be like other people. Public opinion polls provide an excellent means of doing just that. Such a tendency is not limited to the general public but can also be seen in cabinet ministers' statements. They will often respond to questions with statements like: 'The Japanese government will make its position clear after it has carefully considered the positions of other nations.' Curiously, the questioner accepts this reply without further ado. In Japan ministers and bureaucrats alike believe that it is more democratic for the government to guess what the nation desires and act on that basis than to come forth and institute a particular policy it deems necessary or important. And so government agencies and local governments are always taking public opinion polls. That way they can blame the opinion polls for their mistakes.

The Japanese are fond of opinion polls even though they are not compatible with either the Japanese character or the Japanese language. First of all, in European languages people answer questions with a definite 'yes' or 'no'. No American or European could spend an entire day without saying 'yes' or 'no' at least once. 'Yes' in Japanese is *hai*, and 'no' is *iie*, but people do not usually reply to questions using these words. Indeed, it is not unusual for a person to go an entire month without uttering *iie* even once. *Hai* is often used in the sense of 'I see'; it does not necessarily mean that the speaker agrees. For example, to 'Do you support the government's policy?' an American or European might answer 'Yes, I support it' or 'No, I don't support it'. But a Japanese might answer 'I support it, but . . .' or 'I don't support it, but . . .' and then say something to mitigate the force of what he or she has just said. The traditional norm in Japan requires that one avoid directly expressing one's thinking and instead use expressions and constructions that will enable the other party to guess one's real intent.

With negative questions things really become complicated. For instance, 'Yes, I don't like it', 'No, I don't like it', 'Yes, I like it', or 'No, I like it' are all grammatically permissible in Japanese as answers to the query 'Don't you like it?'. Moreover, negative questions are often used in Japan as an indirect way of finding out what other people are thinking.

Second, subjects are often omitted in Japanese. People who use the first person pronoun are considered conceited. Personal pronouns are thus seldom used in Japanese conversation; nevertheless, the Japanese seem to manage quite well without them. By leaving out personal pronouns a Japanese can make his or her statements ambiguous as to whether the opinion contained therein expresses the speaker's own views or merely echoes the views of the public at large. In addition, the Japanese prefer to express themselves as the French would with *on* (as opposed to *je*) or the Germans with *man* (as opposed to *ich*), thereby making it difficult to know whether the opinion being expressed is the speaker's own or that of the general public.

In poll questionnaires it is impossible to avoid using the second person pronoun, the equivalent of the English 'you', for the responder has to know that it is his or her own opinion that is being asked. The Japanese normally use the word *anata* for this purpose. Yet they seldom use *anata* or other second person pronouns in daily conversation or plays. Moreover, the Japanese use different terms to refer to people of different social ranks in relation to the speaker. The different nuances of such terms slightly alter the meaning of what is being said. In public opinion polls such equivocality cannot be permitted. It is thus impossible to avoid using the second person pronoun *anata*. Although the use of *anata* makes the meaning of the question clear, it forces people to listen to questions phrased in a manner unfamiliar to them. Some old people, for instance, resent being addressed as *anata* by young pollsters. But *anata* is the only second person pronoun suitable for polls.

Third, the Japanese hesitate about responding to hypothetical questions. One reason is that the Japanese language has no subjunctive or conditional moods.

Fourth, though the Japanese are very anxious to know what other people think, they are reluctant to express their own feelings clearly. Expressing oneself too clearly is considered strange and even rude.

In conclusion, though public opinion polls do not suit the Japanese, polls will probably continue to increase in number, since many people desire them. Unfortunately, few people realise the seriousness of this contradiction and so perfunctorily write out pat questionnaires with poorly worded questions in increasing numbers. Moreover, advances in computers and statistical analysis make the data of public opinion polls the perfect object of study for those engaged in theoretical games. Government agencies now tend to avoid questions that yield undesirable results. As for the people who have to respond to these polls, more and more have begun to reject the statistical surveys and public opinion polls inundating their lives. Clearly public opinion polls are now approaching a turning-point.

NOTES AND REFERENCES

Generally, the results of opinion polls and articles about the study of polling are written in the Japanese language. Two periodicals are published by *Naikaku Sôridaizin Kanbô, Kôhô-situ*, the Public Relations Office, Prime Minister's

Cabinet. One is the *Gekkan Yoron Tyôsa* – 'Monthly Review of Public Opinion', about 68 pages, and the other is the *Yoron Tyôsa Nenkan* – 'Public Opinion Yearbook', about 660 pages.

Over the past several years, I have sent all results of opinion polls carried out by the *Asahi*, the *Mainichi* and the *Yomiuri* to the Survey Research Consultants International, Inc., Williamstown, Massachusetts; the SRCI also takes *Gekkan Yoron Tyôsa*. Thus one can find many results of Japanese opinion polls in the *World Opinion Update* or *Index to International Public Opinion*.

I list here some articles and books in English and French.

1 'Le niveau des connaissances de la jeunesse au Japon – la comparaison avec les pays occidentaux', *Sondages*, vol. 26, 1964.
2 'Are young people becoming more conservative?', *Asian Political Systems*, ed. Betty B. Burch and Allan B. Cole (Princeton, NJ: Van Nostrand, 1968).
3 'L' opinion publique des Japonais, au milieu du vingtième siècle', *Res Publica*, vol. 8, 1966.
4 'Le prestige des différentes proffesions – l'évaluation populaire au Japon', *Revue Française de sociologie*, vol. 9, 1968.
5 'Les élections générales au Japon depuis la guerre', *Revue française de science politique*, vol. 21, 1971.
6 'Changed and unchanged characteristics of the Japanese', *Japan Echo*, vol. 1, 1974.
7 'L'erreur et la precision de sondage au Japon', mimeo., 1975.
8 *Changing Japanese Values* (Tokyo: Institute of Statistical Mathematics, 1977).
9 Herbert Passin (ed.), *A Season of Voting* (Washington, DC: American Enterprise Institute for Public Policy Research, 1979).
10 Kazuo Kojima, 'Public opinion trends in Japan', *Public Opinion Quarterly*, vol. 41, 1977.

Note: Items 1 to 7 on the above list were written by myself and no. 8 is a reprint of several articles by our colleagues.

8 Political Opinion Polling in the Netherlands

JAN STAPEL

INTRODUCTION

In 1970, when political polling was twenty-five years old in the Netherlands, I wrote:

> Predicting election results a few days before an election is a fairly useless sort of prognosis. It is not a basis for decisions and rightly so; a few days later one knows the full facts. It also is a not very useful way of utilising sampling procedures. Within a very short time election results will be known and total counts are more exact than samples.[1]

I then went on to say that the 'news value' of pre-election polls is such that they are likely to be around for a long time to come.

Yet almost every Dutch election has been preceded by several polls showing the popular vote from the latest possible interviewing. In most cases they have been reasonably correct and always at least indicated the trends. Table 8.1 shows the two major published survey findings just before the general election of 25 May 1977, the most recent one for the national parliament (Second Chamber).

The biggest single error was 2.01 per cent, the average errors 0.66 per cent and 0.65 per cent respectively. The figures in both poll columns were based on partly overlapping samples of voters drawn and interviewed by NIPO (the Netherlands Institute of Public Opinion). The first one (*Elsevier's Magazine*) was based on the question of how the respondent planned to vote on 25 May. The second one (VARA radio) used the standard question 'For which party would you vote if there were elections today?', but after adjustment by Dr Maurice de Hond.

TABLE 8.1 *General election 1977*

	Publication in Elsevier's Magazine 18 May (%)	VARA radio broadcast 20 May (%)	Actual election results 25 May (%)
Labour	33.5	31.8	33.81
Chr. Democrats	31.5	30.9	31.91
Liberal (VVD)	17.0	18.1	17.95
Democrats (D'66)	4.5	5.4	5.43
Communist	3.5	3.3	1.73
Radicals	2.5	2.4	1.69
Pacifist Socialist	1.0	0.8	0.94
SGP-Calvinist	2.5	2.4	2.13
GPV-Calvinist	1.5	1.5	0.96
Farmers Party	1.0	1.3	0.84
Democr. Socialist	1.0	0.9	0.72
Other	0.5	1.2	1.89

HOW AND WHEN DID ALL THIS START?

Unbeknown to each other, two small groups of people had been preparing scientific sample surveys of public opinion during the Second World War, that is, under the German occupation, which until May 1945 ruled out any such activities.

One group was headed by Dr Ph. J. Idenburg, then both director general of the Central Bureau of Statistics and president of the Nederlandse Stichting voor Statistiek (NSS), a foundation devoted to promoting the use of statistics. It had been founded in 1940, just before the Second World War brought the German army into the Low Countries.

The others were the men who founded NIPO a few months after the war's end and whose backgrounds were in marketing, business economics and the application of statistics, including consumer sample surveys.

Both met with the same postwar handicaps of devastation, poor communications and, worst of all, population statistics that were hardly up to date, to put it mildly. Both, too, started in commercial consumer research which soon turned out to be the area in which adequate funding was to be found.

Both succeeded in arranging for the financing of their opinion surveys through contracts with newspapers. NSS made arrangements for exclusive publication rights with a new magazine, *Elsevier's Weekblad*. NIPO entered into similar arrangements with what had been an illegal underground paper that soon became one of Holland's major dailies, *Het Parool*.

The first postwar election was in May 1946 and neither NIPO nor NSS was favoured by beginner's luck. The statistics available at the time perhaps explain a large part of the errors in the quota samples both organisations used. Whatever the cause, the magazine terminated its relationship with NSS. NIPO's contract with *Het Parool* still had to run into November of that year. Its polls therefore continued and, much to the surprise of NIPO's managers/owners and their small staff, the newspaper renewed its contract for a further period and close co-operation, though in varying forms after 1947, continued into the early 1950s. Largely thanks to that, there is a record of the Dutch public's reactions during the traumatic experiences of fighting Sukarno's 'insurgents' in the (then) Dutch East Indies and finally reluctantly granting independence to Indonesia on 27 December 1949.

The standard question 'Do you agree or disagree with the government's conduct of affairs in Indonesia?' showed large support only immediately after the successful Dutch military campaign of December 1948 (in which Sukarno's capital of Jakarta was taken by Dutch paratroopers and the whole 'insurgent' government was taken prisoner). The figures are given in Table 8.2.

All through 1947 and 1948 majorities indicated their wish to have all of Java occupied by Dutch troops. Five consecutive polls and the successful campaign of December 1948 found support for this policy among voters for all political parties with the sole exception of Dutch Communists.

These data proved to be a highly useful contemporary history of the late 1940s showing that the short-sighted colonial policies of both Parliament and three successive governments even so were far ahead of the attitudes held by the population. The one man (out of a list of all the major participants in the Indonesian drama) a large majority felt had done a good job was the general who had commanded the Dutch army in Indonesia (in a survey after Indonesian independence had been established).

It is in matters such as these that political polls make their most valuable contribution, even though the findings were hot news when they were published and provided ammunition for politicians, commentators and the like. Belief in the essential correctness of the survey results was enhanced by the election survey NIPO published in June 1948 prior to the general election of 7 July of that year (Table 8.3).

TABLE 8.2 *Poll on government conduct in Indonesia (%)*

| | With conduct of affairs in Indonesia | |
	Agree	Disagree
March 1946	55	45
September 1947	30	70
November 1948	33	67
(December armistice broken and Jakarta taken)		
January 1949	73	27
April 1949	38	62
September 1949	29	71
October 1949	29	71
(December independence agreed to)		
January 1950	46	54
February 1950	43	57
March 1950	46	54

Note: Don't know's varying between 25 per cent and 35 per cent, not indicated above.
SOURCE: NIPO

TABLE 8.3 *General election 1948*

	NIPO survey June (%)	Actual result 7 July (%)
Roman Catholic	30.0	31.04
Labour	25.0	25.61
Calvinist (ARP)	12.0	13.21
Reformed (CHU)	10.0	9.19
Liberal (VVD)	8.0	7.94
Communist	9.0	7.74
SGP-Calvinist	2.0	2.37
Welter	1.5	1.26
Other	2.5	1.64

SOURCE: NIPO

While private organisations like NSS and NIPO had already taught themselves the art of surveying opinions and attitudes on the job, most Dutch universities by 1948 decided there was a need to teach sociology as such rather than as an addendum to other disciplines. The first generation of Dutch sociology professors was then appointed, soon to be followed by teachers of political science (called *politicologie* in the Netherlands).

What could be termed 'official' scientific interest led to a continuous programme of pre- and post-election surveys sponsored first by one, later by all universities in which political science is being taught. It has led to a series of books about every single general election since 1971.[2] The fieldwork has always been done by one of the commercial research agencies and includes panel-type re-interviewing of respondents soon after they have cast their votes. Secondary analysis of the data from these surveys as well as those from NIPO, NSS and other Dutch research institutes founded in the 1950s and 1960s has helped to produce additional scientific publications about political attitudes and behaviour. Most of the survey data are available to serious students at the Steinmetz Archives (Amsterdam) on punch cards and/or computer tape.

Sustained interest in political polls by political parties originated with the Dutch Labour Party whose current leader, Dr J. M. den Uyl (Prime Minister from 1973 to 1977), was guest speaker at the first and founding ESOMAR conference of 1948 in Amsterdam. The Labour Party, followed later by the Roman Catholic Party, occasionally commissioned research. When NIPO started adding a short opinion research ballot to its weekly omnibus operation the Labour Party was quick to subscribe to a service of succinct weekly bulletins of voting preference; other major parties later followed suit.

The weekly omnibus survey was originally a Dutch phenomenon, started by NIPO as early as 1953. Nowadays at least three private agencies run one in the Netherlands. The catalogue of the Steinmetz Archives data shows that one in particular has produced a wealth of political research data most of which have first been published in the Dutch press and/or on radio or television.

Nowadays about half a dozen agencies occasionally, periodically, or even continuously supply various media with political poll figures. One major source is the Dutch national press agency (ANP) which for many years has had a contract with NIPO for the supply of a weekly press release of very recent poll findings. One of the broadcasting organisations (AVRO) regularly publicises political data from the Lagendijk Institute. Another (VARA) has succeeded in making its Saturday presentations (once every one or two months) of political preference figures the most authoritative source of information on the current situation. It is based on time-series of NIPO data, analysed, presented and commented upon by Dr Maurice de Hond.

After analysing the weekly sampling results (starting in 1968) de Hond devised correction procedures based on past and current voting preferences that so far at least have produced highly accurate estimates (see the example in Table 8.1). They have been extensively published in the Dutch political science quarterly *Acta Politica*.[3]

THE FIRST 'SAME-DAY' POLL

An overview of the Dutch political polling scene would not be complete without paying attention to the first 'same-day' or 'intercept' poll. It was conceived and executed by a young Dutch sociologist, Marcel van Dam (who later was to become an MP and a member of the 1973–7 government), who organised handing out white imitation ballot forms to male voters and yellow to female voters immediately after they had actually voted in a limited number of polling stations on a Wednesday of February 1967. They were asked to record the vote just cast, their vote in the previous election and their age. At IBM's major computer centre a prepared program (full of weighting procedures) was ready to process the data and early in the evening Dutch television broadcasted the expected election results that proved to be correct within narrow margins.[4] The presentation of where that day's vote came from, in terms of men, women, age group and previous political preference, consequently became all the more convincing when later borne out by the various post-election surveys.

Later that same year van Dam covered one local election with equal success and continued doing so over the next few years until his political career forced him (regretfully) to leave the game to others. Since then the Intomart Institute has conducted 'same-day' polls for television and has proved that smart sampling goes faster than, and is almost as accurate as, a total count.

POLITICAL POLLING COMES OF AGE

In suggesting to Queen Juliana (after the 1967 election) that Professor Zijlstra should become the next Prime Minister, one of the sovereign's advisers wrote to her: 'Professor Zijlstra in a recent NIPO poll turned out to be the politician enjoying the largest vote of confidence among the Dutch people.'[5] It is not often that such use of poll data becomes public. In parliamentary debates survey figures are often quoted, however, usually by the party that feels its point of view is being supported by public opinion. That, today, is quite different from the early days. It is obvious that the present generation of politicians have been aware of public opinion research all their adult lives and have come to accept its findings as reasonably accurate. Many politicians, however, maintain a somewhat ambivalent attitude about polls. If and when survey findings clearly indicate that the public or even their own constituency is against what politicians feel is right or should be the party line there often is a tendency towards 'the public be damned'.

Even at an occasion where careful research commissioned and paid for by the Dutch Labour Party indicated substantial loss of votes if a certain platform item were to be adopted, the party's research experts turned out to be powerless. The facts proved them right after the event but, as one of them said: 'If political ideology is in conflict with electoral reality . . . so much the worse for reality.'

Missionary zeal and *Realpolitik* probably are difficult to combine. Another reason is the simple fact that the political market place opens only once every few years at election time while the cash registers in the commercial market place ring – or remain silent – every day.

And, of course, politicians more than anyone else fear the 'band-wagon' or 'underdog' effects of published pre-election polls. It is fairly well established that such influences on voters are non-existent or negligible. A NIPO survey in early May 1977 (over three weeks before the 25 May general election) provides some interesting background.

Respondents were first asked which parties they *expected* to gain most at the forthcoming elections. About half of those intending to vote for each of the major parties mentioned their own choice (56 per cent of Labour voters said Labour would be the biggest gainer, 55 per cent of Liberal voters mentioned their own party and so did 44 per cent of the Christian Democrat voters). Later they were asked which party they *hoped* would become the biggest party. Large majorities in each group expressed such hopes exclusively for the party of their own choice and the expectations (first question) and hopes (second question) turned out to be highly correlated. Thus voters' own electoral hopes are parent to their expectations; not published poll figures.

Between elections tiny activist groups tend to be highly visible on television and occupy columns of newspaper space. Pressure groups know their way around the corridors of power while silent majorities are given voice only by means of the polls. (But the tables of percentages are not the most exciting reading matter.) It would seem that awareness of such background factors is growing.

During the 1970s Dutch government agencies and departments became important buyers of research, accounting for something like 10 per cent of the turnover of the major research agencies combined. Much of this has been in areas akin to research for industry and commerce in that the political content is limited or absent. Government-sponsored surveys in areas like housing needs and preferences, traffic flows or consumer savings, for instance, have been both large and numerous.

Polls concerning politically charged subjects or events have been fairly rare events in government research buying. Until the 1970s such studies were few and far between. Only in the most recent decade has the Prime Minister's Office started commissioning periodic research on topics of interest apparently for added guidance towards decision-taking and the public presentation of government policies. In such areas the various Dutch institutes have tended to deal 'at arm's length' with the establishment in The Hague and, at least up till now, phenomena like the President's Pollster in the United States have not occurred in the Netherlands.

The major polling organisations in Holland apparently feel the credibility of their findings is being enhanced by making them available to as many users as possible, be it for publication or internal use. Prior to the 1977 election I was invited to present confidential recent findings, especially voting preferences along a left/right scale[6] and backgrounds thereof, to the top echelon of one political party. Similar invitations from the other main parties were encouraged immediately afterwards. The institute involved was also extremely pleased that a major weekly became interested in publishing a series of articles full of graphs and tables, thus making the same information available to everyone interested.[7]

As far as is known, this is the only country in which past voting, present voting preference, self-positioning on a seven-point left/right scale plus tendency to move to the right or to the left (or to stay put), are being continually registered. This approach has produced a very large body of data showing that movements between the two political extremes take place very slowly indeed but also that dramatic events, more than anything anyone says or writes, are sometimes followed by clearly observable shifts. It tends to confirm one of the 'laws of public opinion' the late Hadley Cantril formulated in the USA as early as 1944.[8]

In the rich material of Dutch poll findings there also is ample evidence in support of Dr Gallup's observation that the public occasionally is ahead of its (political) leadership. One case in point are NIPO figures that over the last half-dozen years consistently show that a majority of the Dutch have been quite willing to agree to a period without yearly income increases (even though they have been used to that since the early 1950s).

Government and Parliament only got around to doing something about wage-push inflation early in 1980 and it was only in that year that the leadership of some (not all) trade unions swung around to publicly agreeing that a small step back in purchasing power might be better medicine than 'more, more, more' every year. There is at least some evidence that survey results helped convince MPs and trade union officials that what almost all Dutch economists were counselling had indeed become 'politically acceptable', as the saying goes.

If that, as we believe, is true, political polling does from time to time make useful contributions to the public good in the Netherlands.

NOTES

1 'Zo zijn wij', AGON-Elsevier, 1970.
2 'Nederlandse Kiezer – 1971/1972/1973/1977'.
3 M. de Hond, 'De meting van politieke voorkeur', *Acta Politica*, January 1977.
4 Marcel van Dam and J. Beishuizen, 'Kijk op kiezer' (1976).
5 Robbert Ammerlaan, 'Het verschijnsel Schmelzer' (1973), p. 259.
6 ESOMAR/WAPOR seminar, Bonn/Godesberg, January 1980: J. Stapel, 'The voters between left and right'.
7 *Elsevier's Magazine*: issues of 23 and 30 April, 7, 14 and 21 May 1977.
8 Hadley Cantril, *Gauging Public Opinion* (Princeton, NJ: Princeton University Press, 1944).

9 Political Opinion Polling in Spain

JUAN ANTONIO GINER

INTRODUCTION: POLLS WITHOUT POLITICS

> For the first time in Spain, *Madrid* will publish tomorrow a prediction of the outcome of the municipal elections in the capital. Two hundred people are working [on this project] for our readers. (*Madrid*, 18 November 1966, p. 3)

On 16 November 1966 the daily *Madrid*, an evening paper which then headed the journalistic opposition to the authoritarian regime of General Franco,[1] published an editorial which posed the question of the possibility of carrying out pre-election surveys in Spain: 'Will it be possible to conduct these polls among us, to serve the public and the politicians and to ascertain their opinions?'[2]

The answer was yes, '*we can ascertain their opinions* provided that, in the political climate to be investigated, certain conditions are present:

1. That there are diverse candidates with well defined programmes,
2. That the public is well informed of this fact,
3. That election fraud is kept to a minimum,
4. That the proportion of votes cast is high – or at least moderately high.'[3]

The editors of *Madrid* decided to test the possibility themselves and contracted DATA,[4] 'an independent private company', to conduct a pre-election survey 'with the most advanced polling techniques known'.[5] On Saturday 19 November, the eve of the municipal elections in the Spanish capital, the paper ran the front page headline: '*Madrid* predicts: 67 % of the eligible voters will cast votes tomorrow'.[6] In addition to presenting the specific calculations and tables corresponding to the survey, the article mentioned that 'DATA's work is strictly professional and independent and, therefore, the data used are the most objective possible – they are not influenced by any type of pressure or ideology'.[7]

But in fact on Sunday 20 November 1966 the first pre-election poll carried out in Spain proved to be a crashing all-round failure. Of the 383 429 voters registered in Madrid, only 32 per cent cast votes. The pollsters' prognosis showed an error of 35 per cent.[8]

In the days following DATA published a series of commentaries about the election campaign and arrived at the conclusion that 'there is no vote without information'.[9] What had happened was exactly what the editorial of 16 November implied – that the conditions necessary *to ascertain* the current of public opinion were not present. In short, the capacity to conduct accurate polls existed, but authentic political life did not.

For more than forty years there had been no free elections by means of universal suffrage in Spain. After the death of Franco, King Juan Carlos I held the first free elections since 1936 and on 15 June 1977 all Spaniards of legal age were able to elect a democratic Parliament.[10] The polls then published were able *to ascertain* with accuracy the results of an election in which voter turn-out was 78 per cent.[11]

The mutual dependence of political freedom and public opinion explains the long and difficult history which public opinion has had in Spain – a surprising and curious history which has culminated today in the existence of a democratic nation, but which had its beginnings in the autumn of 1942 while Europe was at war and Spain was governed by 'a regime of official opinion, single and monolithic'.[12]

THE PRE-HISTORY (1942–57)

Seven years after the founding of the American Institute of Public Opinion (AIPO)[13] by George H. Gallup, Cayetano Aparicio López, a Spanish journalist, formed what would come to be known as the Instituto de la Opinión Pública (Public Opinion Institute, IOP), but which in the autumn of 1942 was known as the Servicio Español de Auscultación de la Opinión Pública (Spanish Service for the Sounding of Public Opinion).[14]

The First Stage (1942–6)

The first IOP was allied with the Vice-Secretary of Popular Education and the National Delegation of Press and Propaganda,[15] political organisms that attempted to 'educate' and 'inform' Spanish society in keeping with the ideals of the mono-political totalitarian regime.[16] At the beginning, progress was slow. Rafael Fernández Chillón, one of the pioneers, recalled 'people were very hesitant to respond – they confused us with the police'.[17]

Cayetano Aparicio, whose brother Juan was then general director of the Press, discovered the existence of opinion polls conducted by the American press which he habitually read every day in the foreign press department of the National Delegation located in a ramshackle old house at 2 Montesquinza Street. The 'auscultations' or soundings at first were the fruit of such labours as 'detecting rumours' and getting hold of confidential information.[18] The first survey consisted of six questions and 'the synthesis and classification of the results obtained took over a month to complete because, due to a lack of funds, the operation was conducted by hand with a very limited number of staff'.[19]

The first stage of IOP lasted scarcely four years since, in 1946, with the war over and the German army defeated, Franco changed the orientation of the regime with the hope of receiving recognition from the Allied forces. The totalitarian line was abandoned and members of the official party (Falange Española) were removed from office. IOP closed and, in 1948, Cayetano Aparicio died.

During that first stage, some 150 interviewers had worked for IOP, the majority being functionaries from distinct provincial delegations of the Vice-Secretary of Popular Education. Their routine work was to conduct 'a monthly poll, of not less than twenty questions, utilising Watson electric machines for synthesis and classification, which were leased for the occasion'.[20]

The results were 'sent immediately to the high state authorities who, naturally, utilised them according to how each could most benefit', given that the questionnaires had 'an eminently political, social or economic hue'.[21] At the end of 1945 the overall number of individuals consulted surpassed 300 000 'from all over Spain and of all social strata'.[22] The same source noted that, at that time, 'the error [was] found to oscillate between 3 and 4 per cent as an average, but increased in proportion to the instability of opinion itself'.[23]

The majority of the results of these investigations were never published and no record or trace was left behind. However, some of these surveys were reported in the *Anuario de la prensa española* (1945–46) and in the *Gaceta de la prensa española* (1942–6). These sources reveal information about 'one of the first national surveys conducted by the Servicio Español de Auscultacion de la Opinión Pública'[24] published on 1 October 1943 and based on the opinions of 5119 people. The analysis of the poll was 'a documented report of approximately 100 pages, with 98 maps and graphs'.[25] Conducted 'during the last ten days of December of 1942 and first of 1943', the poll indicated that 53.17 per cent of those interviewed bought morning dailies and the most popular sections among the readers were those which informed about the Second World War.[26]

In April 1945 the results of another poll directed at how the Spaniards felt about the national press were published: 49.69 per cent of the 4404 consulted also preferred articles about the war while only 6.92 per cent of those interviewed mentioned their interest in 'editorials', a significant rejection during an era of 'slogans' and strong ideological control of the press.[27]

On 1 November 1943 the Servicio published the results of another survey[28] conducted between 18 February and 15 March 1943 with a national survey of 5251 people. The principal conclusion was that 71.81 per cent of the population were 'radio listeners'.[29] As the number of radio reception units at that time was 'approximately 1000',[30] the mean number of listeners per apparatus was calculated to be five. Finally, asked about listening to foreign broadcasts, 6.87 per cent answered that they only listened to foreign newscasts in their respective foreign languages.[31]

But perhaps the most interesting poll of which we have a record was carried out in April 1943 and constitutes, without a doubt, the first investigation about the political culture of the Spanish population by means of a seventeen-item questionnaire.

They asked [it was written in January 1944] those selected to answer the questionnaire about the names of various personalities who played a predominating role in the political, cultural and social aspects of Spanish life. As supplementary questions, they also asked how many ministers were there in Spain, whether they knew the official hymn of the Falange Party or not, and the national slogans 'Por la Patria, el Pan y la Justicia' [For the Fatherland, Bread and Justice], etc., and the concept which the word *Empire* referred to Spain brought to the minds of those interviewed.[32]

On a values grid, with a maximum of 100 points, they established the following system of how well informed the people were:

1. People who were very well informed ('excellent'): 100 points
2. People who were well informed ('good'): 75–100 points
3. People who were informed at a 'medium' level: 50–75 points
4. People who were 'badly' informed: 25–50 points
5. People who were 'without information': 0–25 points

The results arouse suspicion in that they present a panorama of political culture far superior to that which could be hoped for when compared with results of investigations conducted in other countries[33] in similar eras and in much more open contexts, although perhaps not as 'indoctrinated' as the Spain of 1943.The overall results are shown in Table 9.1. These same percentages, distributed in four general professional groupings, offers a revealing profile of the Spanish social structure of this era (Table 9.2). Amongst other interesting information is the fact that 98 per cent of those questioned knew the name of the mayor of their town or city, while only 57.06 per cent knew the name of the civil governor of their province.[34]

TABLE 9.1 *Level of information, 1943 (%)*[35]

Level of information	Total	Men	Women
Excellent	8.36	9.56	3.65
Good	17.74	19.24	5.81
Fair (medium)	24.18	24.36	22.75
Bad	32.62	33.19	28.90
Without information	19.60	13.65	38.89

TABLE 9.2 *Level of information according to social status, 1943 (%)*[36]

Level of informativity	Domestic service	Liberal profession	Administration	Military
Excellent	0.40	17.28	20.00	27.52
Good	8.79	36.41	29.41	22.01
Fair (medium)	7.40	21.60	25.29	26.60
Bad	31.94	17.28	21.76	19.26
Without information	51.47	7.43	3.54	4.61

The Second Stage (1952–7)

The second stage of the primitive IOP began in 1951 with the creation of the new Ministry of Information and Tourism and the appointment of Juan Aparicio as general director of the Press.[37] A long-time associate of Cayetano Aparicio, journalist Rafael Fernández Chillón was appointed director of the IOP. In this new stage, IOP was to develop its activities within the limits of official circles – at the service of the government – until 8 March 1957 when the Council of Ministers removed Juan Aparicio from office and effectively paralysed IOP.

To the new Minister of Information and Tourism, Gabriel Arias Salgado, public opinion was 'an advisory organ whose pronouncements can serve as an orientation for those who govern' and 'a system of signals which public officials cannot disregard'.[38] With this idea as a basis, all surveys conducted during those years were intended to inform the Head of State and the Minister of Information and Tourism about the movements and trends of Spanish public opinion. The 'duty' of IOP was 'to sound out the state of opinion in Spanish society with the end of informing the authorities'.[39]

In this era, IOP conducted 128 surveys which concerned distinct topics of general interest, 170 confidential surveys 'for the exclusive knowledge of the authorities' and 16 'telegraphic climates' – surveys conducted with urgency and reported in coded language to avoid possible infiltration.[40]

IOP published two magazines during this second stage, *Opinión* and *Mercados*, the first being a monthly bulletin which was distributed among the interviewers of the institute, and the second a vehicle of communication for the staff of the Instituto de Investigación de Mercados (Institute of Market Investigation, IIM), an organisation which conducted the first commercial marketing studies for private clients and whose directors were also members of the staff of the IOP. Fifty-four issues of *Opinión* were published, and it was announced as 'the only publication in the Spanish language about technique and informational doxology'.[41] Circulation was 1500 and it was distributed free of charge.

The activity of IOP was very important for the future development of Spanish public opinion research. A reporter for *Time-Life* by the name of Saporiti wrote in 1952, that:

> sponsored by the Department of the Press of the Government, the Instituto de la Opinión Pública, the Spanish version of the Gallup

Institute, has been founded in Madrid. It directs hundreds of *auscultaciones* distributed throughout the country and the Institute claims to apply statistical methods which reveal the pulse of the nation regarding a variety of topics: national politics as well as sports, expositions, education, living, provisions . . . . The curious aspect of the new Institute . . . is that the survey results are not for the public, but rather for the orientation and use of the government organis- ations and newspaper editors.[42]

Actually, the press published only a few of these surveys, and those which they published were about unimportant themes. For example, a poll was published in 1956 which reported that 88 per cent of the Spanish population got up in the morning before 8.30 and that 48 per cent of the population did not depend on any means of transportation in order to get to work.[43]

Rafael Fernández Chillón, IOP's director in this era, was admitted as the first Spanish member of the European Society for Opinion and Marketing Research (ESOMAR) at the annual Assembly held in Lausanne on 4 September 1953. Before his admission several members of ESOMAR had visited Spain to investigate the quality of the techniques used by the IOP in order to evaluate the efficiency of the official institute.[44]

The interest aroused by IOP led to the incorporation of the study of public opinion in the required course plan of the Escuela Oficial de Periodísmo (Official School of Journalism) during the academic year 1952/3. The new academic discipline was planned to be taught in twenty- four sessions and the first professor was Rafael Fernández Chillón.[45] From then on, by means of an Order from the Ministry of Education on 7 March 1953 which established the plan of studies for the school, the 'theory of public opinion' was to be taught in the second year. Thus the study of this discipline was present from the early stages of the development of journalistic education at university level, and continued to be a key element in the journalism curriculum with the creation of the Facultades de Ciencias de la Información (Schools of Information Science) which replaced the School in 1971, although it is now taught in the fourth year under the title 'public opinion'.[46]

THE TAKE-OFF (1958–76)

The second phase of public opinion measurement in Spain coincided with political and economic reforms which marked the close of the autocracy and the beginning of a progressive liberalisation of the Spanish regime. With the new appointments of Alberto Ullastres as Minister of Commerce and Mariano Navarro Rubío as Minister of the Treasury, the government undertook a new plan of stabilisation which effectively transformed the country's economic system within ten years (1960–70). 'The resurgence of the Spanish economy'[47] represented a mushroom of economic growth equal to that from the turn of the century until the 1960s.[48]

With the progressive movement toward a free market Spanish economy, the commercial sector felt the need to re-establish itself in a market in which 'the consumer was once again the core of economic life: the consumer conditions sales, sales condition production'.[49] This led to the creation of the first private market research institutions. In 1958 Nestlé and Unilever promoted the foundation of the Instituto Eco with the help of the Catalonian advertiser Antonio Riviere. The directors, Manual José Sanchez de Celis and Jesús Ibáñez, had worked previously for IOP. In 1961 Arvay was founded in Bilbao, and in 1964 Metra/Ses in the same city. In 1965 DATA was born in Madrid, a company of 'market studies, opinion and applied sociology' and it is part of INRA (International Research Associates). Lastly, the Ingenieros Consultores SA (Engineering Consultants Inc., ISCA), a company founded in Barcelona in 1958, was admitted as a full-standing member of Gallup International at the annual conference in April 1970 in Punta del Este, Uruguay, and since then has been called ISCA-GALLUP.

These developments in the private sector led to the formation of the Asociación Española de Estudios de Mercado y Opinión (Spanish Association of Market and Opinion Studies, AEDEMO) under the leadership of Ramón Masip, then department chief of market studies for Nestlé. AEDEMO, which began with 25 members, now has a membership of over 200.

Little by little the commercial investigation began to direct itself toward social questions – with all due caution necessary in Spain at that time – and the press started to publish these poll results. Dailies such as *Madrid, Pueblo, La vanguardia, Informaciones, Nuevo diario* and magazines such as *Actualidad económica, La actualidad española, Cambio 16* and *El europeo* diffused the results of public opinion surveys which, as the 1970s wore on, concerned themselves more and more with political or ideological themes.

The interest of readers in knowing what public opinion really was in Spain was also awakened in this period of new freedoms brought about by the Law of the Press – which in 1966 replaced the previous censorship – and led to the governmental creation of a new IOP, 'which will have as its mission the carrying-out of studies and surveys about the state of opinion at both the national and the international levels'. To the Spanish administration, IOP was 'an irreplaceable source of information about the national reality with which it must deal, the knowledge of which would be greatly weakened without this instrument due to the well known errors that come about by improvisation – the partiality and confusion between the real and the ideal'.[50]

For the next twelve years, IOP published the *Revista española de la opinión pública* (*REOP*). The trial issue appeared in April 1965, and the last issue, number 50, was published in December 1977. *REOP* closed shortly after the IOP was replaced by the Centro de Investigaciones Sociológicas (CIS) in November 1977. The new organisation replaced *REOP* with the *Revista española de investigaciones sociológicas*.

Other organisations which were protagonists in the dawning of the socio-political surveys were the private Fomento de Estudios Sociales y de Sociología Aplicada (Organisation for the Promotion of Social Studies and Applied Sociology, FOESSA), founded in 1965, and the Fondo para la Investigación Económica y Social (Economic and Social Investigation Fund, FIES), founded in 1967 by the Confederación Española de Cajas de Ahorro (Spanish Federation of Savings Banks).

The social reports of the FOESSA were the most important documents of analysis and investigation during this period. The *I Informe FOESSA* (1966), 'about the social situation in Spain', was a best-seller. Amando de Miguel, Manuel Gómez Reino and Francisco Andrés Orizo, of DATA's investigatory team, were the authors. The survey was based on 4517 interviews and the first edition of 3000 copies sold out very rapidly; 'the appearance of the *Informe* was an authentically news-breaking event . . . . The *Informe*, intended to offer an overall view of the reality of Spanish society, was produced by means of a very rigorous method, and was backed financially by an unprecedented budget for a study of this nature in Spain.'[51]

This era concluded significantly with the death of General Franco in the winter of 1975. In the months before his death surveys had become ever more popular. Themes had become increasingly more political and the 'audacity' of the questionnaires grew in proportion to the expectation of the proximate death of the Head of State and the imminence of a political change. For this reason, on 5 March 1975 the Dirección General de Coordinación Informativa issued a memorandum 'concerning opinion surveys and periodical publications' which ended up in the hands of the Minister of Information, León Herrera.

The government was worried about the proliferation of the political polls. 'Normally', the memorandum stated,

> the IOP should conduct political polls, without leaving an informational vacuum to be filled by pollsters of unknown origin and with doubtful qualifications . . . . Given the level of politicisation that can be seen in the current national press, it appears convenient that the Administration, in this area as in many others, should not be the under-dog in the events reported, but rather should take the lead in this field.[52]

The First Regulation (1975)

As a result of this concern, the government promulgated a Decree-Law which was to regulate 'the activities of the companies dedicated to opinion surveys'.[53] The new law announced the creation of a public register in which all companies that planned to conduct surveys would have to be listed. If the company was not registered, publication of poll results was prohibited (Article 1). It established the obligation to inform the public about the authors of the survey and the techniques used (Article 2) and the Minister of Information was given the power 'to verify the guarantee and the technical reliability of the survey' (Article 7).

But the most highly disputed provision of the new Law was Article 5 which stated:

> the mass media will not publish the results of any survey conducted by any company not listed in the Register, or any survey in which questions posed or conclusions are contrary to the 'Principals and Institutions contained in the Fundamental Laws', to the due respect for the persons to whom they refer, to the demands of national defence, to the rights of the people or to the law, morality and good custom.

This precept was a repetition of Article 2 of the Law of the Press (1966) which established the limits of freedom of expression. The press reacted immediately. *Cambio 16* qualified the Law as 'the sword of Damocles held over the companies which, in this country, have blazed the rugged trail of investigation – a trail which the anonymous citizens want or prefer open'.[54] For Manuel Gómez Reino, the executive director of DATA, the article opposed 'a fundamental right of the citizens, the right to freely express opinions, and to make those opinions known'.[55]

The protests of the institutions affected and the action taken by AEDEMO led to the suspension of the Law, which never had taken full effect. With the death of Franco, the change in government and the rise to power of King Juan Carlos I inaugurated a new era in which public opinion would once again be allowed to function with absolute liberty and in which the surveys would reach their coming of age.

THE COMING OF AGE (1976–80)

On 15 June 1977 the first free elections in over forty-one years were held in Spain. And for the first time, pollsters conducted pre-election surveys. Soon there was talk of 'the polling boom'. But the absence of electoral precedent caused concern among the polling institutions and the mass media began to run such headlines as 'Are the polls reliable?'.[56]

The elections were preceded by numerous surveys distributed by diverse media, but there was a general lack of confidence in the air. The press reflected the atmosphere with the publication of such articles as that by J. F. Tezanos in *Cuadernos para el Díalogo* entitled 'Election surveys, watch out for fraud'[57] and the publication in *La vanguardia* of 'The risky game of opinion surveys'.[58]

A high level of voter indecision augmented fears of manipulation. 'The average Spaniard is confused and disoriented', Juan Díez Nicolás, director of the CIS, said.[59] *Cambio 16* forewarned:

> this is the first election that Spain has known in forty-one years. The standard techniques for conducting polls and surveys, therefore, have not been duly verified and checked in our case. Public opinion is not sufficiently formed – to the point where the possibility exists that there are 'deformed' sectors – due to an excess or defect in the understanding and comprehension of democratic government. The 'market', therefore, is much more difficult to grasp, to penetrate, by means of standard investigative techniques. Political 'marketing' in Spain lacks rules, formulas, techniques; they are being made up as we go along – in these very months.[60]

Some voices were raised in this period in favour of the suppression of surveys and Spanish Radio-Television's control committee for the electoral campaign decided not to broadcast any information based on opinion polls during the last week of the campaign.[61]

The final outcome of this 'baptism by fire' for the Spanish pollsters was highly controversial. The journal *Comentario sociológico* summed up the experience, reproduced in Table 9.3 (overleaf)[62]. According to the journal, the experience demonstrated that:

1. The polling method was not sufficiently explained in the majority of the cases.
2. The samples were not well constructed. In some cases they were very small for questions of such importance, and in general, the regional distribution was left unmentioned.
3. The polling firms hired by political parties or the government to conduct surveys in general were lacking in organisational substructure and sufficient means to attain trustworthy and accurate results on a national scale.
4. In the questioning process, the minor, newly formed parties were often mixed with the major parties representing the popular ideological trends. Had the polls focused on the major trends, the results offered would have been more probable.
5. The statistics and percentages put forth by the pollsters tended to be biased in favour of the party or the government who had contracted the study and resulted in excessive disparity between polls. For example, one survey predicted that a certain party would carry 4 per cent of the vote while another predicted the same party to carry 40 per cent of the vote.
6. Aside from all the technical, commercial and methodological defects, the strategy used to carry out the polls was not scientific and caused the confusion and perhaps in effect the swaying of voters – which *Comentario sociológico* is compelled to criticise.[63]

In the general election of 1 March 1979 the pollsters resumed their role of the protagonists of important controversies. Accusations against the opinion surveys abounded; much was said during the campaign about 'those lamentable surveys' (Fraga Iribarne), 'the fraud of the polls' (Kepa Bordegaray), 'a saucy manipulation' (professors of the University of Deusto), 'distrust and fear of the polls' (Antonio Kindelán), 'the surveys are manipulated and manipulate' (Jesús Ibáñez), 'the surveys obscure instead of giving light' (Augusto Assia), 'the manipulation of the surveys . . . ' (Basque Nationalist Party), 'the publication of the manipulated surveys . . . ' (*Deia*), etc.[64]

Professor Juan J. Linz of Yale University believes that the polls conducted in Spain at that time were 'shameful from the professional

TABLE 9.3 *Polls in 1977 general election*

Institute: Published by:	SOFEMASA El Pais	CONSULTA Cambio 16	METRA/SEIS Diario 16	METRA/SEIS La Vanguardia	SOFEMASA El Pais	ANA Europa Press	ANA Europa Press	ICSA/GALLUP YA	Actual result
Date:	24 May	5 June	9 June	10 June	12 June	12 June	13 June	14 June	15 June
Sampling:	1638	1494	1700	–	15875	5100	1285	1200	
Party:									
Undecided:	25.7	56	–	–	11.2	–	–	–	
UCD	20.1	10	40.5	34.4	30.2	30	31.4	25.6	34.34
PSOE	13.4	12	20.7	24.2	24	20.7	26	28.9	29.12
AP	5.7	4	8.3	4.9	8.2	11.3	9.5	5.7	8.02
PCE	5.8	4	7.8	9.7	7.2	7.1	8.1	5.8	9.12

Note: UCD: Unión de Centro Democrático (moderate)
PSOE: Partido Socialista Obrero Español (socialist)
AP: Alianza Popular (right)
PCE: Partido Comunista Español (communist)

point of view' and that 'professionally speaking, it is inadmissible that those who demonstrate this grade of professional incompetence should so deceive the public'.[65]

What is certain is that there were fraudulent surveys simply because they had never really existed before. Or perhaps, because they had never existed before, they should never have been called polls or surveys. Another example of the same distortion are the results of a poll published by *El Imparcial* (a newspaper of the far right), which was falsely put forth as a 'popular consultation, carried out by recognised and professional means [which are not elaborated], with the aim of learning, in general terms, the opinion of the average Spaniard'. Publishing these results in the issue of 6 February 1979, the paper claimed to have 'interviewed 24 000 persons', but the study conducted cannot be considered as anything but a typical example of a straw poll.[66]

No less suspicious is the survey published by the daily *YA* (moderate) on Sunday 25 February 1979 and supposedly carried out by the Société Française pour la Gestion, la Promotion et la Publicité (SFGPP), 'contracted by eighteen major industrial and financial firms'. In order to give the impression that the French firm had actually conducted the survey, the address of the firm, phone number and name of the director were included in the article. *Diario 16* (Liberal) published the results of the same survey on Tuesday 27 February. But during this period nobody had been able to contact the firm, speak with the owner, or identify the firms which had supposedly assisted in providing the fieldwork. The sources to which the poll was attributed were soon dismissed as 'phantoms' because, as Pedro J. Ramírez then explained, the so-called poll was in fact an attempt to synthesise various surveys of the CIS . . . . From the beginning to end, this was a set up of the Unión de Centro Democrático [Central Democratic Union – UCD – political party headed by President Adolfo Suárez] – even the data reported corresponds with the political strategy of the party in power'.[67]

With confusion created, the readers scandalised, the politicians irritated and the investigators disconcerted over these 'phantom institutes', the manipulation caused by only the partial publication of poll results, and other abuses, the first to be condemned were the professional pollsters. They were immediately accused of 'electoral sorcery'[68] for their contradictions.[69]

The most recent elections, those concerning regional autonomy for the Basque Country, Catalonia and Andalusia, brought the controversy over opinion polls out of the closet. The mood is best summed up by the headline run by the daily *ABC* (Conservative) on the occasion of the

1980 regional elections in Catalonia: 'The polls predict victory for the party who contracts them'.[70]

In order to re-establish credibility, the Asociación Nacional de Empresas de Investigación de Mercados y de la Opinión Pública (National Association of Market and Public Opinion Investigation Companies, ANEIMOP) was founded and soon denounced the following professional abuses:

1. The publication of the results of anonymous pre-election surveys which have never actually been conducted.
2. The distribution of data obtained in pre-election surveys conducted by supposed Association members to the mass media.
3. The publication of pre-election surveys conducted by companies which do not normally engage in this activity or are currently inactive.
4. The publication of data without mention of the source or description of the technique employed, as a necessary demand of our professional code of ethics.[71]

The Second Regulation (1980)

But the self-defence of the professionals amounted to only a swan song of liberty when, just a few weeks later, *Boletín Oficial del Estado* published the Law of 18 April 1980 concerning the Régimen de Encuestas Electorales (Rules for Election Polls). It had earlier been approved in the Spanish Parliament with the support of both the party in power and the opposition party.[72] The new rules were the result of a proposal presented by the Grupo Parlamentario de Coalición Democrática (a right-wing political party headed by Fraga Iribarne) on 3 May 1979. The proposal read:

Bearing in mind the extraordinary importance which the mass media have in a democratic society – and in particular, the special power they have in determining public opinion, by the publication of polls and surveys which refer to calculations and predictions of election outcomes – both on a general level and on the level of the individual voter – it is necessary that this activity be regulated, with the objective, on the one hand, of procuring a better guarantee of the equality of opportunity for election contenders and of fair competition to enable the voter to form his opinion freely, and, on the other, to promote the guarantee, prestige, responsibility and confidence of the specialised companies, centres and organisations dedicated to the preparation and implementation of polls and surveys.[73]

The Spanish Law of 1980 was inspired by the French Law of June 1977 regarding the publication and diffusion of pre-election surveys,[74] though it is slightly less restrictive with regard to the time-period in which the publication of polls is prohibited before an election (one week in France, five days in Spain).

The principal points of the new regulation are:

That the jurisdiction of the new Law includes 'the publication and diffusion, total or partial, during election campaigns, of elements or results of any poll or opinion survey, or those operations which simulate the vote which are conducted by means of opinion surveys, be they directly or indirectly related to a referendum vote, a parliamentary election, a local election, or an election in an autonomous region'. (Article 1)

Those who carry out any survey or poll must, of their own responsibility, include in the report the following specifications:

a) The name of the organisation or entity, public or private, which has carried out the survey, and its address,

b) The name of the organisation or entity or first and last names of the person who contracted the survey,

c) The technical characteristics of the sampling, which must include the following points: the system of sampling, the number of persons polled and the number of those who did not respond, the level of representation of the sampling, the procedure used for polling and the dates on which the poll was carried out,

d) The precise text of the questions posed. (Article 2)

The Central Electoral Council will be granted open access by anyone who has carried out a published poll or survey, to any complementary technical information which it judges opportune to conduct any further investigation it deems necessary. The information petitions by the Council must not include any data which, in accordance with other current laws, are for the private use of the company or its clients. (Article 4)

Those companies which have published or diffused any survey in violation of the dispositions of the present Law will be immediately obliged to publish or diffuse those rectifications required by the Central Electoral Council, announcing the origin and motives for the rectification, and programming or publishing them in the same space or page as the information which it rectifies. (Article 5)

Five days before an election, the publication of any poll will be prohibited. (Article 7)

All infractions of the obligatory norms established in the present Law will be fined not less than 50 000 pesetas (US $700) or more than 500 000 pesetas (US $7000). (Article 9)

Conclusion

At the beginning of 1979 the CIS, directed by Professor Juan Díez Nicolás, organised a conference about data banks for sociological investigation. Professor Juan J. Linz, on this occasion, summed up the Spanish case:

Spain today is a study bank of the social realities of the world. A great part of the interest awakened by the political transition of our country is due precisely to the many problems and phenomena that are currently being debated here. They are of general interest, of almost worldwide concern: regional autonomy, decentralisation of government bureaucracy, the political parties themselves and how to come to grips with communism.[75]

With all the limitations of the past and the present, public opinion surveys constitute a vital instrument for learning about the real situation in Spain. The peculiar political circumstances which have conditioned the origins and recent institutional transformations of polling in Spain have also provoked numerous controversies. But to date, nobody has questioned the viability of these investigations. Professionals in the field are conscious of their responsibility[76] and, in the academic world, more and more attention is being given to the training of future investigators. It is, therefore, fitting to affirm that in Spain, public opinion polls – with democracy – have reached their coming of age.

NOTES

1 Juan A. Giner, 'Journalists, mass media, and public opinion in Spain, 1938–1978', paper presented before the conference on 'Political Culture and Communications: The Iberian Peninsula in Transition', Columbia University, New York, 23–25 October 1978.

2 *Madrid*, 16 November 1966, p. 3.
3 *Madrid*, 18 November 1966, p. 3.
4 Juan J. Linz, who was, in 1974–5, president of the World Association for Public Opinion Research (WAPOR), was then president of this young Spanish company.
5 *Madrid*, 18 November 1966, p. 3.
6 *Madrid*, 19 November 1966, p. 1.
7 Ibid., p. 3.
8 *Madrid*, 21 November 1966, p.1.
9 *Madrid*, 25 November 1966, p. 3.
10 J. F. Coverdale, *The Political Transformation of Spain after Franco* (New York: Praeger, 1979).
11 F. G. Ledesma, I. Grases, F. Pujol and A. Villafané, *Las elecciones del cambio* (Barcelona: Plaza & Janés, 1977).
12 R. Serrano Suñer, 'Autenticidad y corrección', *ABC*, 28 January 1967, p. 3.
13 G. H. Gallup, *The Gallup Poll: Public Opinion 1935–1971* (New York: Random House, 1972).
14 *Gaceta de la Prensa Española*, 1 October 1943, p. 300.
15 M. Fernández Areal, *La libertad de prensa en España, 1938–1971* (Madrid: EDICUSA, 1971).
16 M. Fernández Areal, *La ley de prensa a debate* (Barcelona: Plaza & Janés, 1971) p. 88.
17 Juan A. Giner, 'La regulación ética y jurídica de las encuestas de opinión pública', unpublished doctoral thesis, University of Navarra, Pamplona, 1978, vol. I, p. 295.
18 Ibid., p. 197.
19 M. López Roldán, 'Qué es y cómo funciona el Instituto de la Opinión Pública', *Gaceta de la Prensa Española*, 1 November 1945, pp. 1915–16.
20 Ibid., p. 1916.
21 Ibid.
22 Ibid., p. 1918.
23 Ibid.
24 R. Fernández Chillón, 'Cómo leen los españoles su prensa', *Gaceta de la Prensa Española*, 1 October 1943, p. 300.
25 Ibid.
26 Ibid., p. 305.
27 Ibid.
28 R. Fernández Chillón, 'Cómo escuchan los españoles la radio', *Gaceta de la Prensa Española*, 1 November 1943, pp. 363–72.
29 Ibid., p. 364.
30 Ibid.
31 Ibid., p. 363.
32 J. Peral Acosta, 'Cómo influye en la información de los españoles la prensa y la radio', *Gaceta de la Prensa Española*, 1 January 1944, p. 488.
33 In 1942, after the lengthy negotiations and signing of the Atlantic Charter, 60 per cent of the American people did not know of its existence and 95 per cent were not able to recall any of the Charter's provisions. In 1945 four out of every ten Americans did not know what type of government ruled in the Soviet Union: S. E. Asch, *Psicología social* (Buenos Aires: Eudeba, 1964, 2nd

edn), pp. 545–6. Several years later, according to a survey by the IOP in Spain, 42 per cent of the inhabitants of Madrid did not know the name of the mayor: L. Gónzález Seara, *Opinión pública y communicación de masas* (Barcelona: Ariel, 1968) p. 74.

34 J. Peral Acosta, p. 490.
35 Ibid., p. 498.
36 Ibid., p. 500.
37 Decree-Law, 19 July 1951, and Decree-Law, 15 February 1952.
38 G. Arias Salgado, *Política española de la información* (Madrid: Editora Nacional, 1958), vol. 2, pp. 86–7.
39 R. Fernández Chillón, 'Servicio de Auscultación' (confidential typewritten report) Madrid, 13 February 1961, p. 1.
40 Ibid., pp. 1–2.
41 *Opinión*, June–July 1955, p. 27.
42 *Opinión*, August 1952, p. 15.
43 *Opinión*, May 1956, p. 8.
44 Chillón, 'Servicio' pp. 5–6.
45 *Opinión*, September–October 1952, p. 10.
46 The 'public opinion' course is taught by Professor Alejandro Muñoz Alonso at the University of Madrid (Complutense), and by Professor Juan A. Giner at the University of Navarra.
47 Hudson Institute Europe, *El Resurgir económico de España* (Madrid, 1975).
48 A. de Miguel, *Manual de estructura social de España* (Madrid: Tecnos, 1974) p. 305.
49 P. Creuheras Terán, *Tablas estadísticas para el análisis del mercado* (Barcelona: Agrupación Nacional de Estadisticos, 1963) p. 9.
50 Ministerio de Información y Turismo, 'Actividades y perspectivas del Instituto de la Opinión Pública', Madrid, 1971, p. 4, and J. Díez Nicolás, *Los españoles y la opinión pública* (Madrid: Editora Nacional, 1976) pp. 9–17.
51 FOESSA, *Il informe sociológico sobre la situación social de España* (Madrid, 1969) p. xi.
52 Giner, 'La regulación etica y jurídica', pp. 342–3.
53 Decree-Law, 31 October 1975.
54 *Cambio 16*, 6 October 1975, p. 35.
55 M. Gómez Reino, 'Dificultades para realizar encuestas de opinión', *Informaciones*, 5 December 1975, p. 20.
56 *YA*, 22 May 1977, p. 9.
57 *YA*, 7 May 1977, p. 46.
58 *YA*, 8 May 1977, p. 4.
59 *Arriba*, 3 May 1977, p. 24.
60 *Cambio 16*, 12 June 1977, p. 6.
61 *Informaciones*, 8 June 1977, p. 3.
62 *Comentario Sociológico*, July–December 1977, p. 300.
63 *Comentario Sociológico*, January–June 1977, pp. 509–10.
64 Juan A. Giner, 'Elecciones en España: el periodismo electoral en la jungla de la confusion', *Nuestro Tiempo*, March 1979, pp. 11–21. See also Juan A. Giner, '¡Luz, taquígrafos y sondeos!', *El País*, 27 February 1979, p. 9.
65 *Comentario sociológico*, January–June 1979, p. 310.
66 Giner, 'Elecciones en España', p. 17.

67 P. J. Ramirez, *Así se ganaron las elecciones 1979* (Madrid: Prensa Española, 1979) p. 354. See also Juan A. Giner, 'Sondeos de opinión y falsas encuestas: entre la manipulación y la propaganda', *Campaña*, April 1979, pp. 24–5.

68 Giner, 'Elecciones en España', p. 17.

69 ibid., pp. 18–19.

70 *ABC*, 6 February 1980, p. 9.

71 *Investigación y marketing*, May 1980, pp. 28–9.

72 Juan A. Giner, '? Es peligroso el público para los sondeos de opinión?', paper presented before the I Annual Conference of the AEDEMO, Madrid, 20–3 May 1980.

73 *Boletín oficial de las cortes generales: congreso de los diputados*, I Legislatura, 30 May 1979, pp. 125–6.

74 Juan A. Giner, 'La regulación de los sondeos en Francia', *Campaña*, 15 September 1977, pp. 20–1.

75 *La vanguardia*, 9 January 1977, p. 29.

76 Juan A. Giner, 'La *sondeomanía*, una enfermedad que preocupa', *Nuestro Tiempo*, August 1980, pp. 96–105.

10 Political Opinion Polling in the United States of America

MERVIN D. FIELD

MILESTONES IN US POLLING

Even a cursory historical review of the use of the questionnaire survey method in US public opinion research clearly reveals that the so-called 'modern era' of polling began in 1936, even though there is much evidence of earlier utilisation of the survey method in US history.

It was in 1936 that such pioneers as George Gallup, Elmo Roper and Archibald Crossley achieved public prominence as a result of their presidential election polling efforts. They became widely publicised because their results were running counter to what was considered at the time the most reliable and proven method of 'forecasting' presidential elections – the 'straw vote' operations of a weekly current events magazine, the *Literary Digest*.

The *Literary Digest* was a magazine of wide circulation and for some time it had conducted national 'straw votes' in presidential elections. These efforts consisted of sending hundreds of thousands of question-naires by mail to that portion of the US public listed in telephone or car ownership directories. However, during that era only a minority of the US public had a telephone or a car. This portion of the public obviously was not representative of the whole population, particularly in political preferences.

Before 1936 the *Literary Digest* pre-election 'straw vote' efforts happened to correspond roughly to the election outcomes in 1932 and 1928. These massive quadrennial samplings (about 2 million people were included in the 1936 effort) were highly publicised by newspapers, radio and other forms of mass media. Up until 1936 the *Digest* had acquired an image of reliability, if not infallibility, in forecasting presidential election outcomes.

During the 1936 campaign the *Digest*'s straw vote results portrayed a landslide victory for the Republican presidential nominee, Alf Landon. However, the Democratic nominee, Franklin Roosevelt, won an overwhelming victory on election day. The fact that the *Literary Digest*'s pre-election measures were at extreme variance with the actual election results shocked the American public. As a result, the magazine came in for widespread ridicule. Shortly afterwards the *Digest* went out of business, even though its presidential straw votes effort was only a periodic activity.

Coupled with the 1936 *Literary Digest* débâcle was the highly publicised emergence of Gallup, Roper and Crossley who were conducting polls for newspapers and magazines. They claimed to use more scientific, or at least more representative sampling methods than those of the *Literary Digest*. In 1936 their polls showed Roosevelt leading Landon throughout the campaign. Further, Gallup described in a pre-election report why the *Literary Digest* results were not truly reflective of a cross-section of US voters and why the *Digest* pre-election results would probably not correspond to election day results. In essence, Gallup publicly predicted that the *Literary Digest* would be 'wrong' in what was considered as its 'forecast' and specified the reasons why. Gallup and others pointed out the limitations in 1936 of polling limited to the world of car and telephone owners.

These 1936 events brought a great deal of national attention to the Gallup Poll and to the methodology it espoused, i.e. improved methods of cross-section sampling involving face-to-face interviews with respondents, along with data analysis which was more sophisticated than previous 'primitive' methods. Following his 1936 presidential election successes, Gallup was able to expand the syndication of his polling feature in a large network of US newspapers. He later extended his efforts internationally, lending his name and techniques to indigenous polling organisations in a number of democratic countries throughout the world.

Fortune Magazine began including Elmo Roper's poll in 1935 and featured it even more after 1936. Crossley for a number of presidential election years after 1936 also supplied a periodic polling news feature column to national newspaper syndicates. These three pollsters were able to build on their 1936 successes in subsequent years. Their efforts in the 1940 and 1944 presidential elections as well as their year-round polling on a variety of social and political issues were widely reported.

Their success stimulated other individuals and entities to set up polling within the various states and some cities.

In 1941 Joe Belden started a Texas Poll which was syndicated to a group of newspapers in that state. In 1944 the *Minneapolis Tribune* introduced and still maintains a continuing statewide poll in Minnesota. Two years later a continuing state poll was launched in Iowa by the *Des Moines Register Tribune*. In 1947 Mervin Field and his organisation started its continuing statewide public opinion news feature, the California Poll, which is supported by newspapers, television, and radio stations in that state.

THE RISE OF COMMERCIAL RESEARCH WHICH UTILISED POLLING METHODOLOGY

The growth of media-sponsored public opinion polls during the 1936–48 period and the methodological principles they featured provided an important stimulus to the US market research industry which had its origins earlier than 1936. Most market researchers during the 1936–48 period used political polling as an easily understood and widely accepted example to describe their business survey methods. In promoting these methods, they frequently referred to the 1936 *Literary Digest* failure as an example of what can go wrong in using biased samples and questionnable data-gathering tools. The names of Gallup, Roper and Crossley were invoked as paragons of the new 'scientific' survey method which had many profitable business applications.

However, the confidence in and acceptance of systematic and 'scientific' survey methods, which had reached a very high level by 1948, were severely shaken by the presidential election polls' performance in that year. The 1948 polls showed Republican Thomas E. Dewey as the consistent and clear leader. However, on election day Dewey lost narrowly to Democrat Harry Truman. The belief that the Gallup, Roper, Crossley, California, Minnesota, Iowa, Texas and other state polls could infallibly predict elections was shattered.

The public had been conditioned by the polls to expect a Dewey victory and few people publicly gave Truman a chance of winning. For example, a widely accepted 'insider' publication, the *Kiplinger Letter*, felt confident enough to mail out tens of thousands of copies just prior to the election with a cover story describing the kind of administration Dewey would preside over during the 1949–52 period. The *Chicago Tribune* printed an election evening edition featuring the front page headline 'Dewey wins'. On election night many radio commentators could not believe what was being reported – that the election was very close and that Truman had at least an even chance of winning. Throughout election night, they equivocated their reports with admonitions such as 'when all the returns are in, it is probable that Dewey will win'.

The immediate aftermath of the 1948 presidential election proved to be a grim and painful period for people who were utilising the survey method – pollsters and market researchers. There were all kinds of agonised formal and informal post-mortems among pollsters, sociologists, market researchers and academics who had a stake in the survey method. The most systematic post-election investigation was conducted by the Social Science Research Council which reported a number of methodological errors committed by the pollsters along with recommendations for improved polling methodology.

Pollsters also came in for heavy derision from the press and public. The failure of their 1948 polls was grist for newspaper editorials, cartoons, radio and night-club comedians. Humourist Goodman Ace, on his weekly radio show which had a large audience, mused: 'Everybody believes in public opinion polls – everyone from the man on the street all the way up to President Thomas E. Dewey.' Fred Allen, another widely known radio personality, put it this way: 'Public opinion pollsters are people who count the grains of sand in your bird cage and then try to tell you how much sand there is on the beach.'

What could be called the survey research fraternity in 1948 was much bigger, more prominent and involved more interests than in 1936. The poor performance of the scientific polls of 1948 compared with the 1936 polling débâcle caused a much bigger national uproar and had more serious repercussions for the larger body of survey professionals and users.

By 1948 the market research 'industry' had grown to be much larger than the political polling fraternity. Nevertheless, until 1948, market researchers were careful to nurture the umbilical cord connecting them to the small group of highly prominent political pollsters. The failure of the 1948 election polls put the pollsters and market researchers very much on the defensive. They were repeatedly ridiculed and required to explain why they were wrong. They suffered a big loss of confidence among clients and employers, as well as the general public. Professional reputations, jobs and research contracts were very much on the line following the 1948 débâcle.

The issue was simply: 'If the political polls were wrong in 1936 and again in 1948 can we ever believe them?' Or 'If polling methodology can't get the right answers, why should business continue to rely on the same methods?' The business public which had been sponsoring market research surveys to a rapidly increasing degree expressed doubts about the validity of the questionnaire survey method on which they were staking very important decisions.

Embarrassed market researchers were forced suddenly to change gear with respect to explaining their real and symbolic relationship with political pollsters. Rather than wrapping the hitherto exalted mantle of political polling around them, market researchers began to create more distance between themselves and their political polling colleagues.

One argument market researchers adopted at the time was that market place behaviour was very different from election day voting behaviour. Many acknowledged the fact that market research methods were imprecise in forecasting buying behaviour. They pointed out that reliance on intention-to-buy surveys was fraught with peril, and that pre-election polls were in effect a form of intention-to-buy surveys.

They also argued that political poll results, when considered as forecasts, were 'all-or-nothing' affairs. They pointed out that if support for a candidate in a pre-election poll was shown to be 52 per cent and if that candidate got just 49 per cent on election day the deviation might only be three percentage points but as a forecast it could be considered 100 per cent wrong. A market share forecast of 52 per cent, however, could deviate several percentage points without impairing the validity or the utility of the survey measurement. In essence, a marketer expecting a 52 per cent share of the market would be dismayed only slightly if the eventual share was only 49 per cent. Pollsters also pointed out that they had failed to poll often enough and long enough to catch the big change in public preferences during the later stages of the 1948 campaign.

THE GROWTH OF MEDIA-SPONSORED POLLING FOLLOWING 1948

Despite the heavy criticism and hostile scrutiny, the market research industry survived the 1948 'crisis'. Since that time it has flourished and grown phenomenally by any standard of measurement, e.g. the number of people employed, the number of market research surveys done each year, the degree of sophistication among market researchers, the extent of use of market research input for making a myriad of business decisions and the sizes of market research budgets. Political polling also survived and has grown since 1948, but at a smaller rate than market research. For example, the number of seasoned US political pollsters in 1981 could be counted in scores: however, the number of seasoned market researchers who utilised the survey method was well into tens of thousands.

One graphic way of illustrating the difference between market research and polling in the USA is to compare the total relative dollar volume represented by each activity. It has been estimated that about $20 million was spent in public and private polling on candidates and political issues in the 1980 election campaigns. Compared to that figure there is the huge annual US market, advertising and public opinion research expenditure utilising questionnaire surveys, estimated to range from $750 million to $1 billion. Thus, even in the big 1980 presidential election year, political polling represented only 2 or 3 per cent of the total survey research volume.

Since 1948 a number of other media-sponsored national and state polls have emerged in the USA. Lou Harris, following a period as a private political pollster, started his own national media-sponsored syndicated poll, the Harris Poll, in the early 1960s. He later expanded his polling operations to England and France.

During the late 1940s and early 1950s such newspapers as the *Boston Globe, Detroit Free Press, New York Daily News, Chicago Tribune* and *Portland Oregonian* began sponsoring local and state polls on a regular basis. In the following decades numerous other US newspapers and TV stations in a growing list of states began conducting polls on an *ad hoc* basis covering presidential and local elections as well as other social and political issues. By 1980 virtually every major and many smaller states were featuring media-sponsored polls.

Perhaps the most significant expansion of media-sponsored polling in the USA during the 1970s has been the establishment of national television networks aligning themselves with large metropolitan newspapers to conduct political and issue polls on a regular year-round basis. Some of these media partnerships which sponsor national polls include the CBS–*New York Times* Poll, the NBC–*Associated Press* Poll and the ABC–*Washington Post* Poll. The *Los Angeles Times*, while not affiliated to a television network, sponsors a periodic national poll.

PRIVATE POLITICAL POLLING

Soon after the expansion of media-sponsored polling following the 1936 election, there was an even greater expansion of private political polling in the USA. These efforts, underwritten by political candidates, parties or other partisan groups, involve candidate races as well as initiatives, referendums and other ballot proposition contests. Private polls use essentially the same methodology as media-sponsored polls; however, private polls are used in a different way from the more widely publicised media polls.

Ever since the emergence of 'straw votes' and polls, political interests recognised the value of conducting 'private' canvasses or polls as a way of obtaining information about the mood and disposition of voters. These efforts are specifically designed to help candidates take steps which can influence the outcome of the election in their favour. Media-sponsored polls ostensibly are not designed to change public opinion but are simply an extension of journalistic reporting.

By 1980 private political polling in the USA was most extensive and represented by far the largest proportion of all political polling being done. Private polling was being conducted at every level of political office – presidential, gubernatorial, senatorial, congressional, state legislature, county supervisor, mayoralty, as well as for other smaller offices. The demand for private polls is such that the candidate who does not have access to private polling data is a political rarity. Reliable data on expenditures for media-sponsored polling and private political polling are difficult to come by. However, I estimate that during 1980 private political polling funds were at least three times greater than funds spent on media-sponsored polling.

Private polls have proved valuable to candidates and partisan interests because they deal directly with such measures as the following:

1. Issue strategy: Candidates and partisan groups want to know what voters are most concerned about and what kind of issues will motivate them. For presidential, senatorial and congressional races, these may be national issues, i.e. the economy, energy policy, foreign relations, defence matters, as well as some broad-ranging social issues. In gubernatorial and state legislative races, they may cover such topics as education, state taxes, crime, highways, public transit as well as local social issues. Private pollsters try to find which issues are pivotal – those which can be supported or rejected by a candidate in such a way as to optimise vote differences *vis-à-vis* opposing candidates.

During the 1970s a number of specific issues emerged in the USA which had marked effects on voting. Some of these issues were so potent that a candidate's pro or con stand on one of them could cause important blocks of voters to be firmly supportive or antagonistic. Some of these 'single' issues which were particularly powerful in the 1980 elections and earlier were abortion, the Equal Rights Amendment, gun control, school busing, nuclear power and religious fundamentalism.

2. *Candidate image*: It is routine for private polls to develop image profiles of candidates and opponents which pinpoint respective strengths and weaknesses for each. For example, typical image profiles can include such measurements as the knowledge of a candidate and his or her record; how a candidate's personality is perceived; voters' perceptions of candidates and opponents with respect to honesty, experience, knowledge of issues; degree of a leader's speaking ability; inclination to favour one group over another; and ideological position.

3. *Candidate strength*: While most media-sponsored published polls generally show who is leading in important races, and sometimes will deal with issues and candidate images, they often do not provide information in helping candidates determine their strengths or weaknesses among various voter-groups. Private polls can show a candidate's relative strengths and weaknesses by such subgroups as single-issue partisans, section of country, state, county or neighbourhood, occupation, religion, union affiliation, sex, party preference, income, ethnic background, or any other relevant demographic or political characteristic.

4. *Party preference*: It is possible through private political studies to locate the subgroups within the electorate who are the party's strongest supporters. For example, while Democrats outnumber registered Republicans in many states, there are within both parties many people who consider themselves 'independents'. Over the years there has been a pronounced decline in party allegiance. Nevertheless, with large groups of voters party designation is still important. Private polls are particularly useful in identifying 'swing' voters, those who are inclined to vote for or against their party's candidate because of an issue or some personality aspect, or whatever.

5. *Effect of campaign activities*: Private polls can measure the effect of a candidate's television appearance, participation in debates, the quality of campaign literature offered, speeches, tours and other campaign activities.

Private polling for candidates has reached a level in the USA where for a number of major races campaign organisations set up voter-monitoring operations where preferences and reactions are 'tracked' continuously throughout a campaign. In such tracking studies, representative samples of interviews are taken frequently, perhaps even daily during a campaign. Usually the number of interviews taken in any one day is not of sufficient size to provide statistically reliable findings.

However, interviews conducted over a two- or three-day period are combined to provide substantial enough statistical bases for separate readings and analysis.

During the 1980 presidential campaign the private pollsters for both major candidates (Richard Wirthlin for Ronald Reagan and Patrick Caddell for Jimmy Carter) were polling continuously on a national basis as well as over-sampling in a number of large states to provide frequent periodic 'read-outs' of voter reaction data.

The position and power of these pollsters in presidential and other election campaigns has reached a point where they are part of the small powerful group of top campaign managers and advisers. Following the 1976 and 1980 presidential elections, the pollster who worked for the winner of the presidential election became a regular adviser to the President and his staff, devoting considerable time to this activity.

6. *Collateral values and effects of private polling research*: Private political studies are frequently useful within the state or local party organisations or political action groups which have access to significant campaign funds. Surveys on voter reaction to potential candidates have helped foster agreement on the best candidate for a party or a group to run. A strong image profile has sometimes convinced a reluctant candidate that his chances of winning are good. Support for basic campaign strategy has been won with the aid of study findings on the concerns of voters as expressed in polls.

7. *Private pollsters' conflicts*: There are unique and special pressures placed on the professionalism of private pollsters. During a campaign, private pollsters are called upon to advise candidates how to win. This entails identifying with the candidates and being subjective about campaign events. Many observers are uncomfortable about the conflict of interests that results when a political pollster offers advice on how to use survey results on behalf of a candidate or a cause. There have been many instances where pollsters have failed to do justice to one or the other of their disparate roles. Political campaigns are intense pressure cookers. A person who is both a researcher and a counsellor during a political campaign often finds the research component of this hybrid combination the first to be impaired.

There is also an uneasiness when private pollsters poll on public policy issues on which their political clients have strong adversarial positions. When a private pollster declares his bias by choosing to work only for candidates of one party or ideological position, it may seem to enhance his image for personal integrity, but it raises the question of how professional and objective he can really be.

THE INCREASED USE OF POLLING IN PUBLIC POLICY RESEARCH

The original incursion of survey research into public policy terrain started when political pollsters found that their media clients were interested in receiving poll reports not just during the height of election campaigns, when interest in the candidate races was most intense, but during other periods as well. This development was further encouraged by corporate interests who were beginning to find that the survey method could not only be used for market research, but could be applied to public policy issues where corporate interests were at stake. In addition, government agencies and other institutions sensitive to their accountability also found it desirable to sponsor *ad hoc* public policy surveys. Public policy research involves public opinion polls being taken by a variety of sponsors on a variety of complex and important issues such as foreign relations, environmental legislation, energy program- mes, abortion, gun control, racial equality, school busing, educational opportunity and other vital issues concerning US society.

Despite the failures of the 1936 and 1948 polls, acceptance of polling methodology and confidence in political candidate polls were restored in large degree in the three decades or so following the 1948 election. Periodically the efforts of one national poll have come in for some public criticism, if not censure. However, there was no widespread recognised failure of the national polls between 1949 and 1979 and as a result the US polling trade or 'profession' enjoys an increasingly high level of public and client confidence.

One development in the way poll results are being presented by the media has resulted in imputing to poll and public policy research data more precision than they justify. For example, some media people and pollsters themselves have been featuring a simplified explanation about the statistical or sampling tolerance of the survey data being presented. Frequently a well-known national newscaster may appear on nation- wide television announcing that a poll shows that '65 per cent of the American public supports the latest Supreme Court decision on abortion and this figure has a tolerance of plus or minus four percentage points'. The only qualification being offered is the simple reference to sampling tolerance. This explanation leaves the public with the impres- sion that the outer limits of the true or correct figure are 61 and 69 per cent – a rather narrow range. Leaving aside the large question of sample representativeness, there are many situations where a number of other non-sampling errors (question wording, data processing mistakes, etc.)

produce numerical variances many times larger than the variance inherent in sample size.

These reporters of public opinion data are not deliberately trying to deceive the public. But in their attempt to caution the viewer or reader they have unwittingly added unjustified credibility to fragile sample data rather than putting the public on guard, which presumably was their intention.

CONTROVERSIES SURROUNDING POLITICAL POLLING AND PUBLIC POLICY RESEARCH

The wide acceptance of polling in the USA has come about because it is generally recognised that polls can provide a unique service to a democracy of 230 million people spanning a large continent. However, the growth of political polling and public policy research has fostered a great deal of public criticism, hostility and unresolved controversy.

A good deal of the controversy surrounding polling has to do with the ambivalent way it is viewed. Ever since 1948 most responsible opinion polling organisations have tried to emphasise that their political pre-election preference polls are not predictions of election outcomes. Despite these disclaimers, nearly everybody, including many pollsters themselves in private, considers late opinion poll results as forecasts of who or what will win an election.

The rationale offered by most pollsters in explaining how their efforts should be viewed generally goes like this. In a scientific sense a poll is simply a description of the public mood at the time of the survey. It has no intrinsic meaning, and certainly no predictive status. Thus, when pollsters offer poll results, what they are saying is simply that their surveys have been conducted in accordance with tested procedures intended to impart qualities of scientific objectivity. Therefore, an accurate poll simply measures public opinion and the facts observed at one point in time.

A 'fact' of the kind pollsters deal with in the case of polls is an observation of an empirical event, i.e. of expressed opinions. Before an observation is given the status of a fact in science, however, it is customary to submit to others the procedures and methods used in the measurement so that they can replicate the procedures and confirm or refute the accuracy of the reported observations.

In modern opinion research, this procedure is well understood. Most pollsters follow a probability procedure in drawing their samples; they try to frame questions in an unbiased manner; they have trained interviewers to administer the questions uniformly; they perform periodic data-processing checks at various stages of the research; and they conduct their analyses according to accepted scientific standards. All such research canons are intended to make it possible to assert the reliability of the measuring instrument, i.e. to claim that another person following these same procedures should get the same results, within the limits of sampling error. This enables pollsters to make the claim that the poll is an accurate observation which can be projected or generalised to the set of all persons who were not sampled. In other words, they report a fact at the time of the observation.

While there is much in the literature which tries to distinguish the difference between a 'fact' and a 'prediction', the two are often muddled. Facts take on meaning only when placed in perspective. A 'significant' fact is one that fits into some meaningful relationship which the analyst can interpret. In this light, then, the interpretation of 'facts' in social science derives from understanding of the way the world of human social action works. A prediction is one kind of interpretation, and it can only be made by fitting previous 'facts' together in such a way as to establish causes and effects.

In public opinion research, understanding of causation in human behaviour, or voter behaviour, is so limited that it is almost a presumption to speak of 'predictions'. However, should anyone be disposed to use a pre-election poll as a basis for a prediction, the analyst is obliged to offer some additional interpretive justification. For example, to attempt sucessfully to combine pre-election poll facts into a prediction, a number of other considerations must be taken into account, e.g. the impact of subsequent campaign events, assumptions about how undecided voters will behave, etc. In short, while a pre-election poll may be used by some to form their prediction, the poll itself is only one 'fact' or bit of information used in making that prediction. Analysts who intend to offer predictions must therefore articulate their argument in a more complete form than simply citing the results of one public opinion poll.

Simple and logical as this reasoning is, it is often lost by those who assume that there will be a close correspondence between a final pre-election poll and an election day event. Unfortunately many pollsters tend to undermine the logic that a pre-election poll report by itself is not a predictor of an election outcome. They do this by being inconsistent in what they say before an election and what they say afterwards. For example, often a pollster will be very careful in pointing out that the result of a pre-election poll is not a prediction, that it is a measurement taken at one point in time, that many things could intervene after the poll is taken to produce an election result at odds with the poll report, etc. However, after an election that same pollster is often prone to exult publicly when the pre-election poll report corresponds closely with election day results.

Most of the criticism about polls falls into five different areas:

Effects: this criticism claims that the publication of a poll report will influence voters in one way or another.

Relevance: this kind of criticism questions the usefulness of published poll results. The argument is put that polls pre-empt attention and tend to create a popularity contest atmosphere, that they are disruptive interventions into the stream of important information about candidates and issues.

Morality: this criticism presumes that voters are relatively vulnerable and holds that it is immoral to interfere when they are in the throes of making what should be a private decision.

Social Control: this criticism suggests that research data can be used to achieve one's private ends through manipulation of the public mind through the selective use of appeals. It casts doubt on the ethics of using survey intelligence.

Technique: this criticism expresses doubt about the competence of persons doing the polling and/or about the validity of the technique itself.

Over the years pollsters and others have tried to answer these criticisms in a variety of ways. The following is an attempt to describe their reactions.

Effects

In talking about 'effects' what is meant is that a voter will act in some new way as a result of reading a poll report. The effect may be direct, or it may indirectly influence the reader only in concert with other information. The effect may be either systematic or unpredictable. In the systematic case, poll reports are claimed to produce certain predictable results on voters; in the other case, there are effects, but they are not predictable and it is impossible to tell whether a given candidate will be hurt or helped by the publication.

An enumeration of some of the general campaign-related effects or outcomes that could be caused by publishing poll results would include:

Direct effects on the voter

1. A poll which shows one candidate leading will discourage voters supporting his opponent from voting at all.
2. A poll which shows one candidate leading will diminish the enthusiasm of his supporters.
3. A poll which shows one candidate leading will cause undecided voters to flock to his banner (sometimes called the 'bandwagon effect').
4. A poll which shows one candidate leading will cause undecided voters to move toward his opponent's banner (sometimes called the 'reverse bandwagon' or 'underdog effect').

Indirect effects on the voter

5. A poll which shows one candidate leading will encourage workers to work even harder, and put the campaign staff on guard to combat over-confidence.
6. A poll which shows one candidate leading will redouble the effort of an opponent's workers to effect a change.
7. A poll which shows one candidate leading will dry up financial support and group endorsement for an opponent.
8. A poll which shows one candidate leading will make it difficult to recruit workers because an intense campaign seems unnecessary.

Over the years there have been various theories about the influence of the foregoing 'effects' on elections. However, there is little evidence to support any of them which would qualify under scientific rules of evidence. Whether voters conform to the consensus shown by a poll or not is still an open question. Some psychological studies of conformity demonstrate the existence of pressure to conform, but only under conditions which do not resemble the effects created by poll reports (i.e. sometimes we go along with the crowd, but this usually occurs only when we know, and are known by, the crowd).

Any mass conformity theory therefore runs counter to reference group notions, which hold that an individual's behaviour and attitudes are influenced greatly by the values and norms of the family or social group to which he belongs, or to which he aspires to belong. The formal evidence here suggests that acquainting a voter with news about the majority vote of his reference group would be more likely to affect his vote than simply describing the voting preferences of the public at large.

There have been instances, however, where each of the four direct effects could be invoked to explain – after the fact – some particular campaign or election outcome. Therefore, an observer could cautiously conclude that direct effects probably exist. But since they are not predictable by any extant theories, they must be treated as random effects which do not clearly favour one candidate or the other.

So far as indirect effects are concerned, it is sometimes claimed that a candidate who is trailing badly in the polls finds it difficult to obtain campaign financing. The implied causal relationship here should be questioned, however. Do the poll results influence backers, or is the poll simply a reflection of the candidate's lack of appeal, not only to the general voters, but to financial interests as well? Experience has shown that attractive, articulate candidates, even those previously unknown, have succeeded in raising campaign funds even when polls showed their lack of identification. In fact, the purpose of raising campaign financing is to obtain exposure for the candidate and to build the identification he needs to compete. A candidate who cannot compete effectively for initial financing may also not be able to project a personality to the public which successfully competes for voter support. The polls in such a case merely reflect this state of voter perception, which happens to be matched by potential financial backers' similar perceptions of the candidate.

It is argued that even if all the supposed public opinion poll effects happen to some degree, the poll results published over the campaign period give voters an opportunity, in real time, to see how the candidates in success and adversity manage their campaigns in response to changes in the public mood. The manner in which a political leader responds, makes changes and meets challenges while his or her campaign generalship is being periodically measured may act as a useful and revealing piece of information which all voters can assess and use to draw their own conclusions.

Relevance

The second complaint about poll reporting maintains that polls are irrelevant. The charge is that valuable time and energy is wasted discussing and reacting to poll results instead of to the 'issues'. However, the results of more than forty-five years of studying voting behaviour appear to show that the vast majority of the US electorate is not primarily issue-oriented, at least in the terms in which social scientists define issues. Certain groups of people are attentive to certain issues, but they are also less likely, by virtue of their involvement, to be influenced one way or the other merely by poll reports of how others feel, just as they are also less likely to be swayed by advertisements, or anything else short of events which radically alter their basic set towards the issues. 'Political man' is as fictitious an entity as 'economic man'.

Indeed, it might seem that voters' perceptions of the 'issues' are less important than their perceptions of the candidate. Issues tend to be short-lived, while the candidate remains in office for a full term. Historically, US voters may have been concerned with issues because they did not have direct access to the candidate or officeholder. In recent years, the electronic media have given voters a chance to 'see' the candidate close up. This has enabled voters to make a judgement about a candidate's style or personality, thereby determining the weight of the issue. Voters' interest and involvement is more readily captured by the human struggle of the candidates. Voters are powerfully affected by the personal and human characteristics of the candidates. A campaign manager seeks to highlight a candidate's best personality attributes; how well the manager is doing is assessed periodically by the polls.

It is frequently claimed that few issues of profound substance are ever discussed by candidates during the campaign. If this is true, then it can be argued that public airing of these is less 'relevant' to the democratic process than the progress of the personal drama. The popularity and interest accorded to pre-election polls is very probably evidence of their 'relevance' to this human struggle.

Morality

Another category of poll criticism holds that reports of pre-election decisions reached by some sample of voters invades the essential privacy of decision-making by the individuals. It is a moralistic argument that arises from the implicit premise that all voting decisions should be made in the absence of information on how others feel.

In spite of such moral strictures, however, it seems quite natural for voters to check their perceptions of a candidate's personality and character against those of fellow voters. Except in special cases, voters see candidates as individuals rather than as issues, and they are curious about how other people see these individuals.

Students of democratic government have long recognised the need for an accurate way to find out what people are thinking. Abraham Lincoln once remarked: 'What I want to get done is what the people want to have done, and the question for me is how to find out exactly.' Somewhat later, in 1893, in *The American Commonwealth*, James Bryce said: 'The obvious weakness of government by public opinion is the difficulty of ascertaining it.' Woodrow Wilson is quoted as having said: 'The people of the United States are thinking for themselves . . . and you do not know what they are thinking about. I have the most imperfect means of finding out, and yet I have to act as if I know.'

While survey research and polls are far from being a perfect means of finding out what the public is thinking about, they are more nearly so than the pronouncements of self-styled, self-appointed spokespersons. Therefore, if the real outcome of published poll results is to convey the state of public beliefs and opinions to public officials and candidates in a way that exerts moral force on their behaviour, it could well be argued that polls serve the democratic process in the very ways they are supposed to harm it.

Social Control

Arguments found in this area of criticism are based on the premise that information, or the knowledge of facts, is power. To the extent that business, government, or special interest groups acquire information about the public mind, and do not share this information, they acquire a kind of power which enables them to manipulate or take advantage of the public, either directly or indirectly.

The claim here is that even when poll results are publicly disclosed, the public is duped into believing that its voice has been heard when, in fact, all that has been heard is the public's answers to questions put to it by the researcher or the special interest group. Most such questions, the argument goes, are actually reflections of the non-conscious ideology which guides the society, while specific issues and alternatives are never explored. For example, questions about busing schoolchildren may assume that children should be compelled to attend the existing public school system, which some believe is a bad experience to start with. In the consumer marketing area it has been argued that research on preferences for dolls advances the sex-role typing of little girls, etc.

The answers to such arguments are complicated by another tenet of science, namely, that knowledge of objective reality is tentative and can only be defined in terms of its usefulness and testability for some purposes. Most marketers and politicians recognise intuitively, if not explicitly, that the public is composed of individuals, each of whom is unique with a personal point of view and set of attitudes. When a question is written for a survey questionnaire it only reflects the purpose or interest of the researcher and his sponsor, who want to know the public's reaction to that question. There are many other questions that could just as well have been written covering other purposes or interests. In this respect a poll question is much like an election choice: there may be many alternative solutions to the problem which a ballot measure seeks to solve, but the one presented is the only one judged.

Therefore, the danger may lie not so much in the publishing of poll results themselves as in holding to any interpretation that implies or states that the public mood has been definitively described by the single poll reported. Here again, what seems needed is thoughtful, critical interpretation of the opinions reported. These would include other possible and plausible explanations beyond the ones implied by the poll report. Journalists, commentators, political pundits and others are certainly well equipped to do this. They need not be technical experts in polling to criticise an interpretation; in fact, they are probably better qualified than most researchers, who tend to be specialists rather than generalists.

In a democratic society the watchdog function of the press serves the people by providing information about one segment of society to another, and about the activities of government to the people. The idea of a democratic society is one where all citizens have equal access to all information about the society. Much of this information is provided by the press. Therefore, research information will not lead to manipulation and control, unless the public does not have access to such information. To provide this access, more sources of information with different points of view are needed. Toward this end, more poll reports and interpretations are needed, not fewer.

The attention which the media have accorded polls is, of course, responsible for their success, but only in a superficial sense. A poll is sometimes described as being simply rigorous quantitative reporting and, therefore, not unlike other journalistic activities, but there is a deeper reason for this alliance. It is the recognition that information about the public mood can be used for social control unless it is made public. Thus, opinion surveys should be made and reported freely as a safeguard against control. If special interest sponsors do not disclose their results, the media can, and should, sponsor and publish their own polls. To answer troublesome questions about the underlying ideology of one survey, another survey is needed with a different ideology and motive. This airing of public opinion, and the public education that arises out of the debate it engenders, is the highest value of freedom of access to information.

Technique

The techniques used for polling by responsible practitioners are anchored in the canons of disciplined inquiry and the rules which govern scientific evidence. Polling is often questioned, however, on sample size with a question such as 'How can one thousand or even two thousand respondents represent the views of 160 million US adults?'. Mathematical statistics and probability theory can answer this specific question completely, but because it has been answered so often and yet still arises, even among responsible and friendly critics, the question may be symptomatic of certain fears.

Much popular suspicion of polls arises not so much out of misunderstood sampling techniques as from the fear that somehow published findings are misrepresenting the 'true' state of affairs. This fear is most likely to be expressed when polls are reported on social issues more complex than voter preference, such as US relations with the Soviet Union, how best to plan a country's energy future, abortion, immigration, racial equality, school busing, arms control, or educational opportunity.

Such fear seems to centre on the idea that somehow the whole story is not told, and that poll reports are incomplete and oversimplified. An interpretation of this accusation is to imply that the attitudes measured are biased in some way, or that the public attitudes reported are not the most relevant attitudes *vis-à-vis* the topic. In other words, the questions which respondents have been asked have failed to cover the range of alternative views or the various shades of opinion. Such criticism also suggests that the analysis falls short of properly qualifying the opinions reported so that only a narrow interpretation or understanding of the issues is really possible.

THE PERFORMANCE OF THE NATIONAL POLLS DURING THE 1980 PRESIDENTIAL ELECTION

The performance of the US national political polls during the 1980 presidential election resulted in another of those periodic upheavals which shake the public's confidence in the ability of polls accurately to reflect public opinion.

The 1980 presidential election campaign featured more pre-election polling activity, both public and private, than in any previous presidential or off-year election season. This polling was most visible on the national level, but there was also considerable polling done at a state and smaller area level.

On election day US voters chose Republican Ronald Reagan over Democrat Jimmy Carter by a margin of 51 to 41 per cent. Reagan's margin of victory was even more one-sided in the electoral college. He won 44 states for a total of 489 electoral votes while Carter won 6 states and the District of Columbia for a total of 49 electoral votes.

Despite Reagan's impressive victory, the expectation created by virtually all the published national polls right up to the final days of the campaign was that the outcome was going to be quite close and that Carter probably had an even chance of winning. While a number of published national polls showed Reagan ahead in the national popular vote, the margins were very small and the results were presented in tentative terms.

Table 10.1 is a summary of the final pre-election results of the five leading media-sponsored national polls. The dates in brackets indicate the interviewing periods. These late poll results were featured prominently in their respective media as well as in nationally distributed wire service reports. They were published and re-broadcast throughout the country. Usually presentations of the data were made with the standard methodological caveat that the percentage differences between Reagan and Carter were within the statistical margin of error inherent in any poll

TABLE 10.1 *1980 US presidential election*

	Reagan (%)	Carter (%)	Anderson (%)	Others/ undecided (%)
Results of the popular vote (4 Nov.)	51	41	7	1
Final poll results:				
Washington Post (29–30 Oct.)	39	42	7	12
CBS News/*New York Times* (30 Oct. – 1 Nov.)	41	40	7	12
Gallup (30 Oct.–1 Nov.)	46	43	7	4
ABC News/Harris (22 Oct.–3 Nov.)	46	41	10	3
NBC News/*Associated Press* (22–4 Oct.)	42	36	9	13

result. The presentations either implied or explicitly stated that the presidential race was 'too close to call'. This phrase became almost a national refrain echoed by headline writers and television newspeople as well as followers of the polls during the final weeks and days of the campaign.

As a result of the substantial Reagan election victory, categorised as a landslide by many observers, most of the national pollsters found themselves in the uncomfortable position which all pollsters must face periodically of having to explain why late pre-election poll results conveyed a different impression from the actual election result.

While most of the public and many political analysts were focusing on the national poll findings, there were a handful of observers[1] who, relying on private and published state poll reports, were getting a different, and what in retrospect would have to be regarded as a clearer, picture of campaign voting trends as well as the outcome of the Reagan–Carter race.

This was because of a simple, unremarkable fact that every student of the US election process learns early on. The USA does not have one national presidential election, but fifty-one separate elections with the outcome decided by the total electoral votes gained by the winning candidate in each of the separate elections. Presidential elections are 'national' only in the sense that voters in all fifty states and the District of Columbia go to the polls to vote for a president on the same day.

During every presidential election campaign there is always some discussion about the vagaries of the US electoral college system; about how the national popular vote could easily differ from the sum of the state-by-state results, producing a situation where a candidate might win the popular vote but not get the required 270 electoral votes to be declared the winner.

During 1980 most of this discussion occurred early in the campaign, when independent candidate John Anderson was achieving a relatively high standing in the polls. When Anderson's popularity began to slide in September, continuing through October, attention paid by the press to candidate standings at the state level diminished.

The amount of 1980 polling activity that was conducted at the state level was much more extensive than it had ever been in previous presidential elections. A steady flow of state data provided a much sounder base for making assessments as to who was ahead and projections of the election outcome. To those who followed these data, a clear picture was presented of a steady trend in Reagan's favour culminating in his resounding victory.

A number of analysts, reporters and pollsters followed the day-by-day developments within the various states throughout the campaign. One writer, Richard Cattani of the *Christian Science Monitor*, regularly reported the race from this vantage-point. In Cattani's 15 September column he highlighted the disparity between national poll findings and state-by-state counts – a disparity which was to continue during the final seven weeks of the campaign and particularly in its closing days. He reported how 'the average of five major national polls showed Reagan ahead by just two percentage points in national vote totals', whereas *Newsweek*'s state-by-state estimate (based in part on state poll data) showed 320 electoral votes for Reagan and 91 for Carter, with 127 rated a toss-up.

On 6 October, in a subsequent round-up of state poll data, Cattani reported another *Newsweek* state-by-state analysis which showed Reagan leading in states representing 321 electoral votes, Carter with 142 and 75 in doubt. At about the same time a *New York Times* count gave Reagan 314 electoral votes and Carter 136, with 88 in doubt, and a *Washington Post* tally showed 283 electoral votes for Reagan and 151 for Carter, with 104 rated a toss-up. Cattani also quoted another state poll watcher, Michael Barone, whose polling organisation, Peter Hart and Associates, was active in a large number of states for Democratic gubernatorial and congressional candidates and where presidential preference measures were being regularly obtained. Barone's analysis on 6 October had Reagan with 334 electoral votes and Carter with 204.

In his 10 October 1980 issue of the *American Political Report*, Kevin Phillips reported a summary of poll results in the ten largest states (California, New York, Ohio, Illinois, New Jersey, Pennsylvania, Florida, Michigan, Texas and Massachusetts) which represent an aggregate of 259 electoral votes. In seven of these states Reagan was ahead as shown by a variety of published and private state polls. Phillips reported conflicting poll reports from Texas: a CBS–*New York Times* state poll which showed Carter leading by 40 to 39 per cent, compared to 'GOP' polls (Wirthlin's) which had Reagan leading by 17 points. Reagan carried Texas by 15 percentage points on 4 November.

For most of the campaign, New York and Massachusetts were considered to be strong Carter states expected to capture 55 important electoral votes. From a national poll watcher's position, it was these two large-population states where it was assumed that if Carter was close to Reagan in the national polls, it would have to be the heavy pluralities coming from New York and Massachusetts which were contributing disproportionately to Carter's national position in the polls. However, even as early as 10 October, based on the reports he was receiving, Phillips classified the Carter–Reagan races in New York and Massachusetts as 'tight'.

On 11 October, in an analysis based on these and other state poll reports presented to a meeting of the Business Council at Homestead, West Virginia, I reported the following:

> Reagan is now in a stronger position than he was two weeks ago. He has strong leads in 17 states representing 126 electoral votes, another 12 states with 159 electoral votes are leaning toward him. The combined total of states currently in Reagan's favour is 29 and they represent 295 electoral votes. Carter on the other hand is strongly ahead in just 6 states (and the District of Columbia) representing only 54 electoral votes and there are another 8 states representing 100 electoral votes leaning to Carter, giving him a total of 154 electoral votes.
>
> Seven states with 89 electoral votes are fairly evenly divided at this time, but even if they break in Carter's favour, he still would not win according to current measurements.
>
> What we may be seeing is the development of a trend which would give Ronald Reagan not just a close and narrow win [on election day] but a victory of substantial proportions.

From 11 October onwards there were fluctuations in the state-by-state charting done by the individuals and polling organisations cited above and others. But the consistent findings from these electoral vote estimates led one to the same general conclusion: Ronald Reagan was continuing to maintain a significant and comfortable lead over Carter in most of the states representing a large portion of electoral votes up until the final presidential debate on 28 October.

Following the 28 October Reagan–Carter television confrontation, there were reports of new polling in a number of pivotal states including, among others, Ohio, Illinois, New York and Pennsylvania. Results of these post-debate polls showed Reagan's states becoming even firmer, Carter's states weakening and the previously 'too close to call' states breaking in Reagan's favour. Thus on the Friday before the election the consistent and clear lead that Reagan had had before the debates appeared to be growing even larger.

Periodically in the course of the campaign, and particularly during its final week, some of those who were following the state polls closely were struck by the contradiction between the large amount of national poll data showing the national popular vote very close and the very different picture being revealed by the state-by-state analyses.

At that time I, among others, in the absence of any other explanation, assumed that the national polls were presenting an accurate picture of the nation's popular vote division. On this basis, the apparent contradiction between the national polls and the state polls was explained as a reflection of the anomaly of one candidate (Carter) being ahead in a few heavily populated states but behind in a large number of less populated states. However, upon closer examination, there were not very many large-population states where Carter had leads that could offset his vote deficiencies in the other states, some of which were also large-population states. Thus, during the final week of the campaign, a sophisticated observer of the state polls had to be troubled by the measurements being offered by the national polls proclaiming the race 'too close to call'.

After the election the explanation given by a number of the national pollsters was the standard argument that their findings reflected public preference at the time of the polls and that there was a big shift to Reagan after they stopped polling, presumably on the Saturday or Sunday before the election. However, this 'late big shift' explanation does not square at all with the consistent picture conveyed by the state-by-state polling analyses during the course of the campaign.

This leads one to raise the rather serious question of why more political observers and reporters did not make greater use of the extensive and available state poll data during the campaign. One reason presumably is that it was not clear during the spring and summer months of 1980 that there would be enough polling at the state level to provide an alternative to the traditional national cross-section surveys. While a number of media sources provide round-ups of state poll data, they were presented irregularly and there was no assurance that they would be updated during the final week of the campaign.

Another inhibiting factor perhaps was that while a few states have had longstanding reputable media-sponsored operations, polling efforts were relatively new and not in the hands of long-tested practitioners in many of the other states. (However, the media polling operations in a number of these states were in the hands of young practitioners who had had academic training in polling methodology. In many cases the findings of these new state polls were being confirmed by 'leaked' private poll data produced by other seasoned researchers.)

In addition, the previous relatively close correspondence between the results of the national cross-section surveys and the outcomes of most of the recent presidential elections obscured the basic fact that the popular vote estimates reported by national cross-section surveys, even if accurate, do not always reflect actual presidential outcomes because electoral votes do not necessarily follow popular vote.

There were other reasons. One was that the sheer over-abundance of national poll data tended to pre-empt the available time and space for the interpretation and presentation of other survey data in the national news media. Another was that the 'too close to call' impression that a number of analysts were conveying was more congenial to their private expectations that the incumbent, Carter, while behind in the race, would in the final analysis emerge as the winner.

There was also the presumption that the elements which made up the traditional Democratic Party coalition (e.g. rank-and-file labour, minority groups, the educational establishment, old-line Democratic Party organisations) would in the final stages of the campaign 'come home' and give Carter the votes that he needed. Further, there was a widespread belief that Reagan would at some point commit a major campaign blunder which would turn voters away from him.

Perhaps a significant reason could be that the weight of the frequent national poll data produced by the big national media and 'media combines' (e.g. CBS and the *New York Times*, NBC and the *Associated Press*, ABC–Lou Harris, the *Washington Post*, *Time* and *Newsweek*) may have tended to undermine the judgement of the editors and political writers who worked for these media poll sponsors and who may also have been overwhelmed by these prestigious poll data sources.

It must have been difficult for political writers not to rely on their own organisation's poll results as the most authoritative account of what was going on. Many of them had immediate access to their organisation's poll data through handy computer terminals and a frequent flow of impressive computer print-outs. The close proximity of a large amount of continuous internally-produced poll data tended to inhibit the review of other alternative poll data sources. Since other national poll data from competing sources seemed to corroborate internally provided national findings, this tended to diminish any need for further validation.

One example of the conflict that editors had in treating national *vs* state poll data is what appeared in the Monday (before the Tuesday election) edition of the *Washington Post*. On page 1 the *Post* featured its final national cross-section poll which showed Carter leading by three percentage points. However, David Broder's column which dealt with a state-by-state analysis and described Reagan's big lead in the states and electoral votes appeared on page 4 of the same issue.

What about the polling methodology of the national polls? Was there anything particular to the national polls that could have contributed to the disparity between national poll data portraying the race as 'too close to call' when the state-by-state analysis showed Reagan to be well ahead for many weeks? Before this question can be discussed, some comments need to be made about the perennial dilemma of pollsters with respect to the issue of measurement and prediction.

During every election campaign, pollsters take great pains to warn the public that their published poll results are not forecasts of the election outcome, for reasons which have been well aired. These include such factors as campaign events occurring after the completion of a poll which might affect voters' perceptions of the candidates, disproportionate rates of voter turn-out on election day, undecided voters breaking disproportionately for one of the candidates, certain small trends that had been in evidence during most of the campaign gathering extra steam in the days or hours just prior to the election and after polling has been completed, and the fact that any survey has statistical margins of error. Pollsters have long argued that to make a flat prediction from poll results requires a higher order of analysis than can be provided by a simple poll report, no matter how accurate it may be.

Despite the logic of these facts and arguments, pollsters have learned that in order to maintain their credibility and reputation they cannot rely on the simple pre-election caveat of 'don't treat my results as a forecast' and expect to be judged fairly by the public or to maintain the financial underwriting of their media sponsors who, no matter what they say, still expect if not require that their pollster's last report correspond to the election outcome.

As a result, pollsters have contributed greatly to their own public relations problem by adhering to contradictory pre-election and post-election positions. Typically, the pre-election pollster stance is to cite all the reasons why his poll report is not a prediction. However, if an election result corresponds closely to his pre-election poll, the pollster is quick to broadcast that 'we were right on the nose in calling the election'.

Pollsters have not yet been able to resolve completely this conflict about how the public should treat their reports. During the 1980 presidential campaign pollsters made considerable efforts to deny that their polls could predict. But, at the same time, they spent a lot of effort on data analysis and data presentation which could only be to give predictive status to their measures.

There has always been considerable if not unavoidable pressure on pollsters to fulfill the explicit or implied requirement of producing data which relate to an election result. At the very least, a pollster is expected to produce a model of those citizens found in samples restricted to the 'likeliest' of voters and offer some clues as to what will happen with those who are undecided.

In confronting the problem of modelling the electorate in a presidential election from public opinion samples, pollsters have available some reasonably reliable parameters in respect of the expected overall rate of national participation. In recent presidential elections, the participation rate by US citizens has been slightly more than 50 per cent. That is, almost one-half of the citizen public in each election has not voted. To produce a representative model of election day participation from public opinion samples of all adults or all registered voters requires a system of reducing larger overall samples to smaller ones; the reduced samples are then held in the judgement of the pollsters to reflect those who are most likely to vote.

One method used extensively by pollsters in this effort involves a series of intention or likelihood-of-voting questions administered to poll respondents. This 'screening' process used by pollsters takes a variety of forms. Generally, an early question determines whether or not a respondent is eligible to vote. Most pre-election polls start with general public adult samples and rely on a respondent's testimony to obtain that person's registration status. If a respondent maintains that he or she is registered, the pollster generally accepts this.

However, there are many people who say that they are registered when in fact they are not. This is not necessarily a case of respondents 'lying'. Registration laws from state to state vary a great deal. There are frequent changes made in registration requirements and there are differences in the way registration lists are produced from time to time. Many people are not clear about their registration status because of a residential move or because of a failure to vote in a previous election. In addition, some people, if they are ineligible to vote at the time of the interview, may believe this condition will be corrected before election day. Finally, there still exists the tendency for some people to feel a loss of self-esteem if they admit to not being registered to vote. All these reasons combined lead to the unreliability of many pollsters' basic assumption that their registered voter subsample is limited to those eligible to vote.

The apparently simple expedient of pollsters limiting their sample universes to published registration lists is not necessarily the answer to this problem. Sampling from registration lists poses a different set of problems. For one, obtaining up-to-date registration lists is not an easy task. The deadlines set for citizens to register have been extended in many states to dates very close to election day and it is difficult to get final lists in time to do pre-election polling. Relying on previously published lists means that they will include ineligible people who have since been purged from the list because they have not voted in recent elections. In addition, lists exclude other eligible people who have moved into an area and whose registration status has not yet been recorded.

However it is derived, a pollster's base of registrants is next subjected to a series of election day 'turn-out' questions, ranging from one or two simple direct queries of how likely it is that a respondent will go to the polls to a complex series of scale questions measuring degree of involvement in the campaign, the importance of voting or not voting, previous voting history, knowledge of where the polling place is, etc. At some stage, cut-off points are established when all respondents are arrayed or 'turn-out' probability weights are applied to each re-spondent. This process allows the pollster to eliminate or weight down from his analyses those people considered to be less likely or unlikely to vote.

Seymour Martin Lipset reported in *Public Opinion* (August/ September 1980) that the resultant range of respondent retention reported by some national polls after screening questions had been applied varied from 54 to 75 per cent. Lipset was referring to a considerable body of data and literature which shows that 'nonvoters tend to be drawn from the more democratically disposed strata, the poor, minorities, the less educated, and the young'. These groups would contain more Carter voters than Reagan.

Relying on even the most sophisticated screening system in national cross-section surveys in order to obtain a national composite of the electorate is still a chancy thing. Registration criteria and voting turn-out rates vary considerably from state to state. It is quite hazardous simply to average all these factors in producing national estimates of voter preferences and electoral counts.

There are a number of reasons why most national polls have not developed state-by-state parameters for the purpose of qualifying respondents as to registration status or likelihood of voting. First, to date their primary scope has not been focused on the state level in presidential election campaigns. There has not been the need to investigate and develop the state-by-state parameters because in a typical national cross-section sample the number of interviews allocated to any one state is not large enough to provide for any significant statistical treatment.

The dollar expenditure involved for one polling organisation to do this is perhaps the chief deterrent to enlarging national cross-section samples to provide findings and analyses on the state level. However, the television networks spent huge sums of money covering the 1980 presidential election. The competing networks and their print medium partners polled in many states during the primary season; they conducted frequent national polls and some state polls during the general election campaign. On election day they underwrote a massive exit poll operation in virtually every state. It would seem that in the face of these huge expenditures all that would be required to incorporate a schedule of pre-election polls on the state level would be a reallocation of funds. If the goal was to provide a more reliable quantitative portrayal of the presidential race, it would seem that this change would be the first order of business for those media poll managers now planning their 1984 coverage.

Another methodological problem which might help explain why some national polls may have under-reported Reagan's and over-reported Carter's strength during the 1980 campaign was the fact that they relied on personal face-to-face interviewing. Historically, in-person interviews have been considered as the optimal method of gathering survey data. In recent years conditions have changed, and it is generally conceded by most pollsters that, when properly implemented, telephone interviewing is technically superior and more efficient than personal interviewing. In making estimates of voter sentiment in presidential elections, there are some inherent problems in personal interview sample procedures which tend to make this method inferior to a well-designed and well-executed telephone interview survey.

In a typical national cross-section survey involving 1500 in-person interviews, a pollster generally has to cluster his interviews to something like 300 or so sampling points. This would mean that at each of these sampling points or clusters, an average of five interviews would be taken.

The effect of interview clustering on data quality in national presidential elections is particularly acute. There may be wide distribution of thought and expression among neighbourhoods on a variety of marketing and social issues but there is a tendency for homogeneity in neighbourhood political preference and voting patterns. Thus the example cited above is better described as a 300-unit sample rather than a 1500 sample.

The use of unrestricted, non-clustered samples in telephone interviewing can avoid biases associated with clustering. However, the implementation of some of the telephone sampling designs used in the 1980 presidential election fell short of any ideal. For example, the NBC–*AP* Poll (*Public Opinion*, January/February 1981), which used the telephone, reported that it made no callbacks except when the interviewer encountered an engaged signal. Limiting any sample to those people who are at home at the time of the first call can produce highly questionable findings.

Because of the accelerated reporting requirements under which many media-sponsored pollsters operated during 1980, short interviewing time-periods were imposed. Even with callbacks, limiting interviewing time-periods to one or two days poses dangers that the public reached may not be sufficiently representative of the electorate.

There may be other reasons which contributed to the national polls not correctly gauging the actual levels of voter preference for Reagan and Carter during the last election. Presumably if an examination along the lines of the 1949 Social Science Research Council review of the 1948 polls were made the explanation might be clearer.

In summary, the negative public reaction to the national polls' performance in 1980 was perhaps as serious as the 1948 presidential polling experience. It could be argued that the 1980 situation was more serious because polling is now so much more extensive and there is a greater reliance and commitment to polling and survey methodology by a wider variety of public and private interests than ever before.

The presidential elections have become the time when the public pays more attention to polls and polling methodology than at any other instance. For pollsters, a presidential election year poses a unique test of measurement and public relations which occurs only once every four years. If polling methodology and the judgement of polls are to be subjected to this test, then those engaged in this effort should be sure operating conditions are optimal.

The performance of polling in presidential elections can be improved simply by viewing a presidential election not through one big national prism, but through fifty-one smaller prisms. Superficially, it would seem that to do this the polling budgets of national organisations would have to be expanded in the order of fifty times. This does not need to be the case, however. A programme of monitoring state polls and augmenting their efforts on a selective basis would do the job for the big media combines without too large an increase in dollar expenditures.

Each of the three television networks and their print medium partners spent huge sums of money covering the 1980 presidential election. They polled in many states during the primary election season. They conducted frequent national polls and some state polls during the general election campaign. During the primary election season, they underwrote massive 'exit' poll operations in most states where there was a contest.

A lot of polling money spent by the television networks and their newspaper partners could be more judiciously spent at the state level. There is already considerable state polling underwritten by local television stations and undertaken independently of network head-quarters involvement. More and more influential state newspapers are committing respectable sums of money for polling in their areas and are performing quite creditably.

During future presidential election years the media-sponsored national poll organisations might consider taking the step of adding to their staff one or two polling specialists who could systematically extract and evaluate private and public polling data at the state and local levels. It is highly probable they would uncover a large amount of valid and usable polling data with much less investment than it takes to undertake independent surveys which often duplicate other efforts. These round-ups of available state poll data could be combined with their own poll data taken in states where none was available. Most important, such a procedure would provide more assurance that presidential voting trends were being more accurately reflected.

So long as US presidential elections are the occasion for inordinate public scrutiny of polling, those who have a stake in this marvellous social invention should be more careful before jeopardising its public acceptance by using a system which has been demonstrated for a long time to have many flaws.

NOTE

1. The people and organisations who supplied me with state poll data during the campaign were Richard Cattani of the *Christian Science Monitor*, E. J. Dionne of the *New York Times*, Gerald Lubenow of *Newsweek*, William Rademacher of *Time*, Alan Baron of the *Baron Report*, Kevin Phillips of the *American Political Report*, Hedrick Smith of the *New York Times*. Other newspapers such as the *Washington Star* featured periodic round-ups of state polling data results. The political editors of *Time, Newsweek, US News* and *World Report* issued summaries of individual state poll results periodically throughout the presidential campaign. In addition, data from other private and public poll sources were available either directly or indirectly.

Appendix: WAPOR Code of Professional Ethics and Practices

The purpose of the World Association for Public Opinion Research (WAPOR) is to establish a worldwide meeting ground for those working in the area of survey research. Through its activities, WAPOR unites the world of survey research within the universities and the world of survey research within private institutes – two worlds which far too often are still strictly separated. It is the express goal of WAPOR to bridge the gap existing between practitioners of social research in commercial institutes and theoreticians of the academe.

The first WAPOR council was composed of three university professors and three directors of private public opinion research institutes. In 1948 it was resolved to alternate the annual meetings between North America, Europe and Latin America. In the past years WAPOR has increasingly held its congresses together with other scientific associations such as the American Association for Public Opinion Research (AAPOR), the European Society for Opinion and Marketing Research (ESOMAR), the International Political Science Association (IPSA), the International Sociological Association (ISA), the International Communication Association (ICA), and the International Association for Mass Communication Research (IAMCR).

This custom of meeting with different international associations indicates that WAPOR and its members are, above all, interested in serving all disciplines of the social sciences by using the common method of survey research. WAPOR members practise their methods in the following fields:

- opinion and attitude surveys
- audience research for papers, magazines, books, radio, television and broadcasting
- market research
- social research

The limitation to public opinion research, as suggested by WAPOR's name, has thus practically become meaningless.

As early as 1948, Hadley Cantril pointed to the cleavage between the work of private institutes and universities in the field of survey research. Cantril saw the key to a full development of survey research methods in a mutually beneficial relationship of university institutes and survey research institutes. There is absolutely no reason to see this differently today. The distrust between the two worlds has even become greater, however, because it has become mutual.

The persistence of such tensions for over some thirty years is due to the peculiarities of survey research. Conducting surveys requires a relatively large staff of scientists, technicians and administrators as well as hundreds of interviewers. Such an apparatus has high overhead costs. On the other hand, only full financial independence can protect researchers from having to accept commissions under conditions which should be rejected from a scientific point of view.

For universities, the running expenses of the organisation needed for surveys are too high. Thus social scientists in universities are in practice often unable to apply the methods of survey research in solving their problems. They often lack the data for analyses and they also often lack the confidence and experience to use this method which is much more complicated and requires more experience and information than many social scientists realise. On the other hand, this very data and experience has piled up in commercial survey research institutes outside of the universities. But the research practitioners in these institutes are generally under such pressure from their clients, financially and as regards deadlines, that barely any systematic development of methods or any analysis provoked by the scientific desire for knowledge could be achieved.

It was therefore one of WAPOR's foremost duties and desires to adopt a 'Code of Professional Ethics and Practices'.

CODE OF PROFESSIONAL ETHICS AND PRACTICES OF THE WORLD ASSOCIATION FOR PUBLIC OPINION RESEARCH

I. Introduction

1. The World Association for Public Opinion Research (WAPOR), in fulfilling its main objective to advance the use of science in the fields of public opinion and marketing research and in recognition of its

obligations to the public, hereby prescribes principles of ethical practice for the guidance of its members, and a framework of professional standards which should be acceptable to users of research and to the public at large.

2. In an increasingly complex world, social and economic planning is more and more dependent upon marketing information and public opinion reliably studied. The general public is the source of much of this information. Consequently, members of WAPOR acknowledge their obligation to protect the public from misrepresentation and exploitation in the name of research. At the same time, WAPOR affirms the interdependence of free expression of individual opinion and the researcher's freedom to interview.

3. Members of WAPOR recognise their obligations both to the profession they practise and to those who provide support for this practice to adhere to the basic standards of scientific investigation.

4. This code defines professional ethics and practices in the field of opinion and marketing research. Adherence to this code is deemed necessary to maintain confidence that researchers in this field are bound by a set of sound and basic principles based on experience gained over many years of development.

II. Rules of Practice between Researcher and Clients

A. Responsibilities of Researchers

5. The objective study of facts and data, conducted as accurately as permitted by the available resources and techniques, is the guiding principle of all research.

6. In executing his work, the researcher shall make every reasonable effort to adhere exactly to the specifications proposed to and accepted by the client. Should the researcher find it necessary to deviate from these specifications, he shall obtain the client's prior approval.

7. The researcher shall in every report distinguish his actual data from observations or judgments which may be based on other evidence.

8. The researcher shall not select tools of data collection and analysis because of the likelihood that they will support a desired conclusion, if that conclusion is not scientifically warranted.

9. Whenever data from a single survey are provided for more than one client or when data are provided to several clients, the researcher shall inform each client of the fact.

10. In the course of a field survey, the researcher shall not reveal the name of his client to respondents or to anyone else, unless authorised by the client.
11. All information and material supplied by the client for the research must remain confidential.
12. Without prior consent of the client, no findings from the commissioned research shall be disclosed by the researcher. However, unless there is agreement to the contrary, the research techniques and methods, such as sampling designs, names of interviewers, field instructions, etc., used for the study remain the researcher's property, if he has developed them.
13. Except by mutual consent, data shall not be sold or transferred by either the client or the researcher to parties not involved in the original contract work.
14. Unless it is customary or specifically agreed to the contrary, all punched cards, research documents (such as interviews and tests of sampled households) or any other material used in the field work shall be the property of the researcher. The practitioner is, however, required to provide for storage of this material for whatever period is customary in a particular country. This obligation shall be considered fulfilled by storage in a recognized data archive, if necessary, with restricted access.
15. Upon completion of a research study and after the researcher has submitted his final report, the client may request, according to previous mutually agreed specifications, a duplicate set of all punched cards prepared from the questionnaire, provided that the client shall bear the reasonable cost of preparation of such duplicates, and that respondents remain unidentified.
16. The practitioner shall be accurate in providing prospective clients with information about his experience, capacities and organization.

B. Responsibilities of Clients

17. Potential clients asking for research proposals and quotations recognize that, in the absence of a fee being paid, such proposals and quotations remain the property of the researcher. In particular, prospective clients must not use the proposals of one practitioner competitively in order to obtain a lowering of the price from other practitioners.
18. Reports provided by the practitioner are normally for the use of the client and his agents. The researcher and the client shall agree in

writing regarding the means of any wider dissemination of the complete or partial results of a research study.

In particular, it should be agreed that:

(a) The client shall ensure that any publication of survey results will not be quoted out of context or distort any facts or findings of the survey.

(b) The researcher must be consulted in regard to the form of publication and is entitled to refuse to grant permission for his name to be quoted in connection with the survey where he considers clause (a) has been violated.

C. Rules of Practice Regarding Reports and Survey Results

19. Every complete report on a survey should contain an adequate explanation of the following relevant points:

(a) for whom the survey was conducted;

(b) the purpose of the study;

(c) the universe or population to which the results of the survey are projected;

(d) the method by which the sample was selected including both the type of sample (probability, quota, etc.) and the specific procedures by which it was selected;

(e) steps taken to insure the sample design would actually be carried out in the field;

(f) the degree of success in actually carrying out the design including the rate of non-response and a comparison of the size and characteristics of the actual and anticipated samples;

(g) a full description of the estimating procedure used for all results which are reported including the sample size on which it was based and weighting procedures used to adjust raw data;

(h) a full description of the method employed in the field work;

(i) the time at which the field work, if any, was done, and the time span covered in collecting data;

(j) the findings obtained;

(k) (where the nature of the research demands it) the characteristics of those employed as interviewers and coders and the methods of their training and supervision;

(l) a copy of the interview schedule or questionnaire and instructions.

20. Technical terms shall be employed in a survey report in accordance with their commonly understood scientific usage.

III. Rules of Practice between Researcher and Respondents

D. *Responsibility to Informants*

21. No informant or respondent must be adversely affected as a result of his answers or of the interviewing process. The practitioner shall use no methods or techniques by which the informant is put in the position that he cannot exercise his right to withdraw or refuse his answers at any stage of the interview.
22. No response in a survey shall be linked in any way to an identifiable respondent. The anonymity of respondents shall be respected, except in rare cases, with the respondent's specific permission. The interview method shall never be used as a disguise for a sales solicitation.
23. For field interviewers:
    (a) Research assignments and materials received as well as information from respondents shall be held in confidence by the interviewer and revealed to no one except the research organisation conducting the study.
    (b) No information gained through a research activity shall be used, directly or indirectly, for the personal gain or advantage of the interviewer in his relations with the respondents.
    (c) Field work shall be conducted in strict accordance with specifications. No field worker shall carry out more than one assignment in contact with the same respondents unless this is authorised by the research organisation.

IV. Rules of Practice between Researchers

24. The principle of fair competition as generally understood and accepted should be applied by all researchers, even in cases where they may be the sole operators in their country.
25. In their personal and business relationships, researchers will be governed by the tradition of common respect among colleagues in the same profession.
26. No outside pressure, political or commercial, can be used by a researcher or research organisation to justify violation of this code.
27. Members shall not try to turn to account or put into evidence the fact of their membership of WAPOR as a token of professional competence. Membership implies no guarantee of qualification, but it does imply acceptance of this code.

EXCERPTS FROM THE CONSTITUTION OF THE WORLD
ASSOCIATION FOR PUBLIC OPINION RESEARCH

Article II – Purposes and Functions

Section 1: The purposes of the Association shall be:
a) to establish and promote contacts between persons in the field of
   survey research on opinions, attitudes, and behaviour of people in
   the various countries of the world, and
b) to further the use of objective, scientific survey research in national
   and international affairs.

Section 2: Functions and activities of the Association may include, but
are not limited to, the sponsorship of meetings and publications,
development of improved research techniques, encouragement of high
professional standards, promotion of personnel training, coordination
of international polls, and maintenance of close relations with other
research agencies. Such agencies include the American Association for
Public Opinion Research (AAPOR), the European Society for Opinion
and Marketing Research (ESOMAR), and other regional professional research associations, as well as the United Nations Educational, Scientific and Cultural Organisations (UNESCO), other
United Nations agencies, and private international organisations.

Article III – Membership

Section 1: Membership in the Association shall be as individual persons,
not as representatives of organisations, nations, or other groups. There
shall be two classes of members, full and associate.

WAPOR does not publish a magazine or journal of its own, but one of
the benefits it can offer to its members is the subscription to *Public
Opinion Quarterly* and *World Opinion Update* at reduced rates.

- WAPOR members can subscribe to *Public Opinion Quarterly* for
  US $15 per year granted to WAPOR members in the USA and
  Canada (surface mail); or US $21 for USA, Canadian, European
  and Mexican members (airmail); or US $27 for all other members
  (airmail).
- WAPOR members can subscribe to *World Opinion Update* for US
  $25 per year or US $30 if living outside the USA and Canada.

Index